When creating a thirst in the hearts of His people for a fresh outpouring of the Spirit, God uses, in addition to His inspired Word, histories of revival, biographies of revival leaders, reports and personal testimonies. In *Sounds from Heaven* Colin and Mary Peckham present a blend of history, biography and reports as well as several testimonies of those blessed on the Isle of Lewis, off the west coast of Scotland, during the 1949-1952 awakening. This will become for those burdened for revival a primary and powerful resource for understanding God's ways in sending 'times of refreshing' for His people. We welcome it most warmly.

Rev. Dr. Ted S. Rendall,
Chancellor Emeritus, Prairie Bible Institute
and Author of *Fire in the Church*

The need for true revival has been very great and is growing daily while the burden of the church for awakening seems to be shrinking. It appears that many professed Christians accept the moral and spiritual decline of the church, so prevalent today, as normal Christianity. Thankfully Colin and Mary Peckham have provided overwhelming evidence and heart-stirring proof that better days can be sought and received by the church. *Sounds From Heaven* provides ringing affirmation that God is still on His throne and delights to make bare His mighty arm in revival when His people get serious with Him.

Rev. Richard Owen Roberts
Author of *Scotland saw His Glory*

If reading about revival can be so thrilling what must it be to experience such visitations of God's grace described by Colin and Mary Peckham as they record those periods of spiritual awakening on the island of Lewis? Both historically and spiritually those accounts are fascinating and challenging. In a time of extreme apathy among Christian people, yet when talk about revival has become trendy, many Christians have no real concept of true God-sent revival. May this publication be used to provide a clearer understanding of revival and also create a longing that God, in His providence, may revive us again and awaken His Church which, in many places, has settled for death.

Rev. Tom Shaw M.A. M.Th.
' Congregational Church, N. Ireland.
·ary President of The Faith Mission.

Most Christians of today's generation know nothing of Duncan Campbell and the remarkable revival that occurred on the Isle of Lewis from 1949 to 1952. This book rectifies that situation and few are better qualified to tell the story, for Mary Peckham was converted in the revival, and her husband Colin has extensively researched the subject, and both of them have served for many years in the leadership of the Faith Mission which was at the forefront of the events in Lewis (and in many other places).

Here you can read Duncan Campbell's own reports, along with eye-witness records (including that of Mary) of those amazing days, and a description of the characteristics of the revival. And although Lewis of fifty years ago may be far removed from our present world, none the less the desperate state of our society and the church which bears the name of Christ should drive us to pray with the Psalmist, "Will You not revive us again, O Lord?"

If this book prompts us to do that, then it will surely have fulfilled its purpose.

Rev. Peter Grainger
Senior Pastor,
Charlotte Baptist Chapel, Edinburgh

Sounds from Heaven

The Revival on the Isle of Lewis, Scotland,
1949–1952

Colin and Mary Peckham

CHRISTIAN FOCUS

Cover picture - Donald MacAulay in his boat, the *Mairi Dhonn*. Donald was later to become the Rev. Donald MacAulay, first convenor of the Western Isles Council whose testimony is in the book.

And when the day of Pentecost was fully come,
they were all with one accord in one place.
And suddenly there came a sound from heaven (Acts 2:1, 2).

Scripture quotations are from the King James Version.

Copyright © Colin and Mary Peckham 2004

ISBN 1-85792-953-5

Published in 2004
by
Christian Focus Publications,
Geanies House, Fearn,
Ross-shire, IV20 ITW, Scotland.

www.christianfocus.com

Cover design by Alister MacInnes

Printed and bound by
Mackays of Chatham

Contents

Testimonies of Those who Experienced the Revivals

Foreword

The last recorded revival in the British Isles ended just half a century ago, but its results are still with us – and that is a mark of authentic revival. The Western Isles of Scotland had experienced a number of short periods of revival at the end of the nineteenth and in the first half of the twentieth centuries, but especially between 1949 and 1952. The story of Duncan Campbell has already been written and therefore is only lightly touched here; but this book is distinctive because whilst most books on revival are written by historians (distant observers), theologians (critical observers), or perhaps by the leaders themselves (immediate observers), here are stories from the heart by ordinary people who were caught up in a magnificent work of God: they have recounted what they saw, heard and personally experienced, and what is notable is the fact that although none knew what the others had recorded, each was telling the same coherent story of the miracle of revival in the Western Isles.

Much of the material in this book should have been available long ago, but we can be grateful to Colin and Mary Peckham for publishing for the first time extracts from the reports sent to the Faith Mission Headquarters by Duncan Campbell during those momentous years, and even for leading us through the labyrinth of the history of the Presbyterian churches in Scotland! This is by no means irrelevant because the historic differences help to explain the tragic suspicion and opposition with which the work of God was viewed by some denominations. There are important lessons to be learnt from all this.

But there are many more positive aspects of the revival, like the first lesson of persistent, insistent, believing prayer ('Many of us pray just enough to ease the conscience, but not enough to win any decisive victory'), the sense of the presence of God ('An overwhelming sense of God invading the atmosphere.... You could feel Him in the homes of the people, on the common and on the moor and even as you walked along the road through the townships'), the chief description of the power of the Holy Spirit being that of conviction of sin ('Strong men broken down and crying for mercy'), and the dynamic of song in times of revival ('Revival singing is anointed

7

singing. It is like a fire that goes through one's whole being').

I cannot recall any book on revival that I have read that has given me greater pleasure, held my attention more, and incited my longing for a new visitation from God more than this one. This is a significant book in the growing library of revival literature.

Rev. Brian Edwards
Surbiton Surrey, England
Author of *Revival*.
Former moderator of the
Fellowship of Independent Evangelical Churches.

Thanks

To all those who were willing to share their testimonies of revival with us from which we were able to glean so much vital information of challenge and blessing.

To the Faith Mission Headquarters for allowing us access to Duncan Campbell's valuable reports from the revival scenes.

To the Faith Mission students who patiently stood at the photostat machine and reproduced Mr Campbell's reports from the Mission's archives.

To Mrs. Sonya Russell, Dromore, N. Ireland, who typed part of the document for us.

To the Lord who has made this a tremendous blessing to our own hearts as we have worked.

Sometimes when reading, translating and typing these thrilling testimonies, our hearts were broken. It has inspired us to cry to Him who is the source of revival to pour out once again His Spirit upon us. May God teach us to pray, to enter into His presence, to learn true soul travail as we bear the burden of the lost.

Colin & Mary Peckham
1 Kilpunt Gardens,
Broxburn, Scotland
EH52 5AT
E-mail: drc@peckham.net
Web-site: www.revival.org

Faith Mission Headquarters
Govan House, 2 Drum Street,
Edinburgh, Scotland EH17 8QG
E-mail: hq@faithmission.org

Faith Mission Bible College
2 Drum Street, Gilmerton,
Edinburgh, EH17 8QG
E-mail: college@faithmission.org

Web-site: www.faithmission.org

About the Authors

Rev. Dr. Colin Neil Peckham, L.Th Hons, BA (Theol), B.Th. Hons, M.Th, D.Th, was born in South Africa where he had ten years of evangelistic ministry and youth work before entering Bible College work in Cape Town. For seventeen years he was principal of the Faith Mission Bible College, Gilmerton, Edinburgh, Scotland. As principal emeritus he now has an extensive preaching ministry in Great Britain and abroad.

Mary J. Peckham (nee Morrison), was born on the Isle-of-Lewis, Scotland. She was converted in the 1949 revival there and soon after her conversion entered The Faith Mission Bible College in Edinburgh. She spent fourteen years in evangelistic and convention ministry in the UK and abroad, seeing true revival on two occasions in her ministry, before marrying Colin in 1969. Together they served the Lord in South Africa for fourteen years before going to the UK to minister in the FMBC, Edinburgh

They have three adult children, two of whom are married, and one grandchild.

Introduction

In order to preserve the testimonies of those who were in Lewis revivals before they passed away, and to give an authentic account of the 1949-1952 revival, we travelled to various parts of Lewis and Harris (and other places as well) to capture their stories. Often the tape recorder was placed on the table and conversations proceeded along the normal lines of the weather, health and other items of the day together with the accounts of the revivals. All this material had to be sorted out, sometimes translated from Gaelic by Mary, and edited from the colloquial manner in which it was gathered. We have the tapes of the conversations, testimonies and any such gathered information.

Duncan Campbell spent five years at the beginning of his ministry in the Faith Mission, and later twenty-five years as a minister in the United Free Church of Scotland. In January 1949, he rejoined the Faith Mission. In December 1949, Mr. Campbell went to Lewis and was involved in a movement of the Spirit from 1949 to 1953. From 1958 to 1967 he was the principal of the Faith Mission Bible College in Edinburgh.

The Faith Mission is an interdenominational evangelistic society founded in 1886, operating in Great Britain and Ireland with its Headquarters and Bible College in Edinburgh, Scotland. It has about 100 workers holding evangelistic missions (or campaigns) mainly in rural districts, and conventions for Christians for the deepening of spiritual life, throughout the country and throughout the year. It holds about 8,000 meetings in any one year. People are trained for Christian service at home and abroad in the Bible College, and any Christian requiring Bible College training may apply.

The workers of the Faith Mission send weekly reports of their work to the Mission Headquarters. The staff then take extracts from those reports and compile a letter called *Pilgrim News* which gives up to date news of all that is happening throughout the work of the Faith Mission each week. This private letter is sent to all the workers so that all are constantly in touch with each other and can therefore pray more effectively for one another.

Realizing that Duncan Campbell's reports were in the Faith Mission archives, we were given access to these and extracted his valuable observations written at the time of the revival straight from the field of action. This material has never seen the light of day and is now released with a prayer that it might be used to inspire prayer and faith for a movement of the Spirit today.

To grasp and understand what occurred at that time it is necessary not only to read Duncan Campbell's reports but also the wonderful testimonies of those who were there. Shafts of light from these testimonies clarify much concerning actions and events of this period and of the revival itself. Mary's testimony has been published in book form three times (*I was Saved in Revival*) and it appears here in an abridged form.

The testimonies glow with an indescribable warmth and the reality of their experience is there for all to see. The gospel is so clear. God manifest among His people is a thrilling reality and the power of the Holy Spirit in the midst, convicting, constraining, converting, confirming, comforting, causes the reader to bend before God in awe and adoration, in love and consecration, in wonder and amazement. One senses the powerful operation of the Holy Ghost.

When we review our own lack of burden, our dim understanding of God's mighty working, we can but cry to God to engulf us with flood-tides of divine refreshing and bring reviving streams to us all, sweeping sinners into the kingdom.

Let us read, ponder, reflect, humble ourselves, pray, seek His face, turn from our wicked ways, and surely He will hear from heaven, forgive our sin and heal our poor land, blighted with the scourge of vulgarity, brutality, nudity, profanity, obscenity, blasphemy, immorality, depravity and spiritual poverty.

May the Lord use this little volume to His great glory.

A day of the ministration of the Spirit would bring many rare and rich blessings along with it; such as discoveries of the Redeemer's glory, convictions of the evil and vileness of sin, many crowns of victory and triumph to Christ, great additions to his friends and followers. Then gospel light would shine clear, saving knowledge increase, ignorance and error vanish, riches of free grace would be displayed, and Satan be bound up. Then ministers and ordinances would be lively, secure sinners would be awakened, dead souls would live, hard hearts would be melted, strong lusts subdued, and many sons and daughters born to God. Such a day would heal divisions, cement breaches, make us all of one heart and mind, and bring down heaven to earth. This would redress our grievances, remove our complaints, and unite Christ's scattered flock. It would make true religion and holy persons to be in esteem, vice to be in disgrace, and iniquity as ashamed to hide its face. Then sabbaths and communions would be days of heaven. Prayer and praise, spiritual converse, talking of Christ and redeeming love, would be our chiefest delight. O then, pray for such a time.

John Willison, *The Balm of Gilead*, 1742

SEND THE FLOOD-TIDES

Send the flood-tides of Thy blessing!
Pour exhaustless draughts of grace;
In the spate of heavenly glory
O, my God, spare me a place.

Come around us, o'er us, on us,
Fill our souls with holy fire,
Come in glory, stand among us!
O my soul, to God aspire!

Cleanse! Thou mighty flood-tide, cleanse me
Purer than the driven snow!
Oh, the precious blood doth reach me,
His blest cleansing I can know.

God is here in matchless splendour,
Gone the glory of earth's sun,
Blinded by the vision glorious,
Lord, in me Thy will be done.

Hallelujah! Glory! Glory!
God in majesty doth sweep;
Gushing forth a mighty torrent
O'er the land His power doth leap.

O Thou Victor – ride in triumph!
Blood-bought riches Thou must claim,
On till we with hosts of glory
Swell fore'er Thy matchless Name!

Colin N. Peckham

Chapter 1

The Island

The Hebrides is a series of islands forty miles west of the most northerly part of Scotland. Lewis is the most northerly island and Harris is attached to it in the south, forming one island about sixty miles long with a population of about 25,000 people. South of Harris the line of islands extends southwards: North Uist, Benbecula, Grimsay, South Uist and Barra as well as smaller inhabited islands such as Bernera (Lewis) and Berneray (Harris). The islands are the first to face the might of the Atlantic gales and their bleak, windswept treeless topography bears witness to the effect of the severe weather.

The stretch of water between the mainland of Scotland and the Hebrides is called the Minch and currents there are such that the seafaring men of Lewis would say that it is one of the choppiest of waters to negotiate. At the time of the 1949 revival the sailings to Lewis were from Kyle of Lochalsh and Mallaig to Stornoway and these journeys would take about seven hours. Seven hours on a small rolling and pitching vessel is something to be endured not enjoyed, so the Hebrides were not the popular destination of tourists and they retained their isolated position. Today there are several sailings to and from different ports and the sailing time has been enormously reduced. The ease now of roll-on, roll-off car ferries makes travel there so much more accessible.

Stornoway, with a population of about 10,000, is the only town on Lewis. Although there are very rural and lonely places on Lewis and Harris most of the folk live in more or less compact villages, mainly in the coastal areas. In several places these villages are so near to each other as to constitute a large community within the compass of a few miles. The general area of Ness in the very north, for instance, has fourteen villages, one of which is Port-of-Ness. It is here that Mary grew up in a home overlooking the harbour and a stretch of beautiful sand.

At the time of the 1949 revival the people were largely occupied in working on their crofts (small-holdings of about six acres) and weaving on looms in sheds on their property, and it is here that the famous Harris tweed is produced. Because very few people owned cars, folk were not able to travel freely and the communities were very much self-contained units where many people knew each other.

Many of the men entered the merchant navy or some other branch of shipping, and Lewismen were to be found on ships all over the world. This was much more so in the fifties than today when many young people migrate south to the cities to find work. Lewis people are instinctively and traditionally religious, with reverence for God, His Word and the ordinances of the church.

Parts of Scotland spoke Gaelic in the eighteenth century. There was a period when the language was actually banned because of political strife, but it recovered and was retained in some parts of the Highlands. All the country areas of Lewis and Harris speak Gaelic, while Stornoway is much more English-speaking. To a large extent Gaelic has died out in most of the Highlands. At present there is a concerted attempt to save and propagate the language through the media and through a few Gaelic-medium schools springing up in various parts of the country.

The 1949-53 revival took place in the country districts of Lewis, so it was conducted wholly in the Gaelic language, using the Gaelic Bible. To the uninitiated, Gaelic is not simply a Scottish dialect of English; it is an entirely different Celtic language, no word of which would be intelligible to an English-speaking person.

The great Uig revival of the early nineteenth century was known on the mainland of Scotland. Many of the revivals which followed in Lewis were also known but because of its isolated position these were not fully investigated nor recorded by the churches nor by any of the local population. The revivals followed one another in different places, bringing great blessing to the people but were not proclaimed abroad in any great measure, lest the people would be deemed to be boastful and would feel that they were grieving the Spirit.

The difference with the 1949 revival was that the man who was greatly used in this movement, Rev. Duncan Campbell, was from the mainland of Scotland. The wonder of it was that although he was from the English-speaking mainland, he also spoke Gaelic, and thus spoke to the hearts of the people in their mother tongue, giving him acceptance with the people far more so than if this had not been the case. When he returned to the mainland, he took with him the story of the revival and this news then burst upon the world scene. It was hailed as 'The Lewis Revival' as if this were the only revival that Lewis had known, which of course is far from the truth.

Chapter 2

Religion in Lewis

Denominations

From 1929 to virtually the end of the twentieth century there were three main denominations in Lewis, all of them Presbyterian: the Church of Scotland (the national church), the Free Church of Scotland (called by some on the mainland, the 'Wee Frees'), the largest denomination on Lewis, and the Free Presbyterian Church of Scotland (called 'the Seceders'), by far the smallest denomination on Lewis.

In 1843, 470 ministers from the evangelical wing of the Church of Scotland broke away to form the Free Church of Scotland (the 'Great Disruption'). In the next decade, feverish activity took place all over Scotland as churches and manses were built for those who, at great sacrifice to themselves and their families, had taken a huge step on high principle. The shock of this severance affected the whole of Scotland, and sadly bitterness was, in many places, its legacy.

In 1874 and 1882 the American evangelist D.L. Moody, with his soloist Ira Sankey, visited Britain. After fairly insignificant meetings in England, he came to Scotland and here his ministry was so mightily blessed that, in the purpose of God, healing took place as people from all denominations worked together for the salvation of souls. Thousands of people came to Christ in Scotland and the name of Moody was heralded across the world. Scotland gave him international repute. Remote Lewis was unaffected by these happenings.

In 1893 the Free Presbyterian Church was formed when two ministers and several thousand people left the Free Church. This denomination has a strict separatist stance and does not expect its members to attend meetings of any other body. Therefore it had nothing to do with any of the revivals experienced by the other churches.

'In 1900, the majority of congregations in the Free Church of Scotland joined with the United Presbyterian Church, to form the United Free Church of Scotland, but most of the Lewis people were against the union, and remained in the Free Church. In 1929, the United Free Church merged with the Church of Scotland.[1] Much of Scotland was now again in the national church. The Free Church, which had consisted of almost a third of the country in 1843, was now reduced to a small number mainly in the Highlands and Islands – hence the name 'Wee Frees'. At the time of the 1949 revival the Free Church was the dominant body on the island and still is.

Communions

Communion seasons took place every six months in every church, and still does. The communion would begin on Thursday morning, which was called the fast day; Friday was the testimony day; Saturday was the day of preparation; Sunday was the great day of the feast; and Monday was thanksgiving day when the final service was held in the morning. It was virtually a convention. Normally two or three ministers would be invited and they, together with the minister of the church, conducted the meetings.

Communion weekends were staggered to allow people to go from one communion weekend to another in different villages. These communion seasons were often times of great blessing and were wonderfully used of God to inspire the faithful and to bring great challenge to the unsaved. They were precious times of fellowship and joy.

The table was 'fenced' or protected when the minister would preach showing, from a biblical perspective, who should be allowed to partake of the bread and wine. This was normally a searching word. The church would be full but only those who took their seats in the designated area, marked off by white cloth on the front of the pews, would participate. The biblical position of allowing only those who knew the Lord to participate in the Lord's Supper was a well-established principle.

The Family Altar

Such was the influence of repeated revivals on the island that in the 1940s and 1950s most homes conducted family prayers at least once a day, when the Bible was read, a psalm was sung and a prayer was offered. This was done in the homes of Christians and non-Christians alike. The only way the unsaved knew to fulfil their baptismal vow to bring up their children in the fear and admonition of the Lord was to read the Bible to them and to offer a prayer.

---

1. Donald MacDonald (1978), *Lewis A History of the Island*, Gordon Wright Publishing, p.115

The whole island therefore knew the Bible, its teachings and its standards, and was committed to the upholding of these things. The groundwork was laid for further movements of the Spirit as the population acknowledged the existence and presence of God and bowed to the authority of His Word. There were very few dissenters.

This attitude and respect for the things of God from nearly everyone on the island is a wonderful tribute to the power of the gospel to change the community. It surely showed Scotland, and indeed other countries, what the gospel could do when it was embraced by so many who were then transformed by the power of God.

Church Attendance

In the 1950s whole communities went to church. It was simply the done thing. If you did not attend church you were regarded as ungodly and would be outside of the spirit of the community. The church was the centre of the community and what the minister said carried enormous weight.

This situation does not pertain today; in fact there has been an increasing polarization between the church and the community, and the church, whilst normally still held in high regard, is not nearly as dominant as it was fifty years ago. Many of those who knew revival have died, others who were influenced by the vital church life have left the island for work in the cities and elsewhere, and there has been an invasion of incomers from the south who have very different values and do not conform to the religious life on the island. Hence church attendance has dropped.

Sundays

Sundays were held in the highest regard. Nothing moved except those who went to and from the churches. If someone was seen on a bicycle, he would be cycling to the village phone-booth to phone the doctor as one of the family would be ill. Quietness descended on the whole island for the whole day. No-one worked on his croft. No clothes were hung on the washing line. People would not even go for walks. Sundays were set apart by God and given to the people to seek the Lord. This instilled into the people the awe of the eternal and the acknowledgement of God. Whether they were saved or not they conformed to the standards of the community.

Singing

The song book of the church on the island of Lewis is the Book of Psalms. No hymns or gospel songs are sung in the church services, with the exception of the English services in the Church of Scotland churches in Stornoway. The people are committed to singing the Word of God, and when sung in the Spirit this is a mighty tool in the hand of God, for He speaks His Word into the hearts of the people.

There are no musical instruments in the meetings, and the people sing without music. The congregations have a 'precentor' (literally from the Latin 'Prae-Cantor' for he 'Sang Before' the congregation) sitting in a slightly raised seat just below the pulpit, from where he leads the singing. In the Gaelic culture, dating back to the days when the folk could not read, the precentor sings one line which is repeated by the congregation; he then sings the next line which the congregation repeats and so on, so that the verses which they sing are actually sung twice. Singing in the revival was mightily used of God and often the power of the sung Word brought great conviction into the meeting.

Prayer

At the time of the 1949 revival all the members of the church attended the weekly prayer meeting. You were not accepted as a member of the church unless you were a true Christian, and the whole membership was in the prayer meeting every week. Many more people attended the Sunday services but they thought that they were not part of the body of Christ and they did not attend the prayer meetings. In fact to attend the prayer meeting was a huge step, for you were telling the community that you were concerned about your soul. It was almost a burning of the bridges behind you.

The prayer meetings were not what one would call 'open' prayer meetings. The minister would call upon three or four men to pray and only those designated men would pray. They would normally be deacons or elders or members in whom the minister had confidence. When these men got liberty there was a tremendous spirit in the meeting. An open prayer meeting where anyone, man or woman, boy or girl, can pray freely was not known in Lewis.

The Reformed Position

Lewis is a stronghold of Calvinism. The five points of Calvinism were well-known everywhere. Children drank in theology with their mother's milk at the time of the 1949 revival. The total depravity of man, the dire consequences of sin, the reality of heaven and hell, the message of God's forgiveness to the penitent and all else that comprises the true gospel were well-known facts. Even when a sinner had drunk too much on a

Saturday night he could reel off as much theology as the minister in the pulpit. They were 'theologians' before ever they were saved.

There were no classes on counselling, no lectures on soul-winning, as are held in many evangelical circles, for such counselling could well be man's work and not God's. The counsellor could give the inquirer false hopes. You had enough of the truth to be enabled by the Holy Spirit to trust Christ for salvation. If you failed in your search for God, then you were possibly not in the elect and you could well be doomed. This brought a tremendous solemnity to the preaching of the gospel, and jokes, clever quips and light stories never came from the pulpit. The sermons were an hour or more of solid theology to which people listened most attentively.

Women

Women did not participate in public ministry. They did not pray in the prayer meetings nor give testimony to their faith on the Communion testimony day when men were able to do so. Women taught in the Sunday Schools and there were those who went out to foreign fields as missionaries, but women do not normally speak to congregations of men and women on the Isle of Lewis.

When Mary, therefore, announced that she was going to the Faith Mission Bible College in Edinburgh, it was a shock to the people, and there was some disapproval. Such knew that the Faith Mission sent out young people to hold missions in which she would then be involved.

Children

Each of the denominations have Sunday Schools where the Word of God is faithfully taught. All the children had a good scriptural knowledge and a good understanding of biblical doctrine as the Bible and the Shorter Catechism were taught at school with the minister examining them once a year.

All this was to prepare them to come to salvation when they were able to understand the deep things of God. Children do not appreciate the theological implications of the gospel and therefore it was generally thought that they would be better able to respond when they came to an age of understanding. During some revivals on Lewis, however, there were quite a number of children who sought and found the Lord.

Few children trusted Christ for salvation in the 1949 revival. Rev. Jack MacArthur, at the age of eleven, was the youngest of any who came to Christ in the revival. He said, 'We think the children can't understand. In revival at the age of eleven, I can't remember ever not understanding what had been said.'

Chapter 3

Revivals in Lewis

A great disadvantage to the Highlands after the Reformation was the lack of the Scriptures in their own language. Through want of schools many of the people had no literary education. The Highlands were so remote that few teachers were available for these duties and 'for a long time, until 1767 the teaching of Gaelic was forbidden'.[1]

In 'the Western Isles we find a deplorable state of matters. Church fabrics were neglected, and had in many cases become ruins.... The people were sunk in poverty, ignorance, superstition...and any religion they had was often...the laird's religion.'[2]

'The first translation of the New Testament into Scottish Gaelic did not appear until 1767, and the entire Bible was not published in Gaelic until 1801.'[3] The Society for the Propagation of Christian Knowledge (SPCK) and other societies did much to bring education and the reading of the Scriptures to the people, so the ground work for evangelical ministry was laid by catechists and newly established schools.

'The majority of ministers in the Western Isles before 1800 were regarded as belonging to the Moderate party of the Church of Scotland.'[4] In Uig, Rev. Munro had a long and unproductive ministry. It was said of him, 'The minister was ignorant of the gospel and of the nature of true godliness.'[5] All over Lewis, and especially in Uig, the spiritual condition was extremely depressing. Liquor was sold on the Mondays after the Communion weekend outside the churches and sometimes even on Sundays.

A lad in Uig learned to read and found salvation in the Word of God.

---

1. Murdo MacAulay (n.d.), *Aspects of the Religious History of Lewis*, Inverness John Eccles.

2. John MacKay (1914), *The Church in the Highlands*, Hodder & Stoughton, p.212

3. Murdoch Campbell (1953), *Gleanings of Highland Harvest* (Christian Focus reprint) p.148.

4. MacAulay, pp.106,116

5. *ibid.* p.105

He went from house to house reading the Bible to all who would hear –
opposed by the minister. There were only a few Bibles in the parish and
only a few could read.

A teacher from the Gaelic School Society named John MacLeod came
to Lewis. He taught the people to read and used the Bible as his textbook.
He exhorted them to seek the Lord and his labours were blessed as numbers
crowded in to hear him night by night. The people were beginning to wake
out of a long, deep sleep.

The 1820s Revival

'Perhaps the man who did more than any other to break up the fallow
ground in Lewis in the 1820s was the famous Highland evangelist, Finlay
Munro. He travelled much in Lewis during the revival and paid at least two
visits to the island, one before the revival which began in 1822 and one
after Mr. MacLeod had been settled in Uig in 1824.'[6]

The 1820s were to revolutionise Lewis completely. Murdo MacAulay
suggests that the revival 'seems to have begun in Barvas and it swept
through the whole island, including Harris'.[7] The movement in Uig certainly
was at the forefront of the great revival in the 1820s, and the ministry of
Rev. Alexander MacLeod in Uig was enormously effective in the movement.
MacLeod, born in 1786, was originally from Sutherland, but came to Uig
from the parish of Cromarty. He was to exercise a powerful and wonderfully
fruitful evangelistic ministry in the island.

When he first came to Uig, he found the people in gross spiritual
darkness. He was the first evangelical minister they had known. At the
communion everybody, that is 800 or 900 people, irrespective of their
spiritual condition, sat freely at the Lord's table. MacLeod's searching,
powerful appeals, as well as the awful reality of spiritual matters, caused
such a change that at his first communion on 25th June 1827, which he had
deferred for two years, instead of hundreds, 'only six communicants were
there from his own congregation, along with fourteen others, but 7,000
attended'.[8]

He continued to preach, teach, catechise, organise and establish schools
throughout the parish. The Spirit applied the Word to the conscience.
People came from neighbouring districts and from further afield to hear,
returning wounded and broken. 'In his diary he records how his sermons

6. *ibid.* p.130
7. *ibid.* p.116.
8. Angus Smith (1992), *The Large Church* (A local Ness production), p.16.

were interrupted by the weeping of the people.'[9] The Spirit was moving in Uig and all over the island, and people were seeking God with all their hearts.

The climax came at the communion in Uig in 1828, when it was estimated that the crowd that gathered numbered 9,000. Remembering that the few roads that there were in those days were in poor condition and that the people had to cross peat bogs and rough ground on foot to get to Uig, it is utterly amazing that so many gathered in so remote a place. People walked for many miles! MacRae says, 'In 1828 the whole island seemed to be moved with one great and powerful emotion.... The spirit of prayer was very marked during this time.'[10] Converts were of all ages, and among the converts were a number who became ministers, evangelists and teachers.

In Ness, the first evangelical minister, Rev. Finlay Cook who was converted in a revival in Arran, was settled there in 1829, and thus began an evangelical ministry in that district which has persisted down the years.

The 1820s placed Lewis firmly in evangelical and biblical truth, gave the people to know the reality of the living God, caused them to experience the presence of God in revival, thus laying the foundation for all the many revivals that followed in many places in Lewis down the years. A new day had dawned in its history and revival was to persist in ebbs and flows from that time on.

From 1825 to 1830 God mightily used the bard John Morrison in Harris as he preached from village to village with great power. The first open-air meeting was held in Tarbert, Harris, when 2,000 people were present. By this time the Uig revival had spread all over the island and every hamlet and village was touched and quickened by the Spirit of life. It was at this time that the famous Dr. Joh⟶   ⟵ld of Ferintosh, the 'Apostle of the North', paid his se⟶   ⟵. The result of that visit was to change the lif⟶   ⟵old things had passed away and all things had b⟶

Later Decades

The Great Disruptic⟶   ⟵in 1843, when over 470 ministers left the Chu⟶   ⟵⟵m the Free Church of Scotland. With the exception o⟶   ⟵...nisters in Stornoway, 'almost the entire population of Lewis joined the Free Church'[11] indicating that they were

---

9. *ibid.* p. 16

10. Alexander MacRae (1899), *Revivals in the Highlands and Islands in the 19th Century*, James Nisbet, pp.83, 84.

11. Murdo MacAulay (1984), *The Burning Bush in Carloway*, Carloway Free Church of Scotland, p. 14.

wholly committed to biblical truth and its proclamation and rejecting the 'Moderate' position of many in the Church of Scotland.

The 1859 revival swept the island and was a means of a great ingathering, particularly in Ness in the north of the island.

In 1900 and 1901 again there was a great move of the Spirit in Uig, and the interest and influence of this revival spread to the neighbouring parishes of Barvas, Ness and elsewhere. Rev. Peter MacDonald of Stornoway, spoke of it as 'one of the deepest spiritual movements that had ever been known in the island'.[12] In 1903 a spiritual movement began in Carloway and the surrounding villages and continued on until about 1912.[13] (This corresponds of course with the Welsh Revival of 1904 and 1905.) 'It would appear from church records that similar revivals took place in various districts of Lewis until the outbreak of the First World War.'[14]

In Ness, under the ministry of Rev Roderick MacLeod, 'at the beginning of 1923 a revival of considerable intensity broke out throughout the district.'[15] This continued until MacLeod left for Dumbarton in 1926. 'There was no outward excitement connected with this movement, but there was much silent weeping and deep contrition of heart. The revival touched persons of all ages.'[16]

Point was particularly blessed with revivals in 1934, 1939, 1949 and 1957 and Rev. William Campbell of the Free Church, who was the minister there throughout that time, was greatly used in this area. In 1950 Duncan Campbell was in Point when a further movement of the Spirit took place in the Church of Scotland.

The island of Bernera experienced a great move in 1936 and another in 1951.

The 1939 Revival

Carloway and the surrounding areas were favoured with an almost continual movement from 1934 to about 1940, particularly under the ministry of Rev. John MacIver. This 'was probably the most impressive and widespread revival in Lewis since the renowned awakening in Uig under the ministry of Rev. Alexander MacLeod in 1824'.[17] 'The revival in Carloway was followed

---

12. *ibid.* p.28.

13. MacRae, p.89.

14. Norman MacLeod (1988), *Lewis Revivals of the 20th Century*, Stornoway Hebridean Press Service, p. 9.

15. *ibid.* p.9

16. *ibid.* p.10

17. *ibid.* p.10

by similar movements in many districts throughout the island, namely in Bernera, Knock, Lochs, Kinloch, Park and Barvas.'[18]

Members of an older generation living in different parts of the island remember the 1939 revival beginning in different places. It certainly had some of its roots in Carloway Free Church under the ministry of Rev. MacIver. The churches were full, and concerning the Carloway scene, Murdo MacAulay reports:

As the movement had spread to other congregations such as Bernera, Park, Kinloch, Lochs, Knock, Barvas and Cross, the number of visitors gathering at the Communion season were enormous. The churches were full, and the solemnity at those services was awe-inspiring as the Word of God went as fiery darts to the consciences and hearts of the unconverted. Wherever the people met, whether in a house or on the road, at peats [the island fuel extracted from moorland], or in the fields, at fanks [sheep-pens], or on buses, the subject of conversation was the work of the Lord in our district and those who had been converted. Some families had four or five converted, others two or one, and a few, none at all. It is remarkable how dark some families remain even in the midst of a revival....I remember one house prayer meeting where seventeen, almost all recent converts, were called upon to engage in prayer. There was such an earnestness and a freshness about these prayers that they gripped the attention of all.

During church services both the minister and the congregation were so visibly moved that the services were veritable Bochims. Some showed signs of great concern and some signs of distress as the Law of God pricked the conscience, constraining them to say, as at Pentecost, 'Men and brethren, what shall we do?' They were thus very reluctant to depart from the church after the service and often sang some verses of their favourite psalms outside the main door of the church, so that the sound of their uplifted praise echoed throughout the surrounding village. What joy was experienced by the Lord's people when these new converts appeared in the prayer meeting!

By the end of the revival there were unusual prostrations, which came mainly as a result of a visit by a busload of young converts and a few old Christians to Shader, Barvas, where raising of hands and praying aloud, almost shouting, had become the custom....When the revival ended the prostrations ended too, and the subjects affected became excellent witnesses for their Master.

The effect on the life and conversation of the young converts was remarkable – a hatred of sin, an abandonment of their former lifestyle, a longing for holiness, with a dread of bringing any blemish on the cause of Christ. They often brought truths which they did not understand to their elders, and very

---

18. *ibid.* p.13

often had clear answers to their problems from the pulpit, so that they felt sure that someone had informed the minister![19]

The widespread 1939 revival was unique in that in various places there was no specific preacher of whom one could say that he featured in the movement. It began in prayer and continued in prayer. It was led by laymen. People would come together in homes and sometimes in churches and meeting halls as the Holy Spirit constrained them, and as the leading elders would arrange.

The 1939 revival was much wider and more influential than the 1949 revival in which Duncan Campbell was involved. It was also unique in that there were far more manifestations in the 1939 revival than the 1949 revival. In fact in the 1949 revival Duncan Campbell sometimes gently rebuked excesses in the meetings.

The 1939 revival in the Barvas, Shader area began when a group of believers went to Point, where the fire was burning brightly, for a communion season. They were greatly blessed and refreshed. On their return journey on the bus, people noticed a young man who was visibly moved and under conviction of sin. This event sparked off a desire for cottage meetings and that evening the local blacksmith, John Smith, sent two young girls through the village (for at that time there were no telephones), with an invitation to each household to gather for a prayer meeting in his home.

The people came and a remarkable movement of the Spirit broke out among them. The meetings continued and soon the house was too small to accommodate the crowds. The Free Church building was not far away so it became the venue for the services. Soon it too became too small. The pews were crammed and some people had to stand. Some sat on the window ledges and on the pulpit steps. There was no awareness of denominational barriers. Believers were united in one desire and passion for the lost. Missionaries of the two main denominations occupied the pulpit and shared in the services. Hearts were bound together in the love of Christ and a great work was done in many lives.

The work continued and many were wonderfully transformed by the working of the Holy Spirit in their lives and by the influence of the revival in the community as a whole.

---

19. MacAulay, *The Burning Bush in Carloway*, p. 33.

Kenina MacLeod (1938 +)

In an article called *Kenina Remembers*, Kenina MacLeod recalls the day when Sandy Mor, who was greatly used in the movements of the Spirit in Point, was converted as Rev. William Campbell preached in the church in Point. She, as did many others, recalls the night when he preached on Ezekiel 37:1 and the resultant blessing.

She says that a revival began in 1937 in South Lochs and on the West Side of Lewis. 'These revivals were very unusual with prostrations, raising of hands and praying out loud. The revival in South Lochs spread to North Lochs where many young men and women were converted. A wave of spiritual blessing passed over these parishes, and many of the older Christians were refreshed as well.... The revival was at its height in the spring of 1938.'

Her husband to be, then a young school teacher, returned from Lochs to Point and organized a prayer meeting in his sister's home that evening. That very night in the packed house God broke through. 'Soon there were many crying out aloud and some prostrate – the same symptoms as on the West Side, and in Lochs.

'After that night meetings were held in other houses and people gathered from other villages. Rev. W. Campbell and Rev. H. MacKinnon of the Church of Scotland attended the meetings, and rejoiced to see young men and women crying for mercy.

'It is very difficult to describe the spirit in these meetings, and especially the singing.... There were many who were sceptical. They remained bitter and censorious, and lost the blessing. They wanted others to start in the same way as they had; any other way was wrong.

'Ministers from both the Free Church and the Church of Scotland were there, and the two churches were like one – except for those who did not believe that it was the work of the Spirit.

'In a nearby village there were some who had been assisting Rev. William Campbell with their prayers for a revival. One day in April a few of them were discussing the revival led by Sandy Mor. He decided that they would hold a meeting, but it would be in a part of the village where there were not many Christians. The woman of the house was the first to go into a trance. Then there was sobbing from many, especially three sisters, one of whom seemed to have convulsions. The elder asked the deacon to pray. The poor man was startled at the commotion and truthfully said, 'O Lord, You know that we were praying for revival – but not like this!' Then he stopped and began again. He praised the Lord because he knew that, although the happenings were unusual, it was the Spirit of the Lord who was present.

'Sometimes more than one house meeting was held on the same evening. There seemed to be a thirst to hear the Word of God, and for the prayers and the singing.... At Communion times, the converts from Lochs and the West Side came. New friendships were made. There was a joy and warmth in these friendships which never died.

'Those who are still living today who frequented these meetings have never forgotten the atmosphere.... Our hearts were so full then! How good to remember the days when our hearts melted under the preaching of the gospel and Christ was made so precious to us and we wished to do something for Him.'

The War

Then came the war in 1939, and some of the lads saved in these meetings were to go and never return. Meetings continued in some places in Lewis during the war, not with the same intensity as in the 1939 movement but nevertheless with nostalgia, desire, hope and prayer for revival to break out again. The war ended in 1945 and the desires of the people were quickened so that by 1949 there were intense and earnest prayers in a number of places for the Lord to come and pour out His Spirit once again. It was at this time that the Lord sent Duncan Campbell to Lewis.

The 1949 Revival

Even before Duncan Campbell came, there was much prayer in Shader and Barvas and the Spirit was moving, saving souls months before his meetings in Barvas in December 1949. The 1949 revival was thus almost a sort-of continuation of a revival which had been interrupted by the sad events in Europe.

Rev. A. MacDonald, a former minister of Ness, reminds us that there, in December 1949, Rev. MacSween from Broadford in Skye held a mission in a packed church situated in the village of Cross. MacSween's brother, a headmaster from Skye, came a few weeks later and held another series of meetings there. In February, MacSween returned for more special meetings. Three missions in so short a space of time! There was a tremendous hunger as the people crowded in, filling the church as they sought the Lord at all these meetings. The Spirit of God was certainly moving in the island. There was an expectancy, an intensity of prayer and a sure hope that God, whom they had known to have worked in revival in the past, would not disappoint them now. Duncan Campbell was at this very time seeing the Spirit poured out in power fifteen miles south in Barvas and Shader at the outset of the movement. Campbell was to come to Ness in both 1950 and 1951 and God was to take a harvest at this time when He manifested Himself in power and glory.

Rev. Kenneth MacDonald tells us that the same thing happened in the isle of Bernera, for even before Duncan Campbell came to the island the power and presence of the Lord were intense in meetings which were filled with believers and unbelievers alike. The revival had not even begun but the whole scene was fully prepared for the great Harvester to put in the sickle for the harvest was ripe. 'It only needs a spark!' as Rev. James Murray MacKay said of Barvas. When Duncan came it was to a people prepared, eager and ready to respond to the gospel challenge and invitation.

The 1949 revival, in which Duncan Campbell figured prominently, was widespread. He was not invited to any Free Church service, so all his preaching was in the smaller denomination in the island, the Church of Scotland. Many Free Church people who felt free to attend the meetings in the Church of Scotland were deeply blessed and a number were saved, but the Free Church people in general were not encouraged to attend. Some did not venture to the church but nevertheless attended the less offensive cottage meetings, where a great deal of the revival work was done.

Later Movements

There were some fruitful times in some congregations in Lewis after 1953, but these were localised and confined to limited areas. There were movements in the Free Church in 1960 in Callanish and after that also in the Free Churches in Back and Knock.[20]

Under the ministry of Rev. Murdo MacRitchie in the Free Church of Stornoway, numbers came to Christ between 1970 to 1974, and later again from 1983 to 1987, under the ministry of Rev. Murdo Alex MacLeod, numbers of new communicants were added to the church. There was blessing too in the 'High Church of Scotland, Stornoway, in the 1990s under the ministry of Rev. Roddy Morrison. But this did not necessarily mean that the power and glory of God were released as has been described by those who testify elsewhere in the book. Here the sense of the presence of God was not widespread and overpowering.

The movement in Lemreway in 1969 in the Church of Scotland, to

---

20. MacLeod, *Lewis Revivals of the 20th Century*, p.16.

which Rev D. MacAulay refers in his testimony, did have the characteristic of that overwhelming sense of God invading the atmosphere, and the term 'revival' would be wholly appropriate in this case.

The last of the widespread movements in Lewis was the 1949-53 movement which began in Barvas and Shader, and in which Duncan Campbell was involved. It was a great pity that the churches did not co-operate and unite in their common desire to see the Spirit of the Lord poured out in all their churches.

Chapter 4

The Life and Ministry of Duncan Campbell

The name of Duncan Campbell is inextricably linked to the movement of the Spirit on the Isle of Lewis from December 1949 to 1953. On one occasion he was billed as 'the man who brought revival to Lewis'. He was extremely upset about this, and so declared strongly on many occasions: 'I did not bring revival to Lewis. Revival was already in Lewis before I came. I thank God that I had the privilege of being there, and, in some small measure leading the movement for about three years, but God moved in the parish of Barvas before I ever set foot on the island.' That statement is completely accurate.

In the research that we have done about this revival in conversation with the people who were there at the time, not one ever mentioned the name of Duncan Campbell until asked. Whilst Duncan Campbell was there and was undoubtedly used in the work of God, taking a leading role in the revival, other preachers were used as well. People were so conscious of the workings of the Spirit that that was the dominant factor. They all majored on the presence of God in the meetings and on the atmosphere that prevailed everywhere. Campbell was often away from the island and on such occasions other preachers simply continued with the ministry and God continued to work. The Communion seasons were great times of blessing.

Doors were open to Campbell in all the Church of Scotland pulpits in Lewis and Harris. He was able to move around from place to place because he did not have a church and congregation of his own where he would be obliged to minister Sunday by Sunday and was therefore free to accept invitations from different parishes.

Because he played such a vital role in the movement, and because interest in him is still strong, we will give a summary of his life and ministry.

His conversion

Duncan Campbell was born on 13th February, 1898, on a croft called Camusliath in the parish of Ardchattan, in the Black Crofts area just north of Oban on the west coast of Scotland. But he experienced the new birth when he was fifteen. It happened like this.

He was away from home, helping someone with practical work in Corpach near Fort William, but returned home to play the bagpipes at a dance in December 1913. During an interlude he played by request, a well-known Scottish tune, *The Green Hills of Tyrol*. Suddenly an amazing thing happened. He was transported, not to the hills of Austria or Scotland, but to the hill called Calvary. Disturbed in mind, he left the dance dressed in his full Scottish regalia to walk the few miles to his home.

On the way he had to pass a small Memorial Hall, and as he approached he saw that there was a light in the hall. How could there be a light in the hall at eleven o'clock at night? He listened at the door to hear the voice of his own father in prayer. He left his bagpipes and dancing swords in the entrance and slipped in beside his father. Two Faith Mission workers, Mary Graham and Jessie Mowat, both from Scotland, were holding a mission in the hall, and he had stumbled in on a night of prayer which some of the Christians were holding with the workers. Mary rose and began to speak on 'God speaketh once, yea twice, yet man perceiveth it not' (Job 33:14). The young intruder was overcome with conviction and soon left, taking his bagpipes and swords with him. On the way home he dropped on his knees time and again in an agony of conviction.

He arrived home about 2 am and to his surprise he again found a light burning. His mother had been unable to go to the prayer meeting but she was on her knees in the house. He poured out his heart to his mother. She counselled him and, because relatives had unexpectedly arrived, advised him to go to the barn and 'tell God what you have told me'. He did so, and in his own words he said, 'Lord, I know not what to do, I know not how to come, but if You'll take me as I am, I'm coming now.' Back in the house he told his mother and together they knelt and praised the Lord for His marvellous salvation. Duncan had had a mighty saving encounter with the living God which transformed his life.

About this time Archibald and Margaret Gray and their family moved into the district. Their youngest daughter was called Shona and even at this time Duncan set his eye upon her. In later years she would become his wife and the mother of their five children.

The Faith Mission continued to conduct missions in that area and

Duncan attended these stirring and challenging meetings. He grew in grace and in the knowledge of the Lord Jesus Christ.

The years passed and over Europe the clouds of war were threatening. Duncan responded to the country's call and saw active service in France. He was in the cavalry division, and in April 1918 took part in one of the last cavalry charges of the British Army. At the command they advanced but in a moment he had his horse shot from under him and he lay severely wounded on the field of battle. A second charge was ordered and the Canadian Horse surged forward. A horse's hoof struck Duncan in the spine and he groaned. That groan saved his life for the young Canadian returned, threw him across his horse and galloped to the nearest Casualty Clearing Station. In that weak state he had a mighty encounter with God and in the joy of this new experience he quoted Scripture in Gaelic. Soon a deep conviction of sin gripped the men and no fewer than seven Canadians trusted Christ for salvation.

The 1920s – Days of Revival

He returned to his home and during the period of convalescence he prayed with people in their homes and encouraged many to seek the Lord. The hand of the Lord was upon him and the call of God within him. He was drawn to the Faith Mission and was accepted as a student in their Bible College and Training Home in Edinburgh. It was then a one-year course. After completing this year Duncan entered the ranks of the Mission on 1st July 1920. After a brief spell in Northern Ireland, he was sent to the Highlands of Scotland where he laboured for the next five years.

In Great Britain the 1920s were days of great spiritual blessing and harvesting, especially the first part of the decade. It was then that the great and unique Irish evangelist, W.P.Nicholson, began his ministry in Ireland with a campaign in Bangor in 1920. In May 1921, he moved to Portadown where 900 people professed faith in Christ, and there his great missions really began. He went to Lurgan in September where over 1,000 professed, and then to Newtownards, and on to Lisburn where 1,950 souls were saved. On to Belfast, Londonderry, Ballymena and other places where thousands of people were swept into the kingdom. His last great campaign of that period was that held in the Assembly Hall in Belfast throughout the month of August 1925, where he spoke to capacity crowds, and hundreds sought the Saviour.

With such an enormous flood-tide of blessing sweeping through Ulster, many sought God in places other than at the Nicholson meetings. The

Faith Mission workers experienced waves of blessing in so many of their campaigns all over the province. There was an awakening all over the North of Ireland.

In 1921, revival broke out in Yarmouth, England, where thousands of fishermen and women were gathered from north-east Scotland for the season, following the annual movement of the herring around the British coast. Rev. Douglas Brown was used in this great awakening which swept the coast of England around Yarmouth, and for two years he laboured ceaselessly preaching to thousands and leading many to Christ.

The fisherfolk had written home to those on the north-east coast of Scotland telling of God's mighty deeds and pleading with them to yield to the Saviour. Scotland was now astir. In October 1921, God directed a Scots cooper, Jock Troup, to leave Yarmouth, where he was with the fisherfolk, and go to Fraserburgh in the north-east of Scotland. He preached along the coast bringing blessing wherever he went and was greatly used in this enormous upsurge of religious revival.

Others entered into the labours and the fire burned all around the coast from Eyemouth, south of Edinburgh, through Cockenzie, Port Seton, Musselburgh and along the small towns to the north of the Firth of Forth. In the villages of Cairnbulg, Inverallochy and St. Combs, out of a population of 1,500, over 600 professed salvation in two weeks. At Portsoy and the surrounding areas about 400 souls were saved at that time. At Peterhead 600 souls professed salvation, at Wick 300, at Hopeman 140. Fraserburgh, Lossiemouth and nearly all the fishing towns along the coast were deeply affected when thousands were brought to Christ. This was no mere superficial emotional upsurge but was a genuine work of the Holy Spirit. Ministers rejoiced in what God was evidently doing and churches swelled with the converts. It has stood the test of time. God worked mightily in these areas.

J.B. McLean, Director of the Faith Mission in Ireland, reported at the close of 1922: 'The revival began last year in some parts of the country, and how we longed for it to spread. We have not been disappointed, for, as we look over our statistics, we find that the results of the year just closed are more than double those of last year and far surpass anything we have previously known.'

In 1923 the Faith Mission had several great missions which took on the characteristics of revival. Pilgrims (as the workers were known) found themselves in the revival tide and shared in the harvest. At Balintore in Easter Ross in Scotland, the mission lasted almost seventeen weeks and 230 people trusted Christ for salvation. Two male workers named McKie and Young began preaching there on 17th December 1922, and ended on 1st April 1923, with amazing results. At Jerrettspass in County Armagh in Northern Ireland, 100 surrendered to the claims of Christ. At Hillsborough, Corlea, Maralin, Ballyrobin, Corby and a number of other places the Faith Mission workers had the privilege of seeing the out-poured blessings of God. In Ireland alone that year 3,602 meetings were held in the Faith Mission work, and that apart from the numerous open-air meetings. There were almost ninety workers in the Faith Mission that year. In his 1923 Annual Report, Mr. Govan, the Founder of the Mission said, 'Statistics will show that this year has been one of the most fruitful and successful in the Mission's history.'

It was in this general atmosphere of anticipation, living hope, expectant joy and vibrant blessing that Duncan Campbell began his ministry in the Faith Mission. In his almost five years in the Faith Mission, which were in this revival period, he, with different colleagues, conducted about thirty missions, all in the Highlands and Islands of Scotland, with the exception of those first few months in Ireland. He was therefore one of those whom God used in so many places in Scotland at that time to gather in the harvest during this revival period when God was so evidently pouring out His Spirit. During that time Campbell saw movements of the Spirit in Ardnamurchan in Argyllshire and in the Isle of Skye. He spent most of 1924 on Skye working with two men, firstly with Fleck and then with Scott. The Lord wonderfully blessed their labours as they worked from village to village. 'Times of Revival in the Isle of Skye' is the title of a report of their work in the *Bright Words* magazine.

Pastoral Ministry

It was from Skye that Campbell retired from the Faith Mission in April 1925, eventually resigning in July 1925, and marrying a few months later, in December. He was asked to care for a small United Free Church in the village of Ardvasar, Skye, where he became the church missionary. In 1930 he was ordained as the missionary to the newly formed United Free Church in Balintore, where eight years earlier a great revival had taken place. His caring ministry, particularly amongst the youth, was greatly appreciated. He was not a trained theologian but a down-to-earth practical one and as such was loved by the congregation which he served so well. In March 1940, he accepted a call to the United Free Church in Falkirk, and after two years there was ordained to the ministry in recognition of the good work that he had done during the past number of years.

In spite of all the excellent pastoral ministry that he had given to the three churches he had served, and although his preaching had been appreciated not only in these churches but also in other meetings to which he had been invited, he felt that he could now be out of the will of God. Somewhere he had lost out spiritually. What should he do? To retrace his steps to the Faith Mission would be a huge move. Would the Faith Mission accept him with his large family? Financially, he would be going from a salaried position as a minister back to 'faith' work. How could he ask his family to share the sacrifice that he would make? What else could he do? He described his heart's condition as 'a barren wilderness' in which he had been 'for years', and felt that he had to make a move from his present situation. This was undoubtedly one of the great crises of his life.

Encounter with God

Campbell, together with Dr. Thomas Fitch, was speaking at the Edinburgh Convention for the deepening of spiritual life. He says: 'As I sat listening to Dr. Fitch giving his last message, I suddenly became conscious of my unfitness to be on that platform. I saw the barrenness of my life and ministry. I saw the pride of my own heart. How very humiliating it was to discover that I was proud of the fact that I was booked to speak at five conventions that year! That night in desperation on the floor of my study, I cast myself afresh on the mercy of God. He heard my cry for pardon and cleansing, and, as I lay prostrate before Him, wave after wave of divine consciousness came over me, and the love of the Saviour flooded my being; and in that hour I knew that my life and ministry could never be the same again...If in any small measure God has been pleased to use me, it is all because of what He did for me that night.'[1]

Campbell remembered that his young daughter Sheena had asked him, 'Daddy, God used you in revival in the past; how is it that you are not seeing revival now?' The question devastated him. Alone with God that night, in a kind of trance he saw thousands from the Highlands and Islands of Scotland going to hell. He had to go to them. There, in the presence of God, he went through an upheaval of enormous dimensions. This was a pivotal point in his life. The battle was on. It was a night of encounter with the Almighty. God touched his life once again and restored him to full fellowship and blessing. He would ever after say how glad he was that God was a God of new beginnings.

---

1. Duncan Campbell (1964), *God's Standard*, The Faith Mission, p.61

Duncan now had no choice but to obey God's leading, resign from his present position and trust God for the future. He wrote letters of resignation and also approached the Faith Mission. The Faith Mission Council was very cautious for they were reluctant to receive a man of fifty years of age with a family. Eventually all the pieces of the jigsaw fell into place and Duncan returned to the Mission on 1st January 1949. A house was acquired for him and his family in Edinburgh and it was from there that he began an evangelistic programme in the Highlands.

It was to the Isle of Skye, from where he had left the Mission, that he returned. In fact, during 1949, execpt for meetings which he had on the mainland, he was involved entirely in missions on Skye, apart from leaving it for a campaign in Barvas on the Isle of Lewis in December. This, of course, was the beginning of the Lewis revival.

Request from Barvas

Because there were so many requests for him to minister at different places, the Faith Mission Headquarters handled his bookings for him and in conjunction with him. When an invitation came for him to minister in the Church of Scotland parish church in Barvas in December,[2] the General Secretary, Percy Bristow, informed Campbell about it, but said that he thought that he should not take the meetings as he was already booked up with so many other engagements. On 3rd October 1949, Campbell wrote to Percy Bristow as follows from Staffin: 'I have written to the Rev. James McKay, Barvas, to say that I am not free to visit Lewis this winter, but hope to do so at a later date, if the door is still open. I take this decision as guidance in the matter, although I must say, it goes against my own leading and judgment. I am however content to rest in your decision, and leave the issues in higher hands.'

Rev James Murray MacKay had actually invited Rev Tom Fitch to speak at these meetings. At the Strathpeffer Convention Fitch informed Mr. MacKay that he could not come but suggested that he should invite Duncan Campbell instead. Duncan could now say, 'I cross to Lewis tomorrow to begin a short mission at Barvas.'

On Wednesday, 7th December 1949, Duncan Campbell crossed on the ferry to the Isle of Lewis. He had never been there before and this visit was to change his life. On 9th December 1949, he wrote: 'I have made a very

---

2. In addition to the communion seasons on the islands, all the churches had a short evangelistic mission each winter called the *Orduighean Beag* or 'little communion'. It was to this Orduighean Beag that Duncan Campbell was invited in the Barvas church.

good beginning here. God is already at work and the opportunity is great but the strain is very heavy. It seems to me that we are on the verge of something grand and glorious here. I just regret my time is so short. I understand that a Conference is being arranged in Stornoway for my last Saturday. As far as I know I shall be leaving Lewis on Friday 23rd December. My next mission is to be in Staffin, Skye, on January 15th.'

Little did he realise that the Lord had purposed to cancel his plans and to keep him on the island of Lewis for longer than he had anticipated for His own great glory.

Ministry after the Awakening

After the three years spent largely on Lewis in the midst of revival, Campbell was much in demand as a speaker and was invited to many churches and conventions all over the British Isles. In 1958 he was appointed as principal of the Faith Mission Bible College in Edinburgh where he remained for nine years. His time there was owned of God and it left a very evident mark on the students. He was held in high esteem in Christian circles all over the country and this had a considerable impact on the College and the Mission as a whole. To some extent he left the running of the College to the staff, and focused on the numerous invitations which came to him from different places. He retired in 1967, but continued to respond to the many invitations for ministry. During Easter 1972, he crossed to Switzerland to speak at a convention there, and it was at this convention, in the midst of ministry, that he passed on to his heavenly reward.

* * * * * * * *

Duncan Campbell was in itinerant ministry when Mary trained at the Faith Mission Bible College, and Mr John Eberstein was in charge at the College. Mary had been in the Lewis Awakening and was united in spirit with all those who knew the mighty workings of the Lord at that time. There is still a wonderful spontaneous understanding and an affinity of spirit with those who are, as it were, the 'children of the revival'.

As she and other workers of the Faith Mission laboured, Campbell would, on occasions, minister with them at conferences, conventions and, sometimes, at missions. Because of Duncan's love for the Highlands and Islands, and because Mary with others, particularly Jean Wilson, worked a great deal in that area, they would at times call on Duncan to come and help them. Mary speaks Gaelic, which was a further bond between them in the ministry, for Gaelic-speaking Scots are clannish. The workers loved, respected and worked gladly with him as he threw himself wholeheartedly into the battle with them. The workers, with Duncan, frequently touched the throne together in prayer.

In 1957 Campbell, even though he was not in the best of health, went to South Africa on a preaching tour . He was speaking at a campaign in the city of Pretoria, when one afternoon and evening a great burden descended on Mary in Britain for him in Africa. She went apart and prayed and immediately wrote to him enquiring if anything was wrong, naming the day and time that she had been so burdened for him. At that precise time he had been on the platform in Pretoria and was in the middle of a message when he suffered a severe haemorrhage and had to be rushed to hospital straight from the platform. It was an amazing communication across 6,000 miles. It reached one so close to him in spirit who would be able and willing to pray effectively for him at the very moment when he so desperately needed prayer.

In 1972 Mary and I came to Britain for six months. In all that time we had an average of a meeting every day. Travelling with two babies was an adventure, to say the least. We arrived in Scotland two days after Mr. Campbell had left for Switzerland to speak at a YWAM Conference. We were disappointed to have missed him but expected nevertheless to meet him in due course in our travels.

Soon afterwards, when at Mary's sister's home in Clifford St., Glasgow, one day she began to weep. She wept for anything and everything. 'What's the matter?' I asked.

'I don't know,' she replied.

'Have I done any thing wrong?'

'No,' she replied.

'Then, why are you crying?'

'I don't know,' she said, and wept again. In fact she wept all day.

The next day we discovered that Duncan Campbell had died in Switzerland the previous day.

Such things might seem beyond explanation. Without realizing that these two had both seen God work in power, both breathed one spirit and were bound together in the Holy Ghost in oneness of heart, mind, objective and purpose in the service of God for His glory.

One humorous incident could be told. Duncan was ill and the reports reached Skye that he was dead. One concerned Christian wrote to him saying, 'Mr Campbell, we hear that you have died so I am just writing to you to find out whether this is true.' When Mary heard it she laughed out loud and said, with a twinkle in her eye, 'To what address did he send it?!'

As far as can be determined from Mr. Campbell's weekly reports submitted to the Faith Mission HQ. the following is the record of his main ministry during the time of the revival.

1949

23 Sept. – 29 Oct. Staffin, Isle of Skye.
9 Nov. – 6 Dec. Culnaknock, Isle of Skye.

7 – 22 Dec. Barvas, Isle of Lewis.

1950

8 – 25 Jan. Barvas, Lewis.
26 – 31 Jan. Ness, Lewis.
22 Feb. – 12 Mar. Carloway, Lewis.
23 – 31 Mar. Galson, Lewis.
1 & 2 Apr. Skye.
23 – 14 May Arnol, Lewis (also some meetings
   in Ness).

16 – 28 May Tarbert, Harris.
11 – 28 June Leverburgh, Harris
29 – 5 July Visit to Lewis
31 Oct. – 5 Nov. Visit to Barvas, Shader, Ness, Arnol, Uig.
6 – 22 Nov. Point, Lewis.
23 – 29 Nov. Harris
5 – 22 Dec. Barvas

1951

9 – 19 Jan. Bragar, Lewis.
25 – 31 Jan. Ness.
9 Feb. – 14 Mar. Kinloch & Leurbost, Lewis
15 Mar. – 2 Apr. Barvas, Uig, Bernera
   Communions
22 Apr. – 6 May Carloway

10 – 24 Aug. Isle of Bernera, (Lewis).
15 – 30 Sept. Barvas & Shader
11 Oct. – 14 Nov. Balli-na Cille (Uig)
15 – 19 Nov. Isle-of- N. Uist
5 – 18 Dec. Balli-na-Cille

1952

6 – 23 Jan. Stornoway
22 Feb. – 17 Mar. Callanish, Lewis.
19 – 29 Mar. Shawbost, Lewis
14 – 27 Apr. Isle–of-Berneray, Harris.
15 – 27 May Bernera, Crulivig, Callanish, Arnol, Shader, Ness.

17 – 27 Oct. Some places formerly worked; also meetings in Galson.
28 Oct. – 12 Nov. Leverburgh, Harris.
13 – 18 Nov. Callanish, Arnol, Ness

1953

27 Jan. – 2 Feb. Visits to different places
on Lewis
3 – 13 Feb. Habost, Lochs, (Lewis)
3 – 16 Mar. Uig area
17 – 21 Mar. Ness

27 Apr. – 3 May Bernera, Lewis
6 – 17 May Berneray, Harris
14 – 20 Aug. Uig, Bernera, Barvas, Arnol.
21 – 31 Aug. Gravir, Lewis.

Chapter 5

Duncan Campbell's Revival Reports (1949-1950)

From the Faith Mission Archives we obtained the *Pilgrim News* letters and extracted all Duncan Campbell's reports which were written from Skye and Lewis at the time of the revival in 1949 to 1953. This valuable material has never been seen in print before. We have taken relevant extracts from these reports and present them here, with explanatory information bracketed in italics.

He writes from Culnaknock, Skye, on 7 December 1949 (Wednesday): 'I cross to Lewis tomorrow to begin a short mission at Barvas.' He must have written the letter on the 6th and dated it the 7th because he crossed over and began the mission on Wednesday 7th.

Barvas, Lewis, 14th December 1949

I began my mission on Wednesday night in the parish church. People gathered from all over the parish and we had a congregation of over 300. The meeting began at 7.00 and ended at 10.45 p.m. I preached twice during the evening. (*He obviously speaks of the meeting in the church as well as the house meeting immediately after the church meeting as one meeting.*) This was repeated on Thursday and Friday. Yesterday I preached in three different churches to crowded meetings. At the last meeting the Lord manifested His power in a gracious way, and the cry of the anxious was heard all over the church. I closed the service but the people would not go away, so I gathered the anxious ones beneath the pulpit and, along with the minister, did what we could to lead them to Christ.

21st December 1949

We are in the midst of glorious revival. God in His great mercy has been pleased to visit us with showers of blessing, and the desert is rejoicing and blossoming as the rose. Some of us will live to praise God for what our ears are hearing and our eyes are seeing these days in Lewis. Meetings are crowded, right up the pulpit steps. On several nights the meetings continued until 3.00 and 4.00 o'clock in the morning in the homes. Already about seventy adults have professed; we are dealing with anxious souls in every meeting. Last night at our fifth service, just as the people were leaving, a young man began to cry for mercy at the gate leading from the church. Just then an elder began to sing the 102nd psalm and the whole congregation took it up, singing verses 13-16. The congregation then came back into the church and before we dispersed twelve men and women sought the Saviour. It is with a heavy heart I leave for home this week, but this work will go on.

After two weeks in Barvas, Duncan went home to Edinburgh for a short Christmas break and returned to Barvas early in the new year for a further two weeks, and yet another week working with Rev. Murdo MacLennan from Carloway in both Barvas and nearby Shader.

18th January 1950

Revival fires are spreading, and at present it looks as though other parts of Lewis are coming under its sway. Buses and vans are bringing the people from all over the island, and each night men and women from other parishes are seeking the Saviour. Six sought the Lord between one and two o'clock this morning; last night was our greatest meeting yet. The message was from Zechariah 9:12, and many 'prisoners of hope' found deliverance. I shall greatly value prayer this week as I am addressing meetings each night in two different parishes twelve miles apart.

25th January 1950

This has been another week of 'God's right hand'. Meetings have been larger than ever; hundreds have been crowded in, and many turned away. I may say, I am now at it night and day, and just getting sleep when I can. The largest meetings are now in the parish of Ness. This is part of Lewis that is thickly populated and, praise God, it is gripped by revival. Among the men who sought God last night there were two pipers who were to be playing at a dance in Carloway that night. At the beginning of this week, buses came to collect people for a concert in the town; they had to return empty for not one person went.

1st February 1950

I have been greatly assisted this week by other ministers, two of them sharing the preaching with me, especially in the night meetings (*i.e. the house meetings*), so that I was able to rest a good deal. Meetings continue to be crowded and souls are being saved every day, with some outstanding cases.

In my last report I mentioned two pipers being saved, who were to have been at a concert and dance that night. A minister from the district where the dance was held, and who was in the meeting, felt led of God to go home and visit the dance and tell what had happened. He did so, arriving there at 3 o'clock in the morning. After some opposition from the leader he was allowed in; he there and then gave out Psalm 50, the last three verses. God's Spirit fell upon the gathering and in less than ten minutes men and women were crying for mercy. The first to be saved was the leader of the concert party. This is just another incident of the many wonderful things happening here just now. This week I shall be visiting four different centres where revival has broken out, and I shall value prayer. This, I think, will be my last report before returning to Edinburgh.

Carloway, Lewis, 22nd February 1950

I arrived back in Lewis on Wednesday of last week. My crossing of the Minch was an experience which I would not like to describe. I certainly was not in a very fit state to address two meetings, one at 9 o'clock and one at 11.00 p.m. Here, as in the other districts, the Spirit of God is at work, although so far we have not experienced the revival blessing that is sweeping the other side of the island, but we believe it is coming.

1st March 1950

I am writing this report at 2 o'clock in the morning. Revival has come to this parish and meetings continue until the small hours of the morning. Among those saved last night, there was a nurse from the Royal Infirmary, Edinburgh, the daughter of the parish minister. One other interesting feature is that all our meetings are crowded with Free Church people. The enemy is at work; pray that he may be defeated.

8th March 1950

This has been another wonderful week of crowded meetings, and souls seeking the Saviour. The crowds this weekend resembled Bangor on Monday of the convention (*i.e. the great Faith Mission Easter Convention in Bangor, Northern Ireland*). I counted fourteen buses (*could be buses and vans*) this morning, with twice that number of cars (*there were very few cars around in those days*). I addressed five meetings today. We simply cannot get the people away and meetings will continue until tomorrow morning. People are here from every parish in Lewis and Harris. Practically every house in Carloway has visitors who have come to stay for the weekend (*this was probably the communion weekend when staying over was common*). Revival has gripped much of the island.

15ᵗʰ March 1950

My mission at Carloway closed on Tuesday. We had large crowds right up to the end, and the same deep conviction as in every part visited. We had conversions up to the end of the mission. I am at present resting in Harris, before opening my next mission in the parish of Ness. Here, as in Lewis, God is at work. I was asked to address a meeting at noon today and fully 800 people gathered, some coming long distances, even from Lewis. Requests for missions already made would keep me going for the next three years.

Galson, Lewis, 22ⁿᵈ March 1950

I begin my mission in Galson, Ness, tomorrow night. This is the only district that the revival has not touched, except for the school-master and his wife and son (*Alan and Jack MacArthur's parents*). They were converted during the Barvas mission. Mr. Black (*of the Faith Mission*) will be with me a week today. I am looking forward to having him.

29ᵗʰ March 1950

We are in the midst of the greatest move yet. The Spirit of God is mightily at work, and many have come to the Saviour. I am writing this report in the early hours of the morning, having dealt with the last lot of anxious ones at 1.30 a.m. Pray that the Lord may undertake and give guidance, as I am due to leave Lewis on Friday, and the work is just beginning here. Mr. Black joins me tonight. I am looking forward very much to his coming.

5ᵗʰ April 1950

Mr. Black and I were in the midst of blessed revival scenes right up to the end. So great was the interest during the past week that it was necessary to hold an afternoon meeting in the parish church of Ness. Here as well as at Galson, God is mightily at work. So great is their conviction of sin, that strong men have even fainted behind their looms (*for making Harris Tweed*). The night meetings have been crowded out and people turned away.

The past weekend was spent in Skye. God has been doing a very blessed work there. The conference at Kilmuir, Skye, was one of the best I have attended for years.

Edinburgh, 19ᵗʰ April 1950

News keeps coming from Lewis of crowded meetings and souls seeking the Saviour. I leave Edinburgh this week to begin my next mission at Arnol, where already God is at work.

Arnol, Lewis, 26ᵗʰ April 1950

I began my mission here in Arnol in the midst of the most bitter opposition. Opposition meetings are being held about 200 yards from the church in which I hold my meetings. But in the midst of it all God is mightily at work, and the revival is spreading. My main difficulty here is accommodation; we were crowded out last night notwithstanding the fact that the island was swept with a snow storm. In view of this, it may be necessary for me to leave Arnol and go to a central district where we can have a larger church. Pray that I may be guided aright in this matter. (*The meetings in Arnol were held in the church hall, for there is no church there.*)

10ᵗʰ May 1950

We are in the midst of a glorious revival here. Opposition has vanished, and the whole district is moved. People are being saved at work, and in shops work is being suspended, churches are crowded, and crowds outside. People were coming to the meeting last night bringing their own chairs to sit on outside. So deep the distress of many, that we had to remain helping them until the morning.

Tarbert, Harris, 17ᵗʰ May 1950

I came to Harris in the hope of getting a few days' rest before beginning my mission, but so great was the interest and expectation that I had to begin on the very first day of my arrival, and already I am preaching to crowded meetings. The closing meetings at Arnol and Ness were mighty. (*It was in these meetings that Mary sought the Saviour.*) Services were held in the afternoon, evening, and on to the small hours of the morning. My last meeting in Ness spilled out into the open air after the house meeting and it finished just as the dawn was breaking. This past fortnight was, I believe, the most fruitful of the revival; one interesting feature was the number in the middle age who found the Saviour. Our arrangements are now complete for the weekend conference in Stornoway; the dates are June 2nd to 5th.

24th May 1950

This has been another week of very blessed meetings. I held meetings in six different centres, and in each place the spirit of revival is abroad with souls seeking the Saviour. Harris is very different from Lewis in this respect, that the townships are small and far apart, and there are districts where there are no roads or any means of transport. Yet our meetings are crowded and so deep is the interest that during my visit to a certain district all work was stopped, and the day regarded as a Sabbath; meetings were held during the day and at night. Yesterday, buses brought the people a certain distance, others came by boats, but most came over the hill and moor on foot. How blessed it is in these dark days to see God so manifestly at work; families are being saved and communities changed; and, best of all, God is glorified.

31st May 1950

Our hearts are full of praise to God for what our eyes have seen and our ears have heard this past week. The Spirit of God is moving in a mighty way in our midst, and each day men and women of all ages are coming to the Saviour. At a meeting in the early hours of this morning, fourteen adults were seeking the Saviour; a husband and wife and a local school teacher were among them. This blessed move in Harris clearly demonstrates that missions can be worked as effectively in summer as in winter, as seasons and seasonable work present no barrier when God is at work. I leave Harris on Monday, 29th, returning D.V. on June 10th, after the weekend Conference at Barvas and the Council meetings in Edinburgh. (*This letter was either dated wrongly, or dated in the report in Pilgrim News on the day on which it was received in Edinburgh.*)

Stornoway, Lewis, 7th June 1950

Mr. Black of the Faith Mission writes: 'The weekend Conference meetings have been times of rich and deep blessing. Attendance started with 400 and has since risen to 700, and on Sunday night every available seat in the Town Hall was occupied. Buses are continually bringing people from all parts of the island, and the meetings are full of grip and power, all the speakers giving of their best with acceptance. These meetings have been the means of breaking down much denominational prejudice and God is working among the people. The closing meeting is tonight, Monday, when we again look to the Lord for further triumph and victory.

'Mr. Campbell reports a good close at Tarbert, Harris, with over forty seeking the Lord for salvation. I continue here until Friday, amongst the Prayer Unions, and will be glad of prayer.'

14th June 1950

Mr. Black reports again: 'Mr Ellis Govan phoned to say he was back from a short weekend in Lewis with Mr. and Mrs. Duncan Campbell. There was a wonderful spirit in the meetings. People continued to get saved and much of the island has been blessed. He asks special prayer for Mr. Campbell as he begins his new mission.'

Leverburgh, Harris, 21st June 1950

This has been a week of hard fighting, but I believe victory is in sight. I have been up against strong opposition from the usual source, but my eyes are toward God, and already the enemy is yielding. My great difficulty is accommodation, as the church is too small for the crowds that are coming. Tomorrow, Sunday, we are taking the people by buses to a larger church five miles away, and we may have to do this every night; some very good cases. The meeting went on from 8 o'clock until 1.30 in the morning; it was really the first touch of revival here.

28th June 1950

This has been a very blessed week. The real break came on Thursday, and since then we have been in the midst of a very blessed move of the Spirit. Men and women have yielded to Christ in every meeting, as many as fifteen at a time, and meetings continuing until dawn, and then buses taking the people home. I closed my mission tonight in a crowded church, when again God made bare His arm in salvation. I leave for Lewis tomorrow, and will address meetings in Arnol, Ness and Barvas, before leaving Lewis on Wednesday night. I look back with gratitude to God for all I have witnessed of the mighty power of God during the past six months.

Monaghan, Southern Ireland

Mr. Campbell had a mission in Monaghan, Eire, during the last three weeks of August.

28ᵗʰ August 1950

He reports on the last week: 'Meetings have been well attended and we have had some blessed manifestations of God at work. On Tuesday we met at 7 o'clock and continued until 2 o'clock in the morning. I do not think that any of us who were present will forget this meeting. Men and women, convicted of their sin and failures, confessed openly to one another, and to God, masters confessing to servants, and servants to masters. Since then the ungodly have been awakened, and a number have sought and found the Saviour.

Partick, Glasgow, Scotland

Mr. Campbell had a campaign in a church in Partick during the first three weeks of October.

11ᵗʰ October 1950 (second week)

Interest continues to increase and a very blessed work is being done. Meetings are crowded every night. I believe that all the Highland congregations in the City are represented. Last Thursday I asked all who were seeking the Saviour to go to the hall of the church, and fifty-three went in. Since then we have had an average of twenty-five each night, some in terrible distress. I began English services this week, as well as Gaelic; we had 300 at an English service last night.

18ᵗʰ October 1950 (third week)

Interest and blessing continued right up to the end and we had great crowds over the weekend. I preached five times on Sabbath in the one church. We had men and women seeking the Saviour every night, some so distressed under the conviction of sin that it was impossible to deal with them. I now rest for ten days before going to Lewis.

Shader, Lewis, 1ˢᵗ November 1950

The communion season at Partick was a time of rich blessing; not for many years were such crowds seen. I was very sorry having to leave such a movement of the Spirit of God, but the work is in good hands. I am now in the island of Lewis and rejoicing to see the work of God going on. The three services which I conducted yesterday were full of the Presence of the Lord, and one soul sought the Saviour. I am to be in Shader until Wednesday, in Ness on Thursday, Arnol on Friday, and with the Faith Mission brothers at Uig over the weekend. I begin my mission at Point, on the 6ᵗʰ November.

8th November 1950

This has been a week of crowded meetings, of souls seeking the Saviour and of much joy among God's people. The revival spirit and blessing is as deep as ever on this side of the island. At Ness and Arnol we witnessed a greater manifestation of God than at any time during the past winter. I shall probably return to Barvas after Point, as Barvas church is large and central to three parishes. I enjoyed my visit to Uig; the brothers there are having a hard fight. I considered the weekend meeting very good, with deep conviction. I begin at Point tonight.

15th November 1950

We have had a good week here, but not revival so far. While we are having very large meetings and souls seeking and finding the Saviour each night, the community is not yet stilled as in revival, but there are signs that it is near; during the weekend we had as many as twenty seeking the Saviour at one meeting, and I addressed four meetings between Sunday and Monday morning.

22nd November 1950

As I sit down to write this report the words of Psalm 107 come to my mind, 'Oh that men would praise the Lord for His goodness.' We are in the midst of revival, and what scenes! The whole district is stirred. I counted eight buses taking the people to church today, not to mention cars and vans — crowded meetings and men and women finding the Saviour. One farmer from Canada was heard to say, 'I had to come home to my native island to find my Saviour.' Men who never went to church, and who were regarded as hopeless, have been gloriously saved. In one community all the young men are saved or in deep distress of soul. I shall value prayer for guidance. I am being pressed to return to this district, but other places are waiting for me to fulfill my promise to them. I leave Point on Wednesday, 22nd, and go to Harris for a week.

Lewis and Harris, 29th November 1950

Our mission at Point closed amidst scenes of revival, meetings continuing all through the night, with souls being saved at each meeting. I hope to return to this district, but meantime meetings are being held all over the parish by Free Church and Church of Scotland ministers and missionaries. During the past week I have been assisting at a communion in Harris. God is mightily at work here. I never in my life witnessed such crowds in the

Highlands. The people came from all over Harris; it was reckoned 300 came for the whole period, apart from the people of the parish. No church building was big enough, so overflow meetings had to be arranged. Conviction and distress of soul was very evident, and one meeting for dealing with the anxious went on until 3 o'clock in the morning.

Barvas, Lewis, 13th December 1950

After spending a few days at home, with services in Kilmarnock and Glasgow, I returned to Barvas and began my mission on Tuesday of last week in the midst of a snowstorm. I am glad to report that the revival movement is very much alive in this part of the island. The crowds attending the services are as large as ever, with the same deep conviction. Every bit of standing room was taken up last night, with the pulpit steps filled. I am addressing two and sometimes three meetings each night, with a final meeting in some home to help the anxious. The Rev. Murdo McSween and his brother are coming to assist next week. Pray that they and all engaged in the gracious movement may be kept in the will of God.

20th December 1950

This has been a week of blessed meetings; interest and blessing is as deep and widespread as last winter. We have had some great cases of conversion this week. Men who were steeped in sin have been gloriously delivered, and our meetings are crowded. People are walking over snow-covered roads, many of them a distance of three miles, and walking back home in the early hours of the morning. There is a remarkable change in the attitude of the Free Church, and most of the converts this week are from that church.

Chapter 6

Revival Reports (1951–1953)

Bragar, Lewis, 24th January 1951

We finished here on Friday night amidst scenes of great rejoicing. I question if the church ever witnessed anything like it. Buses, vans and cars brought the people, and crowds gathered round unable to get in. Word had to be sent to one district to stop the buses, but even then the people gathered and stood outside for three hours. A second meeting was arranged and those outside were allowed in first. Some very old people got gloriously saved last night, as well as young men and women. I open in Ness tomorrow.

Ness, Lewis, 31st January 1951

I am in the midst of my mission in the parish of Ness; but also in the midst of a snowstorm. Interest is as deep as ever; crowds attend the meetings, which continue until midnight. To see the parish church crowded is a great sight, but to see the anxious coming into the prayer meeting is a more wonderful sight. There was a mighty manifestation of the power of God in the meetings last night. Wave after wave of Holy Ghost power swept over the meetings and strong men were broken down and crying for mercy. A number came from Bragar, a distance of fourteen miles. God is working mightily in the latter; converts are holding meetings, and the district is in the grip of revival.

Kinloch, Lewis, 14th February 1951

I arrived back in Lewis on Friday in the expectation of beginning my mission on Sabbath, but found on arriving at my destination that the people of the district had gathered and were expecting a service, so my mission began on Friday night. The interest is keen and already one feels the spirit of revival. I believe we are going to see a blessed move here. God is already at work in the district, and several have come to know the Lord who were not in contact with any of our meetings.

21ˢᵗ February 1951

Our hearts are full of praise to God for what our eyes have seen and our ears heard this past week. The breath of revival has come to this side of the island, and there is great rejoicing among God's people. The movement really began on Thursday in our first meeting and among the Christians. This meeting will not soon be forgotten in this parish. At our second meeting, which went on until 2.00 in the morning, seventeen were seeking the Saviour. Again last night men and women were in great distress. People are coming from all over the island, some a distance of twenty miles.

28ᵗʰ February 1951

This has been a most glorious week, probably the best of the whole revival. Nowhere has there been such a sense of the presence of God or greater interest shown. People have gathered from all over the island, some travelling over forty miles. Meetings have been held in churches, halls, schools and on one night in a shooting lodge; the meetings in the latter place went on until three o'clock in the morning. Over 170 gathered, and many were in great distress with about twenty seeking the Lord. People have been in such distress that they have cried out for mercy in the services; others fainted. Requests have come to me from Free Church communities for a mission in spite of the opposition of some ministers. I close here on Tuesday and go for two days to Uist.

Leurbost, Lewis, 14ᵗʰ March 1951

I was very sorry not being free to go to Uist. The failure of a minister through illness, who was to have carried on for me, made it impossible for me to leave the island. I was to have finished here last week, but the hunger among the people for the Word of God is so great I had to cancel my next mission and continue my meeting at the other end of the parish. People are coming from all over, especially Free Church people. God alone could have brought about the change in their attitude. So eager were they a few nights ago, that on hearing we were to be in a certain church at 11.00 o'clock at night, they secured buses and arrived an hour before the service, filling the church, so that the people of the district had to remain outside for two hours. Another meeting was arranged which continued until 3.00 o'clock in the morning. One man who got gloriously saved this week sat under Professor Renwick's (*of the Free Church College in Edinburgh*) ministry in Peru years ago. I leave Lochs on Wednesday and will be assisting at Communions in Barvas, Uig and Bernera, until the end of March.

Communions in Lewis are just like a convention; hundreds of Christians gather for the five days.

Lewis, 28th March 1951

We had a great finish at Leurbost. Interest was greater than in any other part of the island. On the last two nights, the church was crowded three times, between 7.00 o'clock and 2.00 in the morning, and many sought the Saviour, as many as forty-seven in one meeting. This was a return visit between two communions. I had intended to rest, but so great was the distress among so many, I had to return. I shall probably have to do so again after I am through with the communions. I am just now at Uig; meetings are a bit hard. I go to Bernera tomorrow for a week before returning to Edinburgh.

Carloway, Lewis, 26th April 1951

I am now on my second visit to Carloway, and so far the going has been stiff. The weather is very much against people coming from a distance, and buses do not run as on the other side of the island. There was a decided improvement in attendance today, and a better spirit, but generally the parish is dead and indifferent to all that is happening. A goodly number professed last year and these are very bright. Pray that revival may come, as the need here is desperate and my time is very limited

Bernera, Lewis, 15th August 1951

The Spirit of God is moving in our midst and men and women are finding the Saviour. This is a wonderful island; one can truly say that the praises of God are heard from every village. Ever since the movement began, the Spirit of God has been at work; the young believers are growing in grace and manifesting the power of the Saviour in redeemed lives. Meetings are crowded and full of divine power, conviction and distress of soul as deep as ever, and the expression of praise among the converts in outbursts of song is soul-stirring. We had a praise meeting this morning at 1.30 a.m.; meetings generally begin at 8.00 o'clock and continue until 1.30 a.m. I am assisted by a young lad from Arnol who has been, and is, mightily used of God; he will continue with me until he returns to the High School.

22nd August 1951

This has been another week of much blessing. Notwithstanding very stormy weather, the people have come out in crowds and on several nights refused to go home until morning. Converts from Ness, Barvas, Arnol and Leurbost have been coming in buses, and at 4.00 o'clock this morning we were assembled on the shore singing the songs of Zion as the boats carried them across the sound to the main island.

We have had some great cases of conversion this week; at one meeting nine men came to the Saviour, seven of them heads of families, and three of them key men on this side of Lewis. This has been a week of glorious victory over hell and the devil. One man in his prayer said the following words: 'Lord, we thank Thee for this victory and for giving the devil such a sore head and we know you will not give him an aspirin to ease it!' I hope to return to Edinburgh this week and look forward to the Pilgrims' meetings and the F.M. Perth Convention.

Barvas and Shader, 19ᵗʰ September 1951

Our communion services at Bernera were a time of rich blessing. Crowds gathered from all over Lewis, and many of God's children were richly blessed. The spirit of conviction among the unsaved was as deep as ever, and there was great joy among the Christians in seeing men and women coming into the glorious liberty in Christ. One visitor from London got gloriously saved. I am now at Barvas and Shader. After a few days of hard going, the Spirit of God has again broken through. Yesterday three churches were crowded and the last meeting continued until 1.30 a.m.; it was a great sight. While I and two other ministers were dealing with the anxious inside, crowds gathered outside singing. We left them singing, 'Oh the children of the Lord have a right to shout and sing.'

3ʳᵈ October 1951

This mission did not come up to our expectation. We had crowds of Christian people from all over the island, but after the first wave of blessing, things hardened up, so that we had no-one seeking the Lord for salvation this week. We need much prayer, as it would appear the enemy has got in, opposition is now coming from other quarters. However, we continue to look to the Lord, and He will lead us to victory again. I am resting for a few days before going to the Strathpeffer Convention.

Baile-Na-Cille, Uig, Lewis, 24ᵗʰ October 1951

On Wednesday of last week I began my mission in the parish of Uig. The FM Pilgrims worked this district last winter, and left behind a group of praying people; these, along with the parish minister, gave me a very warm welcome. I was not long in the district until it became evident that God was already at work, as bad roads, stormy weather and no transport did not prevent the people from gathering. Meetings were arranged for 7.30 and 10.30 p.m., and here as in other parts of the island, God made bare His arm. The break came on the second night, and great was the rejoicing. My time here is very short and I shall value prayer that the movement may spread all over this wide parish.

31ˢᵗ October 1951

I find it difficult to put down on paper what our eyes have seen and our ears have heard this week. Revival has gripped the parish. Deep conviction of sin has laid hold upon the people, and many have found the Saviour — as many as twenty in one meeting. Men who were never near a meeting were suddenly arrested by the Spirit of God and had to give up work and give themselves to seeking after God. Places of worship are crowded, and meetings continue until the small hours of the morning. People walk miles through wind and rain, and will wait through three services between 7.30 and 3.00 o'clock in the morning. We praise our faithful God!

8ᵗʰ November 1951

This has been another week of much blessing. The awakening continues, and has now spread to every part of the parish. The FM Pilgrims who worked in this district last year will be glad to know that those who were concerned then have all found the Saviour. 'One soweth and another reapeth.' Our meetings this week were characterized by physical prostrations and swooning, and the agony of godless men whose consciences awoke was terrible to see. Men have been found walking the roads at night in distress of soul; others have been found during the day praying among the rocks. I continue for another week before going to Uist for a few days.

14ᵗʰ November 1951

This has been another week of much blessing. Meetings have been larger than ever, and people have come from all over Lewis to witness the movings of God, some as far as about fifty miles. Whole districts have been completely changed. Social evils have been swept away as by a flood, and a wonderful sense of God seems to pervade the whole district. One elder in his prayer yesterday said: 'The hills and the valleys are shouting for joy.' That was certainly true a few mornings ago when a crowd stood in the Uig valley and sang the late Pilgrim Angus McLean's great hymn on 'The Suffering Lamb'. Yesterday was a day that will never be forgotten in Uig. We began at noon and continued until 3.00 o'clock this morning. In that time I addressed six meetings. I leave today for Uist, returning to Edinburgh next week.

Baile-Na-Cille, 12ᵗʰ December 1951

Extremely wild weather continues here. I do not remember ever conducting a mission under such conditions; yet in the midst of it all, God is mightily at work. It is most inspiring to see the people facing wind and rain, and securing such means as are available to take them to the meetings. Fortunately, four men who have cars of their own were converted this week, and their cars are now at our disposal. We had a mighty manifestation of God last night; one whole family, father, mother, two sons and daughter were among those who found the Saviour. When the congregation realized what was happening, someone started singing Psalm 103, verses 17 to the end, and as the Spirit of God swept through the meeting, the cry of the unsaved could be heard, as strong men wept their way to the Saviour. I am suffering from a bad chill that has given trouble in my chest and throat, and I have found it necessary to reduce my meetings to one each night. I shall value prayer.

19ᵗʰ December 1951

We had a very good finish at Uig, crowded meetings, deep conviction, and souls being saved. I was very sorry leaving such a move, but the meetings will continue under the local minister. I cross to Ireland on Monday, returning on Friday to assist at Highland Conferences. The Stornoway meetings begin on 6ᵗʰ January.

Stornoway, Lewis, 9ᵗʰ January 1952

We had a good beginning in Stornoway. Notwithstanding a night of wind and rain, the Town Hall was filled, and the spirit of the meetings was good. We cannot, however, close our eyes to the fact that we are up against a good deal of opposition, and of a kind we did not experience before, but 'our God is able'. Pilgrim Jamieson (FM) joins me tonight. I greatly enjoyed the visit to Mr. Black (*of the Faith Mission*). It was refreshing to be back on old battlefields again and to find the work of God going on. God is surely working in the district; that was quite evident from the well-attended Conference. Oban, Inverness, Kinlochleven and Broadford were outstanding. One came away with the impression that we are really near to something great in the West Highlands.

23rd January 1952

This has been a mission of hard fighting. Everything seemed to be against us, and for the first week, large gatherings and a few seeking the Saviour was all we could report. But how different when God breaks through! This week we have been experiencing a gracious wave of blessing. The movement really began a week last Friday, and since then we have been in the midst of revival blessing. Last night we witnessed a mighty manifestation of the power of God. As a young lad from Arnol was praying, God swept in, in power, and in a few minutes some people were prostrate on the floor, others with hands raised up fell back in a trance. We were in the midst of it until 1.00 o'clock in the morning. I leave for Edinburgh tonight, to rest for a few days before opening in the Town Hall, Inverness, next Sabbath. Brother Jamieson will carry on in Lewis with a short mission at Bernera, by special request.

Inverness, 30th January 1952

Our mission in the Town Hall began with a fair measure of interest, but one came away from the first meeting with the impression that this is going to be a hard fight. A reception meeting was held on Saturday evening, when I met a number of leaders in church work in the town. They all seemed keen, and I believe they have been doing all in their power to make the mission known. They considered the opening meeting good from the point of view of attendance, the hall being three-quarters full. The Gaelic side of the mission begins on Tuesday. From then onwards I shall be conducting two services each evening. Pray that the weather may improve, as weather conditions just now make it very difficult for people to come out.

His reports of the mission in Inverness on 6th and 12th February indicate that even though the Town Hall was packed with several seeking the Saviour, they did not see revival as in Lewis. They had great closing meetings with extra seats having to be brought in and with God manifestly working among them as Christians re-dedicated themselves to God and as souls sought the Saviour. 'An interesting feature was the support given by the ministers of the town; as many as eight were present at one meeting. The local press also helped by favourable reports. United prayer meetings are to be continued to pray for revival.'

Callanish, Lewis, 27th February 1952

I am now back again to the parish of Carloway; this is my third visit to this district. The revival touched this parish at the beginning of the movement, but bitter opposition and misunderstanding hindered the work, and since then little has been seen here. I began on Wednesday with a very small meeting; we have had an increase every night, and last night the church was full. I believe things are now beginning to move, but we need much prayer. The enemy is busy on the island, and the revival spirit is being restricted. A real break through would set it ablaze again, so pray hard.

5th March 1952

The spirit of revival has gripped this parish, and we expect to see great things happening. Already souls are in great distress and are coming to the Saviour. Our meetings are crowded, and there is an air of expectancy in the whole district. We had a meeting on Saturday night in a house and it was crowded with unsaved young people. The four beds in the house were packed with them! All the rooms were full and beds were used for seating. We never witnessed anything like this in Carloway before. It will be necessary for me to again change my programme and remain in this district.

12th March 1952

This has been another good week. The Spirit of God is working in the parish, and it is evident that a deep hunger for God has laid hold upon the people. This is seen in the effort they are making to get out. Buses and vans have brought the people, and every night this past week, souls have sought Christ. We had a mighty meeting on Friday night. Several young men from Arnol came to our assistance, and as one of them prayed, God came down in mighty power, and before his prayer ended souls were rejoicing in deliverance. This meeting will stand out as one of the great meetings of the revival. I am to be assisted this week by the Rev. Kenneth Gillies, Partick, Glasgow.

19th March 1952

This mission is now closed, and we have much to praise God for; interest and blessing continued up to the end. We did not witness the same move as in some other districts, but souls were seeking the Saviour every night this week. Meetings were held in the afternoon, evening and on until the morning. People came from Crulivig by boat and vans, and some who were deeply convicted while Pilgrim Jamieson was there came out brightly on the Lord's side; one young man is an outstanding case. I begin in Shawbost tonight (Monday) where I look forward to having Brother Dale (*FM*) with me.

Shawbost, 26ᵗʰ March 1952

Interest is good, and a number have come to know the Lord, nine this week, but so far the revival spirit has not reached us. We are having very large meetings, with buses coming from distant places, but the deep spirit of conviction that was manifest at Callanish is not yet in our meetings. I am again being bitterly attacked by [elements in] the Free Church, and this has caused a measure of unrest among the converts. Pray that they may be kept in the liberty wherewith Christ has made them free. I hope to have two meetings in Crulivig where brother Jamieson worked, and will value prayer. Although brother Jamieson did not see the fruit of his labours, the fruit was there, and I believe we are going to see much more in that district. I believe that a busload is coming this week to Shawbost. As far as I know I close here on Thursday night and join brother Black at Kyle for the weekend, before returning to Edinburgh. (*Willie Black was the Faith Mission Superintendent for the Highland District.*) This will probably be my last effort in Lewis for the time being. Bernera, Harris, will be my next mission. I go there after the Easter Bangor Convention.

2ⁿᵈ April 1952

This mission closed on a grand note of victory, with men and women seeking the Saviour right up to the end. The crowds at our closing meeting exceeded anything we saw in Lewis. People who could not get in sat in the buses outside, while many had to return home. My only regret is that I had to leave to fulfil a promised engagement in Skye. The end of the mission at Shawbost brings to a close my labours in Lewis for the present. I look back on the past two years with deep gratitude to God for allowing me to labour in the midst of revival, and I pray that this gracious movement may continue and spread. I am now at home for a short rest before going to Bangor, N. Ireland.

Berneray, Harris (a small island between Harris and North Uist), 30ᵗʰ April 1952

We are in the midst of a blessed awakening here. God broke through in revival blessing on the second night of our mission, and since then the whole island has been moved. Humanly speaking, this is the most unfavourable time of the year for meetings, as the people are busy on the land, but today, work on the land has a secondary place and all who can move are at the meetings. One of the elders assured me last night that every person on the island who could be out, was in the church. I am dealing with anxious souls every night. On my way home last night I met a group by the roadside in great distress; others had met in a house and were there until 4.00 o'clock this morning. Word has just come in to say that the fire has spread to the island of Uist, and that a fishing boat has been secured to take the people over to Berneray tomorrow (Sabbath). How sorry I am that I must leave on Monday morning, for Edinburgh.

28ʰ May 1952

Since my last report I have done a bit of travelling around. A weekend in Glasgow proved to be a fruitful time; we had the joy of helping a number who were seeking the Saviour. My visit to the Western Isles along with Mr. Black was interesting and inspiring. A grand bit of work has been done in Uist by the Pilgrim brothers. It was a real joy to meet so many who were brought to the Lord during the past year. I was greatly impressed by the solid nature of the work. I visited Bernera (*off Lewis*), Crulivig, Callanish, Arnol, Shader and Ness, and in each place preached to crowded meetings. It was a great joy to find the converts going on so well. Two-and-a-half years have now passed, and there has been practically no backsliding; only four of the hundreds who professed. For this we praise our God. I leave tonight, Tuesday, for Oxford and London, where I shall (D.V.) be addressing meetings for ten days.

Later that year he was involved in meetings in various places on the mainland, including Oxford, the Keswick Convention, the Isle of Man and Glasgow. In October he returned to Lewis.

Leverburgh, Harris, 29ʰ October 1952

I am back again to the Western Isles, and happy to be in the fight again. Several days have been spent visiting districts touched by the revival, and in every place we saw much to encourage and praise God for; the converts are going on well and growing in grace. We had a crowded meeting in Galson. Buses brought the people from far and near, and there is every sign that God is going to break out here again. The mission at Leverburgh opened yesterday, with a well-filled church in the morning, and a crowded church at night. This was followed by a prayer meeting which went on until midnight. I shall greatly value prayer for this mission, as this will be my only contact with Lewis or Harris until February.

1st November 1952

We have not yet seen revival as witnessed in Lewis, but we believe we are very near to it. The weather has been very much against us, but the people have come against wind and rain, and God has been in the midst. We've had some great cases of conversion. God broke in among the self-righteous sinners on Friday night, and it was grand to hear them confess their sins. One man in great distress of soul was heard to say, 'Lord, I never knew until this night that I was such a sinner.' We praise God for such deep conviction.

Yesterday (Sabbath), I was preaching in a church ten miles from Leverburgh. The parish minister of Leverburgh decided to close his church and three buses were engaged to take the people to this other church. Most of those who went were unsaved. At night this church at which I preached in the morning closed for the evening, and buses were engaged to take them to Leverburgh. I preached three times between 5.00 and 9.00 p.m. to a crowded church. We believe for great things this week.

8th November 1952

This has been another glorious week, for which we praise God. The weather has been very severe, making it difficult for the outlying places, where buses could not reach them, but night after night they came; it was an inspiration to watch their torches flashing as they came across the moor or over the hill. This is the greatest move we have witnessed in Harris; some terrible characters have been saved. So great was their distress that we had to leave some of them lying on the floor last night. There has been a most blessed ingathering of men. One young student, just home from the army, some days after his conversion heard the call of God to the ministry; his father was among nine who sought the Saviour at 1.00 o'clock this morning. Yesterday I had four phone calls from ministers asking for missions. I leave here on Monday to address three rallies in Lewis, before going home.

Lewis, 19th November 1952

The movement in Leverburgh has caused a great stirring in the whole of Harris. We are on the verge of another great movement, I believe. I returned to Lewis on Monday and addressed crowded meetings at Callanish, Arnol and Ness. One church was so crowded that chairs had to be brought in from nearby houses, and even then crowds were outside. A late meeting was arranged for those who were not able to get into the first meeting. I am now home resting for a few days before going south with Mr. Eberstein to address Conferences arranged by Mr. Fox. I then go to Hastings, Oxford, London, Corsham, Bristol, Bath and Stoke-on Trent, returning to address a conference of ministers in Glasgow, before beginning in Dunfermline on Sunday, 7th December. I shall greatly value prayer for these engagements. (*Reports of these meetings are given in the Pilgrim News. He returned to Lewis early in 1953.*)

1953 Onwards

Habost, Lochs, Lewis, 4th February 1953

During the past week I visited several districts in Lewis and Harris, and in each place had very good meetings. God is working in the parishes of Barvas and Ness; meetings on Sabbath and weeknight are largely attended and souls are seeking the Saviour. This movement began without any special effort. In Barvas, at a weeknight meeting, held in one of the churches, fully sixty were turned away the church was so packed. On the same evening, I was addressing crowded meetings in Ness, so God is on the move again. In Habost, Lochs, where I began yesterday, we are met with a very different situation; but God is able. Our opening meeting yesterday was largely attended and the spirit was good, but I am up against opposition, so there is much need of prayer. The minister and office bearers of the Church of Scotland in whose church I am holding the services are doing all in their power to help, and we are believing for victory.

11th February 1953

This has been a good week. Although we have not witnessed revival, we have seen men and women coming to the Saviour. The first break came on Friday night. Since then there has been a real seeking after God. Our meetings are crowded, with a great sense of God. I have been preaching in the afternoon and at 7.00 o'clock in one parish, and at 9.30 p.m. in another. The latter is a Free Church community; here the church is so crowded that people bring chairs and forms and even then we cannot accommodate them. Tonight, Sabbath, we had five seeking the Saviour. We believe we are going to see a great move this week. Unfortunately I must finish on Thursday night, as I am due to begin my mission in Dunfermline on Saturday 14th.

18ᵗʰ February 1953

The mission in the parishes of Lochs and Gravir finished on a grand note of victory; the last few days were wonderful, and that in spite of much opposition. Buses, lorries, vans and cars brought the people that crowded the church, and each meeting people came under deep conviction; in one meeting alone twenty-seven men and women were seeking the Saviour. On my last night I addressed two meetings in the parish of Lochs, assisted by two Church of Scotland ministers. Buses brought people from other parishes as far away as Bernera and Stornoway. There was also a bus full of converts from Gravir. This meeting was regarded by many as one of our best; it certainly represented many districts in Lewis. God is moving in several places on the island just now, and churches are crowded; these movements are quite independent of any outside agency. I began in Dunfermline on Saturday with a very good meeting; there is a spirit of expectancy abroad, and we are believing for a move. Yesterday's meetings were most encouraging in number and spirit.

Lochcroistean and Crowlista, Uig, Lewis, 11ᵗʰ March 1953

This has been a week of fighting but one of victory. On Friday evening we had a great manifestation of the power of God in the hall at Crowlista. I had to stop preaching, until the cry of the people who came under the power of God became more subdued. Some burdened sinners were greatly distressed and since then have found the Saviour. This surely is an answer to prayer, as I have been much the subject of bitter attacks by the enemy through the local press, and this fresh manifestation of God's power will, I believe, silence this opposition. While writing this report a man came in praising God and saying he found the Saviour last night; only two are left in this village unsaved.

9ᵗʰ April 1953

Since my last report, I have witnessed God's gracious hand at work in different places. My report about the movement in the parish of Uig was late in reaching Edinburgh and consequently did not appear in 'Pilgrim News'. There, in spite of much opposition, God broke through and we witnessed a most gracious move. Some very ungodly men got gloriously saved. I then went to the parish of Ness for a few Christians' meetings; here again we witnessed the power of God moving among His people and several men came to know the Saviour. I am at present in the south of England, addressing meetings in different places. We had a most blessed time at Oxford among Chinese students; at one meeting the Spirit of God was so manifestly in our midst and His power so evident that I just stopped preaching and gave the meeting over to prayer. I am now at St. Albans, at their annual Convention. It has been a real joy to meet a few Lewis converts here. I go tomorrow to assist Mr. Fox (*FM*) at his conferences and then to Norwich, before returning to Bernera, Lewis.

Lewis, 6ᵗʰ May 1953

The week of meetings at Bernera, Lewis, was a most blessed time. What a joy it was to meet the converts of the move in June 1950, all going on well with God. Here again God has broken through in revival blessing, although not so intense as formerly. I felt the FM Glasgow Convention to be a helpful time; numbers were larger than for some years and the spirit good. A crowded meeting in Gardiner Street Church of Scotland last night was among the best I ever had in Glasgow; quite a number came to an after-meeting seeking the Saviour. I begin in Berneray, Harris, on Wednesday 6ᵗʰ.

Berneray, Harris, 13ᵗʰ May 1953

I began here on Wednesday 6ᵗʰ, and since then we have been in the midst of a very blessed move. The ground was well prepared by the converts of last year, and I found myself in an atmosphere as tense as ever before. Every person that could move was out today and an extra meeting had to be arranged in the church. Between midday and 11.00 at night, I addressed five meetings. I had a powerful meeting down by the shore before the boats left to take the Harris people home, followed by one to help those in distress of soul. How we praise God for being in the midst of revival again. Seeing the people coming over the hills and along the roads, others coming in boats, was a sight to be remembered, and to listen to the singing of Psalm 122 from the boats leaving the shore was soul-inspiring. For the next few days I shall be addressing meetings by day and night – pray for much-needed strength.

Meetings in Oxford were particularly blessed in May, and later he had a tent campaign in Motherwell, Scotland, in August, at the end of which he said, 'I now begin what will probably be my last mission in Lewis.'

Gravir, Point, Lewis, 26ᵗʰ August 1953

Before opening what I expect will be my last mission in Lewis, I, along with several ministers from the south, visited Uig, Bernera, Barvas and

Arnol, and met with the converts of the movement. We were greatly cheered and encouraged to find them all going on and growing in grace, and to God's glory we can report that no-one in the districts mentioned has gone back. At Arnol we had a crowded meeting, when they gathered from far and near. There is, however, much need for prayer, as the enemy is at work, causing division. Preachers from churches with different emphases have been here, from Brethren to Pentecostal, causing confusion. I am at present in the parish of Park, in the district of Gravir, and here we are witnessing a gracious move of the Spirit, similar to what we saw in other parts of Lewis; crowded meetings, deep conviction of sin, and souls seeking the Saviour. Another headmaster has been added to the number already witnessing for Christ. Now that God is moving, buses and vans are bringing the people from other parishes, from as far as Leverburgh in Harris. Our meeting continues each night until midnight. I am arrested each night by a group of ministers from the south of England who are rejoicing in seeing revival.

After this Mr. Campbell went South and spoke at meetings in many places, for instance, Westminster, Sheffield, Bolton, Southport, London, High Leigh, Ireland, Birkenhead, Manchester, Westbury and St. Albans. He returned to the Highlands and worked a mission in Skye. This he found to be extremely hard but experienced victory as the mission progressed.

Duirinish, Isle of Skye, 4th November 1953

This has been one of the hardest battles it has been my lot to face; it seems almost incredible to think that any part of Skye could be without a prayer meeting or anybody to engage in prayer, yet such is the case here. Meetings are small; however last night saw the first real move. God was in the midst at both Gaelic and English meetings, and we believe for greater things.

18th November 1953

We have witnessed a most gracious move of the Spirit, and today men and women are rejoicing in salvation, who, a short while ago, were strangers to grace and to God. This breath of the Spirit came after a very hard fight, in answer, I believe, to the cry of those who dared to believe that 'God was faithful who had promised'.

On Tuesday of the second week, people came from all over the parish, and of them it could be truly said, 'they were seeking for Jesus.' During the singing of the opening Psalm, one felt an awareness of God coming over the gathering, but it was after the address and while singing Psalm 147:3 that God broke through; from then until I left we were in the midst of men and women of all ages seeking the Saviour. There were as many as fourteen adults in one meeting who publicly acknowledged their acceptance of Christ, but the most remarkable feature of the movement was the sudden change that came over the community.

He then preached in other places such as Shetland, where he saw a gracious move of the Spirit in Lerwick, and then in Swinton, Durham, Sunderland, Bromsgrove, Birmingham, Wales, and probably many other places not mentioned in the reports. In August 1954 he returned to Lewis for a short period.

Lemreway, Lochs, Lewis, 25th August 1954

This mission is at the invitation of Free Church people and promises to be a good one. The interest is already really great and the spirit in the meetings is good. We are well supported by the converts from the Gravir movement of last year. Their steadfastness has made a great impression on this stronghold of the Free Church – there are no Church of Scotland people. The mission has been made possible by the kindness of Mr Rudkin who has brought his car to Lewis and is with me here. If I had not his car I could not mission these parts, as the townships are so far apart and the only available lodgings four miles from the place of meetings.

1st September 1954

This has been a very good week; the interest of the first week was well maintained notwithstanding a change in the weather and the commencement of the Lewis communion season. We could not say that we saw revival such as we witnessed in the other parishes of Lewis but on every night this week we saw men and women seeking the Saviour. At least fifteen men and women sought the Saviour since last Sunday evening. I now rest for a few days before going to Capernwray Hall and Highleigh.

A fitting quotation to close this chapter would be that which he wrote on 2nd April 1952: 'I look back on the past two years with deep gratitude to God for allowing me to labour in the midst of revival, and I pray that this gracious movement may continue and spread.'

Mr. Campbell returned to the Faith Mission Convention held on the island every year since the revival. In 1969 he had a remarkable move of the Spirit in a special series of meetings in Lemreway. This is described by Rev Donald MacAulay in his testimony.

The Lewis Awakening of this time centred at the beginning in Barvas and Shader and took place mainly in the years of 1950 and 1951 and also 1952. By the end of 1952 it was decreasing in intensity. We praise God for the revelation of His mighty power during this period.

Chapter 7

Rev. James Murray MacKay
(Minister of the Church of Scotland, Barvas)

After the war, Gaelic ministers were scarce, and an appeal went out from the church authorities that if any Gaelic ministers on the mainland could give some time to ministry in the Gaelic-speaking islands it would be appreciated. Rev. MacKay went to Barvas, which was vacant at that time, for a month's locum early in 1949, and was deeply impressed with the earnest spirit of prayer and expectancy in the area. Many people in the parish of Barvas were giving themselves to prayer and were crying to God for an outpouring of the Spirit. They were aware of the fact that the 'tide was out'. There were diminishing numbers in public worship and the youth were careless and worldly. The blessing of the 1939 revival, before the war, was still fresh in their minds. Was it not the case that ten years previously the 1939 revival had been born in cottage prayer meetings and continued in this way? They knew what God had given and they knew what they wanted!

When Mr. MacKay returned to his parish on the mainland, he said to his wife: 'It only needs a spark!' She told us that he repeated this often when speaking of the tremendous sense of prayer in the Barvas area: 'It only needs a spark,' he would say, 'It only needs a spark!' He himself was a product of a revival in Uig years before and was sensitive therefore to the movings of the Spirit.

Not long after this, he was called to fill the vacancy in the parish of Barvas and in April 1949 he was inducted to the charge. He became the much-loved pastor of the church, having a heart for evangelical truth and for revival. The normal programme of the church was backed up with spontaneous cottage prayer meetings. Prayer was woven into the very fabric of the church and at that time the whole membership of the church would be present in the weekly prayer meetings. You would not be accepted as a member of the church in Lewis if you did not have the testimony that Jesus Christ was your Saviour and Lord.

It was customary for the Lord's people to gather after the church prayer meeting in one of their homes for a further time of prayer. These occasions were not organized but were spontaneous and were characteristic of island life at the time and in some areas this is still the case. No doubt Mr. MacKay would attend these gatherings, for he had the spiritual well-being of the community at heart. Many spontaneous prayer meetings took place as the people of God visited each other in their homes.

Much has been made of the two old ladies in Barvas and the part they played in preparing the way for the revival, as well as the seven elders who prayed. Yes, they did pray, but they were only a very small part of the whole burdened, praying community who were earnestly and constantly seeking the face of God for His mercy to be revealed. Margaret MacLeod's amazing sentence, which all who were there would heartily endorse, sums it up, 'It was a community at prayer!'

Mr. MacKay entered into the whole prayerful and expectant scene with heart and will. It was he who brought Duncan Campbell to Lewis when Rev. Tom Fitch could not come. He reports as follows:

This spiritual awakening began under the hand of God through the preaching of Rev. Duncan Campbell who was used by the Lord in an amazing way in awaking never-dying souls. He began to hold meetings in the district of Barvas on Wednesday, the 7th December 1949. Meetings were held every night in the churches of Barvas and Shader for three weeks. It was at these services that the awakening began, which, from that time and in particular through this preacher, has spread to many places in Lewis and in Harris.

How the Work Began
The awakening broke out in the church in Shader on the night of Sunday, 11th December 1949. It was a real privilege to worship in the church in Shader on that night – listening to the large congregation singing heartily and tunefully at the beginning of the service:

> From out of Zion, his own hill
> where the perfection high
> of beauty is, from thence the Lord
> hath shined gloriously.
> Our God shall come,
> Keep silent shall not he:
> Before him fire shall waste, great storms
> shall round about him be (Psalm 50:2-3).

Following this, the preacher, under the power of grace and the anointing of the Spirit, proclaimed the gospel; and finally the singing of Psalm 132:3-6:

> I will not come within my house,
> Nor rest in bed at all:
> Nor shall my eyes take any sleep,
> Nor eyelids slumber shall;
>
> Till for the Lord a place I find,
> Where he may make abode;
> A place of habitation
> For Jacob's mighty God
>
> Lo at the place of Ephratah
> Of it we understood;
> And we did find it in the fields
> And city of the wood.

At the close of the service some came back to the prayer meeting seeking the Lord as Saviour of their souls, and following this a glorious time was enjoyed at the house meeting in the home of Donald Morrison that night. (*The ministers were not present at this latter meeting.*) More people sought the Lord at the house meeting than at the church, and many a blessed meeting was later held in this house after that night. Many of the Lord's children triumphed in prayer in the meeting on that night. The Lord revealed Himself in saving power and found His servants awake. They recognized Him and they heartily welcomed His gracious work. No wonder they tunefully sang:

> Thy goings they have seen O God;
> The steps of majesty
> Of my God, and my mighty King
> Within the sanctuary (Psalm 68:24).

The Spread of the Awakening

That was the week when the awakening spread from Shader to Barvas and Borve, and even young people from Ness and Kinloch came to know the saving grace of Christ in the meetings in Shader and Barvas.

The Spirit of God was resting amazingly and graciously on these two townships at that time, and His resting was glorious. You could feel Him in the homes of the people, on the 'machair' (common) and on the moor, and even as you walked along the road through the two townships.

On Saturday night, at the end of the service in the Barvas church, there were many souls who were seeking Christ as their personal Saviour – more than at any time in the awakening. In a short time they all found peace of conscience and soul rest in the Saviour whom they sought so earnestly. They were there from each denomination who received the blessing that enriches the soul.

The awakening followed Mr. Campbell, his helpers and the converts in each area where they laboured, but the awakening was not as powerful there as in Barvas, Shader and Arnol.

It was in 1950 that the meetings were held in Arnol, and there were blessed happenings in that village. The services in the Arnol church were good and blessed but it seemed that the house meetings were even better. Very often those who were awakened in the church service would find rest of soul in the house meeting. Many souls have sweet memories of the house meetings in Borve, Shader, Barvas and Arnol. Who will ever forget the one that ended with John Smith, the blacksmith from Shader, leading in the Psalm 107:1-4:

> Praise God, for he is good; for still
> his mercies lasting be.
> Let God's redeem'd say so, whom he
> from th' en'my's hand did free;
> And gather'd them out of the lands,
> from north, south, east and west.
> They stray'd in desert's pathless way,
> no city found to rest.

That was Arnol's big night!

It is God Himself who does the work and it is seen and assuredly evident in Arnol – the living, radiant witnesses on the Lord's side. The place that was as hard as the rocks and as unfruitful as the wilderness – now transformed by the power of God to become a garden for the Lord.

The Hallmarks

We are asked to give some of the hallmarks of the awakening. We will relate them as evident in this district.

To begin with, the *preacher*. He is one who has a saving knowledge of the Lord and an experience – personal experience – of His power to save. He keeps close to the Lord and is totally dedicated to Him. He has a burden for never-dying souls and is zealous to win them to Christ. A humble man, pleasant, loving, and one to whom Christ is everything.

Another thing that helped the blessed work of the Lord in this area was the oneness and co-operation of the *elders* and many others of the Lord's people who were happy, and ready to help when the awakening began. 'They all hold swords, being expert in war: every man hath his sword upon his thigh because of fear in the night' (Song of Solomon 3:8). They love the Lord and the souls of those who have no saving knowledge of the Lord. They are always ready to help wounded souls who are weak and needy. Wherever they were aware of a seeking soul, a meeting was held in their home as soon as possible.

And now, a word about the *converts* themselves. They came to the Lord as lost sinners on the path of repentance. You could not hear a sound nor was there any movement around them, but throughout the service tears flowed from their eyes, betraying the fact that the Spirit of God was striving with them in a saving way and that the solemnity of Eternity was dawning upon them.

The Prayer Meeting (the after meeting)
In the prayer meeting after the services, those who were seeking the Lord remained, as did the Lord's people. Usually, three men would be called upon to pray and Mr. Campbell would preach for fifteen minutes on the simplicity of the way of salvation from such texts as Isaiah 1:18; Isaiah 55:6; John 10:27. He would shed light on the fact that seekers should be sincere in this solemn and personal matter – that they must believe the Word of the Lord and be obedient to it.

Many of the awakened found the Lord at these prayer meetings; others left the prayer meeting without getting any relief from their burden but rather feeling worse, though longing with all their hearts to follow the Lord. And then, as the lepers of old 'as they went, they were cleansed' (Luke 17:14), on their way home, they found the Saviour.

There are over 100 in this district who have come to saving faith since the beginning of the awakening. God is keeping them all; not one of them has gone back. These lambs, trophies of grace, are being shepherded and nursed gently and lovingly by the Lord's people who have a loving concern for them.

This can be said of the lambs of the flock: their behaviour is fragrant, their fellowship blessed, their love living and warm – trophies of grace as beautiful as ever seen by men. Many of them are upholding the cause of

Christ strongly in their homes, while others who have now left the island, being scattered all over the world, are subjects of our prayers. May the God of grace keep them in each place and circumstance 'until the day break and the shadows flee away'.

> And now, if I never see you again
> Farewell to you all, and my love:
> And I wish you well at the end of your days
> At that time when the Universe will burn.

Rev James Murray MacKay came to the parish of Barvas a few months before the awakening began (April 1949), and he passed into the presence of the Lord when the revival ended in 1954. This gives fresh meaning to the last paragraph of the above article which he wrote.

Chapter 8

Preparation for the Carloway Campaign
Rev. Murdo MacLennan [1]

25th December 1949, Sunday

(Items 1 – 4 were the usual congregational business)

5. Thank God for the success of the Barvas Campaign.

6. For some years I have been trying to get Rev. Duncan Campbell to assist at our communion, but he was engaged on all occasions and was sorry he could not come. Now that the Lord has opened the door, in a marvellous way, I have secured his services for a special evangelistic Campaign in February.

He is coming back to Barvas in two weeks time and hopes to be there for a month – then Carloway.

Till then there are about six weeks; almost the time that the disciples waited in the upper room, on their return from Olivet, for the promise of the Father. Six weeks of prayer until the day of Pentecost was fully come; then suddenly the Holy Spirit came upon them like a rushing, mighty wind and in cloven tongues of fire.

So – to your knees God's people! Remember the stone-breaker by the roadside who said, 'I break them on my knees!' 'This kind goeth not forth but by prayer and fasting.' Therefore you must take this to heart. Before you will receive a full blessing, the following conditions must be met:

1. First and foremost, God's glory from first to last!

2. Confession of, and putting away of all known sin!

3. Full dedication to God of our bodies and spirits so that we may become channels of blessing.

---

1. Rev.MacLennan was the minister of the Church of Scotland, Carloway, at the time of the 1949 revival and was greatly used in so many of the meetings. He worked with Duncan Campbell and was a strong supporter of the movement. This is a copy of the intimations which he gave to his congregation just before Duncan Campbell came to Carloway. We include this brief exhortation as it could well be an inspiration for laymen and pastors alike as we see how whole-heartedly he prepared his people for blessing.

Channels only blessed Master,
Yet with all Thy wondrous power
Flowing through us, Thou canst use us
Every day and every hour.

4. Absolute faith and utter dependence on the power of God to raise the dead. (spiritually)

5. Prayer and intercession day and night on behalf of :

(a) Duncan Campbell, that God would use him in the salvation of precious souls in this parish.

(b) That he will come in the fullness of the blessing of the gospel of Christ and endued with power from on High.

(c) That he will be kept in health and strength.

If these conditions are fulfilled, I will guarantee you that God will open the windows of heaven to pour out His blessing, and there shall be no room to contain it.

'The time has come when the dead will hear the voice of the Son of God and those who hear will live.' This is the truth that spoke to me before the last revival and it has come to me again.

Finally, in a previous revival, the Spirit of God was moving in the congregation at harvest time. I was awakened at the Barvas and Carloway communions. The Spirit did not depart from here or from Barvas. There is a need for preparation! 'The fields are white already to harvest.'

Oh, my friends, don't be a tool of the devil. He went into Judas Iscariot, and he tempted Peter. He has no power but through people. Therefore, people of God, pray, pray, pray!

His assurance that the Lord would work was based on the Word which God had given him and upon his observations of the mighty workings of the Spirit just fifteen miles away in Barvas. He could thus exhort his people with confidence and courage to storm the gates of glory until the blessed answer came.

Chapter 9

Characteristics of the Revival

The characteristics of which we will be speaking are mainly those of the 1949 –53 revival. Undoubtedly many of these characteristics would be found in the other revivals which have been mentioned, but we are concentrating on the 1949 revival.

The Influence of Scripture and Former Revivals

The young people knew the Bible, as this, together with the Westminster Shorter Catechism, was taught at school. Virtually the whole community, at that stage, honoured the Word of God and respected the things of God as a consequence. They were theologically educated and many tried as much as they could to live up to that which they knew to be true, keeping the Sunday strictly as the day of worship when no work was done. There was an acknowledgement and an acceptance of spiritual things. The influences of past revivals had an enormous effect upon the lives of the people.

Mary says, 'Successive revivals in the island, since the great revival in Uig in the 1820s, had brought the Scriptures into prominence in the schools and there we were taught to honour the Word of God and to memorize it. We all memorized many psalms, and whole chapters in both English and Gaelic.... In our own home my unsaved father would conduct family worship each night.'

A righteousness and a decency prevailed throughout the island. In Ness, in the north of the island with its fairly dense population, there was only one policeman, and he existed mainly to fill in papers and sign forms! In Barvas fifteen miles south of Ness there was another single policeman who cared for the interests of those in Barvas and the surrounding villages. Even today piles of peat sit at the side of the road but no-one would dream of taking them. Large bales of woven Harris tweed are placed beside the road waiting for the truck to pick them up, and no-one would think of stealing them. Few people bother to lock their cars and many even leave the keys in them. Things are changing now though, for the increasing number of tourists do not have the same sense of morality and honesty.

This knowledge of the Word of God and the attitude to the things of God throughout the island formed a basic foundation for the Spirit to operate in unusual power. The preacher would not have to explain who Moses or Abraham or Philip or Nicodemus were. These things were known. He would not have to instruct the people in the rightness of biblical morality, for that was accepted. They knew, acknowledged and believed the Word of the Lord and accepted its standards.

The Use of the Word of God in the Revival

The 1949 revival was Bible centred. Duncan Campbell preached the Word of God. Everyone who heard him will gladly bear testimony to this fact. Mary says, 'He seemed to go from Genesis to Revelation preaching the Word. He quoted so much and applied it to our hearts. We were confronted with what God said. This was his authority and this was the strength of his preaching.' He said, 'Preach the Word! Sing the Word! Live the Word! Anything outside of this has no sanction in heaven!'[1] He was a Bible preacher, and this was central to the revival.

On occasions Duncan was given just the right word to fit a specific need, without knowing about that need beforehand.

A lorry was bringing a number of folk to a meeting, but it broke down on the journey. The road wound around a loch and they realized that if they took a boat they would still be in time for the later meeting. This they did. Duncan knew nothing of this but took as his text: 'They also took shipping, and came to Capernaum, seeking for Jesus' (John 6:24). They too were seeking for Jesus and found Him that night. As dawn was breaking a large crowd accompanied them to the shore and they set sail for home amid singing and rejoicing.[2]

When Mary and four other teenager girls arrived late for a meeting, she said to them, 'Watch and see, he'll be preaching on the five foolish virgins.' Great was their astonishment and awe to hear his booming voice ring out, 'Tonight we will turn to the 25th chapter of Matthew and we will consider the story of the five foolish virgins.'

Mary and her cousin Catherine were seeking God and began to read

1. Andrew Woolsey (1974), *Duncan Campbell*, Hodder & Stoughton. p.152.
2. *Ibid.* p.125

the Bible but had *The People's Friend* handy to disguise their intentions should anyone approach. As he preached, he seemed to look at them and state emphatically, 'You're holding the Bible in one hand and *The People's Friend* in the other' – a rather unnerving and disturbing experience.

Norman MacLean says that Duncan preached as if I were the only person present. 'He spoke about my sin,' he says. When he went back on another occasion, it was the same. 'It was my sin that he was speaking about.' God gave guidance and pin-pointed the areas in different lives by the Word of God.

Prayer

Roderick MacKay tells of the many prayer meetings in the Carloway district before and at the time of the 1934 revival.

Sandy Mor (*Mor in Gaelic means Big*) recalls the 1934 revival: 'There was a oneness of spirit as we engaged in prayer and an increased burden as we interceded for an outpouring of the Spirit in the community.... There seemed to be a compulsion to pray, and we all felt it.'

Norman Campbell says: 'There had been a revival in 1939 – a revival in which prayer was the dominant factor. No preacher led the movement but people came to the Lord in the prayer meetings in the homes.'

Catherine Campbell recalls, 'The 1939 revival was still fresh in the memories of my parents and their friends and they were very burdened for the lost – always! The 1939 revival was born in prayer and that spirit of prayer continued, eventually increasing until the 1949 revival broke out.'

Annie MacKinnon (Kintyre) says of the 1939 revival: 'A minister who visited there stated that at that time the very fields were hallowed. The sea was hallowed. Wherever people worked, they prayed. The place of solitude was precious to them. Out on the moor, caring for the cattle, they prayed. Prayer was not a burden to them but a delight. They loved to pray; they were constrained to pray.'

Donald John Smith recalls of the 1949 revival that 'there was a great spirit of prayer everywhere, and that was actually the beginning of the revival'. He tells how that in the mornings when he would go to the smithy, he would often find his father on his knees at the anvil.

John Murdo Smith says, 'There were watchmen on the walls of Zion who resorted to prayer and would not accept things as they were. Prayer meetings for revival were held in various Christian homes. The cry that went up from many hearts was 'O! that Thou wouldst rend the heavens and that Thou wouldst come down.'...Those who engaged in prayer and believed that God would answer, continued to pray until the power of God came. We know of the two old ladies who prayed, but more people than those two ladies were constantly praying. I met them, I saw them and heard them, and I know how diligently they prayed that revival would come.'

Margaret MacLeod says: 'Christians met often and would pray and sing in the homes. That is my abiding memory of that time; in fact I do not remember the children of the Lord behaving in any other way... *It was a community at prayer!* There was great expectancy and much prayer. After a visit to a home up the road where the conversation would invariably be on the things of God, they would drop naturally into prayer. In April 1949, Rev. James Murray MacKay accepted the call to Barvas. I had just been converted before he came. People had great expectations and prayer intensified in the community. Everyone was looking forward to his ministry and looking to the Lord to work mightily in great revival power. People were praying, singing, praising. Much prayer was made and great supplications ascended from home after home in the district. Much is made of the two old ladies in Barvas who prayed. Well, there were many old ladies, and younger ones too, as well as the men, who poured out their souls to God to visit Lewis again... We prayed mightily. We believed that the Lord would work – and He did!... The atmosphere was full of joy and expectancy, but we were praying all the time; praying, praying, praying! Sometimes we were burdened for specific individuals, and sometimes it was prayer for the whole community.... We had such enormous liberty in prayer and testimony and this was the result of God's presence in the midst.'

Agnes Morrison says: 'There were some godly people in the district and they held prayer meetings. They were always getting together and praying in the house meetings.'

Chirsty Maggie from Arnol says: 'And the prayers! So many of the elders who prayed were so inspired of God that we were overwhelmed with the consciousness of the presence of God as they prayed. I remember Ruairidh Alex! He was powerful in prayer.'

Donald MacPhail records: 'It must also be said that it was the people who were saved in the '39 revival who spearheaded the '49-'52 revival and who were the prayer warriors. It was these people who followed Mr. Campbell around the island and on whom he depended to pray through. They knew how to pray and to travail for souls.'

Jack MacArthur says: 'There were men there who recognised that although God had come and revival had come, it didn't absolve them from further prayer. It placed them under a burden to pray more. When Duncan Campbell had a hard time and was to have another meeting, some men went home. They knew that they had a mission to fulfil, and so when Duncan was preaching they were at the house praying through, broken before God – supporting!'

Donald MacPhail tells of how Duncan Campbell involved both seasoned intercessors and young converts in his meetings. 'On one occasion he took a team of us to Bernera.... He would call us to prayer at 4.00 p.m. and we would pray through for the meeting in the church building and also for the after-meeting in one of the houses in the village.'

Donald MacAulay tells how the ground was prepared in the Isle of Bernera in 1951: 'There was an air of expectancy and a lot of prayer before he came. Some of the elders in the Free Church and in the Church of Scotland encouraged us to go and hear the man whom God so blessed elsewhere.'

Expectancy

William MacLeod says that the conversion of several folk 'caused great anticipation. Interest in the things of God quickened and all around us folk were expecting great things from God. Everywhere they were praying, trusting and waiting on God to work.... When we were swept into the kingdom, our expectancy rose and we were looking for new converts and praying that more would come and join us in our joy.... An atmosphere of excited expectation and certain hope possessed us as we watched the Spirit of the Lord in the community breaking down barriers, bringing conviction and leading one and another to salvation.

Jack MacArthur says: 'Those who were praying were looking around and thinking, who is it going to be tonight?'

Donald John Smith says, 'The presence of God was so powerful that you were constantly living in the expectation that something was about to happen. You would feel a sort of excitement inside yourself.'

Chirsty Maggie says, 'It seemed that the only thing we spoke about was God and the things of God. We went through the day waiting for the evening meetings. The converts followed the meetings from village to village, gathering strength as they went on. It was a wonderful time.'

John Murdo Smith speaks of the expectancy that prevailed. 'God's people were waiting and longing just as they were at Pentecost – united and waiting for the coming of the Lord in their midst.'

Conviction

This was no easy believism. There was deep conviction as the solemnity of eternity fell on the people. People wept and were broken over their sins. They knew that they had to stand before Almighty God and give account. Eternity was real; heaven was real; hell was real. Their plight was terrible, their judgment certain and eternal. How wretched their condition, how unenviable their position before a just and holy God. They knew that they were doomed and damned. Outside of Christ they knew that there was no hope. Truths which they had known and believed in their minds were now living realities as they realized their desperate need of God's mercy and salvation. Campbell's insistence on the true knowledge of sin and of needed repentance from it produced a deep conviction of sin which characterised the movement.

Mary wandered for three months having a form of godliness without its power and being convicted of her need. She heard her father weep in his room and cry repeatedly, 'Oh God, be merciful to me, a sinner!' He went down to the harbour and wept behind the boats. Donald MacPhail wandered amongst the sheep with deep misery and conviction dogging his every footstep. In fact he spoke to the sheep envying them that they did not have the torturous thoughts that he did. Norman Campbell tried to drown his conviction in drink at the pub – but he could not escape it; it was there! Men and women, broken in spirit, wept over their sin.

Sandy Mor speaks thus of the conviction during the 1939 revival: 'As we came from the meeting we came across young men and women on the road weeping and praying that the Lord would have mercy upon them.' And again, 'We went on a little further and we heard singing and then further along the road another group were crying and asking the Lord to have mercy on them. What a wonderful night that was!'

William MacLeod says: 'I began ticking off the things that were keeping me from the Lord. I was now under conviction of sin.'

Annie MacKinnon says of the 1939 revival: 'I recall how that in the church in Kinloch the conviction of sin was so intense that some of the people collapsed in their pews. They had to be carried out of the church at the close of the service.'

Jack MacArthur recalls how his brother had been the Master of Ceremonies at a local dance, when the minister, Rev. MacLennan, walked in and spoke a few words before leaving. He says: 'My brother who had been so angry couldn't be found anywhere, but was ultimately found in the back of the bus that had brought them to the dance – broken before

God.... Revival had broken into the community.' He relates how that, later, even those who were against the revival were 'coming under the power of the Holy Ghost – under conviction.'

Catherine Campbell says graphically: 'The meeting was mighty and I was overwhelmed with conviction. As I came out of the meeting, I just fell on my knees outside the door. I didn't care who was around. That night I came to Christ.'

Concerning a house meeting, Mary remembers that 'every room was full. I was sitting beside the kitchen but could not hear the preacher for the strange noise that was coming from the kitchen which was crowded with teenagers. They were not hearing what the preacher was saying for they were sobbing. They were gripped with the impression of the presence of God and the fact of their sins. The Word which they had learned at school suddenly became alive and they knew that they stood guilty before the bar of God. These were days of great conviction and outpoured grace. Sometimes at the close of a meeting the preacher's voice could hardly be heard for the sobbing of the people.... In another house meeting on Bernera one night, the power of the Lord was so mighty that a number of girls sitting on a bed just bent towards one another and wept. Duncan Campbell passing by looked at the weeping girls and said, "What a beautiful nest!" They were weeping their way to the Cross.'

Some would come to a meeting and be swept into the kingdom with great joy. Many, smitten with conviction, would carry this terrible burden for days, weeks, months before they got through to God and knew the joy of His forgiveness. One man was in such a state of mind with terrible conviction that Duncan Campbell was called to the house. His wife opened the door of the bedroom and let Mr. Campbell see him writhing and weeping in anguish of soul. 'There he is, Mr. Campbell, there he is, the mighty sinner,' she said, 'and let him take his bellyfull!' as she closed the door on him in his grief. The next day he came through to a glorious experience of salvation.

Mr. Campbell reports (18.10.50): 'We had men and women seeking the Saviour every night, some so distressed under the conviction of sin that it was impossible to deal with them.' And again (29.11.50): 'Conviction and distress of soul was very evident, and one meeting for dealing with the anxious went on until 3 o'clock in the morning.' Of meetings in Barvas he says, 'The crowds attending the services are as large as ever, with the same deep conviction' (13.12.50). He says of meetings in Kinloch, 'People have been in such distress that they have cried out for mercy in the services;

others fainted' (28.2.51). Of Bernera he says, 'Meetings are crowded and full of divine power and conviction, and distress of soul as deep as ever' (15.8.51). He writes again: 'Men who were never near a meeting were suddenly arrested by the Spirit of God and had to give up work and give themselves to seeking after God' (31.10.51). Of Baile-na-Cille he says, 'Men have been found walking the roads at night in distress of soul; others have been found during the day praying among the rocks' (8.11.51). And again, 'as the Spirit of God swept through the meeting, the cry of the unsaved could be heard, as strong men wept their way to the Saviour' (12.12.51).

Of Berneray, Harris, he says, 'On my way home last night I met a group by the roadside in great distress' (30.4.52). From Leverburgh he writes (8.11.52): 'So great was their distress that we had to leave some of them lying on the floor last night.'

The Consciousness of the Presence of the Lord

Without question, this was the outstanding characteristic of the revivals in Lewis and particularly that of the 1949 revival. Without exception everyone to whom we spoke mentioned this as the outstanding feature of the movement.

This was the cry of the prophet when he said, 'Oh...that Thou wouldst come down, that the mountains might flow down at thy presence' (Isa. 64:1). Mountains of sin and difficulty flow down at the presence of the Lord. Duncan Campbell said, 'Revival is a going of God among His people, and an awareness of God laying hold of the community,'[3] and this was exemplified in so many places where the fires of revival burned.

Norman Campbell says: 'The outstanding feature of the 1949 revival was the presence of God. This was also the case in the 1939 revival. You could sense and feel the presence of God everywhere. Even the children sensed something. It was the power of God let loose! People went on their knees anywhere.'

Annie MacKinnon (Kintyre) says: 'I felt as if the Spirit of the Lord was in the very air one was breathing – and it was just wonderful! The atmosphere was not just in the church but everywhere.'

William MacLeod says: 'I shall never forget the intensity and blessing of those days. They made a mark upon me that has never been erased and for which I shall thank God for ever.'

---

3. Colin N. Peckham (1986), *Heritage of Revival*, The Faith Mission, p.165

Agnes Morrison says: 'Whatever we were doing and wherever we were, we were conscious of the presence of God. We had no desire to go to sleep. Even though we had so little sleep we were not tired.'

God was in the meetings bowing the hearts of the people. Things which would have been spoken of easily and without any special significance were suddenly imbued with spiritual meaning and power. When young Donald MacPhail rose to his feet to pray and said 'Father' it was enough for a congregation to burst into tears.

God was in the homes; God was speaking to people at their daily work. The consciousness of the divine was everywhere. Mary speaks about walking on the road and being conscious that the place on which she was standing was holy ground; of going out in the boat with her father and looking down at the fish, realizing that it was God who made all these creatures; of sitting in a cinema and being brought face to face with God even by the subject shown on the screen – *The Wonders of the Deep*. She, and others, have described the presence of God as a canopy overhead. She says, 'Everywhere I went I was conscious of God.'

Donald MacPhail tells of the convicting presence of the Lord when he was out in the fields with the sheep. Kenny MacDonald says: 'Wherever you went you could not get away from the presence of the Lord.' Chirsty Maggie claims: 'God was everywhere, in the very atmosphere. Whether they were godly or godless, people knew that God was there.' An unsaved man in Arnol said, when invited to the meetings, 'I don't need to go to the meetings to know that there is something supernatural going on in the village. I feel it in my own home.'

John Murdo Smith says, 'Now, if I were to tell you the outstanding features of revival it is this. There was a universal consciousness of the presence of God – a sense of the Lord's presence was everywhere. On the streets, in the shops, in the school – wherever people gathered revival was the topic of conversation. It was by no means confined to revival gatherings – wherever people met, even in the public houses, the revival was the topic of conversation. On the buses, and I know of even two of the bus drivers who conveyed people to the meetings being converted. Everyone seemed to accept the fact that the Lord was working in the parish – a universal consciousness of the presence of God.'

Catherine Campbell says, 'The presence of God was everywhere, not just in the meetings. We could not get away from the working of the Holy Spirit. God accompanied you everywhere. This is the abiding memory of the revival.'

On one occasion several men were walking home from a meeting in the early hours of the morning. They stopped and looked back at the area from which they had just come where numbers of the lights in the homes were still burning. Instinctively they removed their caps and stood in the darkness in the presence of the Lord whilst one said softly, 'My brethren, God is everywhere.'

Of the Lemreway movement in 1969, Donald MacAulay says, 'When the revival broke out the presence of the Lord was felt all around Lemreway. It seemed to be a circle around the village or a canopy over the area. Outside of this circle there was nothing; it was just so ordinary.'

When God appears on the scene and makes Himself known as a felt reality, repentance, return, yielding is easy, for He is seen as the One to whom all honour is due. Gratitude then becomes the irrepressible fountain of consecration and service. We come gratefully and gladly to pledge allegiance to the One who died and lives for us now. *God* becomes our salvation. It is not merely clever arguments which draw the soul; it is the presence of God. He is unspeakably precious and we fall in worship before Him in true and utter dedication, giving Him our all. Christians are restored, refreshed, quickened and revived and the unsaved are drawn by the revelation of His presence to trust Him for salvation. His presence is everything and it certainly makes the feast.

The Power of God

Donald MacPhail remembers that 'there was a solemnity that settled on the community and we were convicted whether we attended the meetings or not.... On the Thursday we had an after-meeting at 11.00 p.m. at number 28. The atmosphere changed and we were very conscious of the presence of God. Something happened – it was as if the power of God swept through the house. Most of us sensed the awesome change and a number came under deep conviction of sin.'

Of a meeting in Bernera, Donald says, 'The power of God was intense. It was a wonderful evening of the revelation of God's presence and power.'

Mr. Campbell reports on 28.6.50: 'I look back with gratitude to God for all I have witnessed of the mighty power of God during the past six months.' Of meetings in Ness he says (31.1.51): 'There was a mighty manifestation of the power of God in the meetings last night. Wave after wave of Holy Ghost power swept over the meetings and strong men were broken down and crying for mercy.'

Early in the New Year (23.1.52) he reports: 'Last night we witnessed a mighty manifestation of the power of God. As a young lad from Arnol was praying, God swept in, in power, and in a few minutes some people were prostrate on the floor, others with hands raised up fell back in a trance. We were in the midst of it until 1.00 o'clock in the morning.' Of Callanish he says (12.3.52): 'Several young men from Arnol came to our assistance, and as one of them prayed, God came down in mighty power, and before his prayer ended souls were rejoicing in deliverance.' Of Uig he reports (11.3.53): 'On Friday evening we had a great manifestation of the power of God in the hall at Crowlista. I had to stop preaching, until the cries of the people who came under the power of God became more subdued.' He says of Berneray, Harris (13.5.53): 'I had a powerful meeting down by the shore before the boats left to take the Harris people home.'

Singing

Singing was a mighty instrument in the revival. They were singing the Word of God and this, filled with the presence of God, made the singing mighty in the Holy Ghost. The people sang with all their hearts and meant every word they sang. The words became arrows in the hand of the Almighty and many were the slain of the Lord as His Word penetrated the hearts of the people with enormous power in song.

Of the 1945 revival in Harris, a lady reports of the journey from the island of Scalpay, next to Harris: 'In the morning as we travelled back in the boat, the people began to sing the psalms while the precentor led. The singing was wonderful!'

Different expressions describing the singing in the 1949 revival were used: 'the words went straight to my heart;' 'the singing was like fire going through my whole being;' 'the singing was out of this world, I had never heard anything like it;' 'the glory of God was in the singing;' 'revival singing is anointed singing;' 'I could never describe what the singing meant to me;' 'the singing was powerful;' 'the singing was dynamic;' 'As we sang from our hearts often the atmosphere would change dramatically and it seemed that heaven itself was present.' Kenny MacDonald or 'Ban' (*ban* in Gaelic means *fair* or *blond*) says, 'they sang – oh how they sang!' Margaret MacLeod reports: 'And the singing! It was simply glorious. It was almost supernatural, full of joy and spiritual power.' John Murdo Smith recalls, 'And the power of God in the singing! A foretaste of heaven!' Mary says, 'When the people sang, oh, the shivers chased themselves up and down my spine. I had never heard singing like this.... The words rose to heaven in a power that could only be sensed but not described. The singing was fire! It went right through you.' Paddy says, 'To hear an awakened congregation singing this Psalm (132) in an atmosphere pregnant with the presence of God was an experience which one could never forget.'

Often they sang **Psalm 126:**

When Zion's bondage God turned back,
As men that dreamed were we.
Then filled with laughter was our mouth,
Our tongues with melody;

They 'among the heathen said, The Lord
Great things for them hath wrought.
The Lord hath done great things for us,
Whence joy to us is brought

As streams of water in the south,
Our bondage, Lord, recall,
Who sow in tears, a reaping time
Of joy enjoy they shall.

That man who, bearing precious seed,
In going forth doth mourn,
He doubtless, bringing back his sheaves,
Rejoicing shall return.

Another favourite among the many favourites was **Psalm 72:17-19:**

His name for ever shall endure;
Last like the sun it shall;
Men shall be blessed in Him, and blessed
All nations shall Him call.

And blessed be the Lord our God,
The God of Israel,
For He alone doth wondrous works
In glory that excel.

And blessed be His glorious name
To all eternity;
The whole earth let His glory fill,
Amen, so let it be.

Donald John Smith reports, 'As you sing in revival you sense the Spirit's presence and know the reality of the subject of which you are singing to the extent that you want to reach out and touch it. And of course we were singing the Word of God, for the psalms are the hymn-book of the church in the islands.'

He tells of how in the summer they would go out to the shielings (small huts) on the moor and be awed at the sound of the singing coming over the loch, 'There is a loch beside our shieling and on a quiet night the singing at the worship in our shieling seemed to echo across the loch. Singing from other shielings wafted through the silence. It seemed to spread far and wide.'

The singing outside of the meetings was challenging, inspiring and full of joy and victory. They sang everywhere. They sang on the public transport buses, they sang on the buses coming to and going from the meetings; they sang after the meetings in the street outside the churches; they sang in groups as they walked; they sang after the house meetings in the small hours of the morning.

Some of the girls from Shader, called the Shader singers, often began the singing and many would join them as they praised the Lord from the depths of their hearts. Agnes Morrison, one of the Shader singers, says: 'In the small hours of the morning, on returning from a meeting, we stood on the street, loathe to part company, and we would sing and sing and sing!'

Catherine Campbell says: 'After the meetings we would make a circle on the street, holding hands and singing at the top of our voices. It was heaven on earth. Everything was made new.'

The night that Mary came to Christ, after the after-meeting, a number of the young people went down to the beach at the Port-of-Ness harbour, and walked along the shore singing above the sound of the waves. One of the few English songs they knew, and which they sang with full hearts, was

> Now none but Christ can satisfy,
> None other name for me;
> There's love, and life, and lasting joy,
> Lord Jesus, found in Thee.

It was all a wonderful expression of the touch of God upon them and of the blessing which they were experiencing. They praised the Lord!

Joy
This was one of the outstanding features of the movement – joyfulness! The spirit of joy was infectious.

In the gatherings of the saints there was spontaneous and exuberant joy. When they met at the roadside or in the meetings, there was always the evidence of God's thrilling presence and their joy knew no bounds. 'Wilt Thou not revive us again that Thy people may rejoice in Thee?'

Here are some of the expressions: 'We were thrilled to be involved in the meetings.' Kenny MacDonald reports: 'I was filled with unspeakable joy; my heart was absolutely free.' Norman Campbell says: 'I was flooded with inexpressible joy.' Norman MacLean says: 'it was the most glorious period of my life.' Margaret MacLeod says, 'I couldn't stop crying, but I was crying for joy.' Donald John Smith (Balantrushal) comments: 'And the joy! Even in the fields you felt an inward urge to sing.' John Murdo Smith reports, 'I have never in my life experienced such rejoicing.... When people were converted – the rejoicing! When those who were praying and labouring saw it happen they rejoiced!' William MacLeod says: 'Joy welled up within me. The joy of it all was beyond explanation. This was one of the unspeakable gifts which we as the Lord's people had at that time – this indescribable and overwhelming joy.'

When Mary's father trusted Christ in the middle of his formal prayer at evening prayers in the home, he was filled with irrepressible joy and wanted to go out into the street and shout abroad, 'I'm saved!' Joy was the wonderful privilege of those who were in Christ and who, with joyful expectancy, watched as others trusted the Lord in meeting after meeting.

Fay Hay says, 'Oh! The singing in her house that night! The rejoicing! It was just beautiful!'

The cottage meetings were times of great rejoicing when all were welcomed whatever their denomination. There was such a unity and a bond among those who were there that it still exists today. They are, as it were, 'the children of the revival'.

Mr. Campbell says of Barvas, 'there was great joy among the Christians in seeing men and women coming into the glorious liberty in Christ' (19.8.51). He says of Baile-na-Cille, 'One elder in his prayer yesterday said "the hills and the valleys are shouting for joy"' (14.11.51).

Love and Unity

So many spoke of the love that existed among the people of God. Bonds were formed – forever! Numerous quotations could be given from many people to confirm the fact of this wonderful unity amongst those who were heart and soul in the meetings. They loved one another! Jack MacArthur speaks of preachers staying with them in their home and of the love which embraced these who were really an extension now to their own family. 'Love was shown,' he says, 'by all sorts of people.'

Chirsty Maggie from Arnol says: 'We loved everybody! It did not matter to which church anyone belonged. They were all enveloped in the wonderful love of God! We just loved them all.'

Catherine Campbell says, 'Our hearts were so full of love that we could not keep it in.'

Fay Hay remembers that when she entered the home of some Christians, her friend's 'dear parents flung their arms around me and scooped me up saying, "Oh my love – you will not leave here until you find Christ." '

John Murdo Smith says that 'the older Christians cared for the converts. They were so supportive, so caring. They were so well nurtured.'

Hunger – Late Hours

People in Lewis do not normally go to bed early, and at the time of the revival meetings continued well into the night. Normally they would have the meeting in the church and then another following it in someone's home. In the more friendly relaxed atmosphere of a home, much of the revival work was done and it was here that many came to the Lord.

The house would be filled with people; every room would be full; the staircase would become seats for many. At the height of the revival there would sometimes be yet another meeting, making three meetings in one night. People would be caught up on the warmth and intense fervour of it all and would sometimes arrive home for but a few hours sleep before starting off for work. Amazingly they did not get tired.

Mary says, 'What a waste of time it seemed to go to bed! Often we would come home and creep up the stairs to our rooms in the early hours of the morning. I can recall returning home on one occasion at six o'clock in the morning!'

Sandy Mor recalls: 'Sometimes, because of the meetings, we did not go to bed at all, yet we did not feel tired. We would arrive home from the meetings at 3.00 a.m. or even 5.00 a.m.' He says of the 1949 revival in Point under Rev. William Campbell, that 'the minister would normally preach until 9.00 p.m. and then he would go to the manse for a cup of tea. From there he would go to the cottage meeting until midnight or 1.00 a.m. every night.'

Norman Campbell recalls: 'We would be out at the meetings at 7.00 p.m. and then go home at about 9.00 p.m., have something to eat, then off to the next meeting in Aird or somewhere else until 11.00 p.m. or midnight. After that we would go to a house meeting until 4.00 or 5.00 a.m. This would go on night after night! Imagine Duncan Campbell going to all these meetings. He was not young! Amazingly, we kept going and did not get tired. The power and presence of God strengthened us. It was supernatural for it could not have happened without the Lord strengthening us for the task.'

Roderick MacKay says: 'Although we were in house meetings nearly every night we didn't seem to get tired at all. One night I was in a house meeting until 6.00 a.m. and, without having any sleep at all, I started on the croft work as soon as I got home.'

Annie MacKinnon (Kintyre) remembers: 'I will never forget how the "gillies" would come home in the morning – radiant. "We were not in bed last night. We had an all-night prayer meeting and we are not even tired," they said.'

William MacLeod recalls: 'During and after the third week, at the very height of the movement in Barvas, there were three or four meetings nightly; the first at 7.00 in the church, and then in the homes at 10.00, midnight, and even later.' His wife Margaret says: 'There was an after-meeting every night and after the ice had been broken people were being converted every night.'

Donald John Smith says: 'We were up until 3.00 or 4.00 a.m. at the meetings and then up again between 7.00 and 8.00 a.m. to go to work, and we were not tired!' Alistair MacDonald joins the chorus: 'Usually we did not return home until the early hours of the morning, but still we went to work at 8 a.m. without feeling tired. One seemed to have received supernatural strength!'

Of the movement in Lemreway, Donald MacAulay says: 'We had services in the church every night at 6.00 p.m. Nobody wanted to leave. We would go to the nearby manse, have a cup of tea and then return to the pulpit for another hour-and-a-half. The people still would not go home but gathered in the manse for yet more preaching, singing and fellowship. People left the manse for work in the morning before they went home.'

In Duncan Campbell's reports there are numerous records of people seeking God at all hours of the day and night. He says: 'On several nights the meetings continued until 3.00 and 4.00 o'clock in the morning' (21.12.49); 'Buses came to collect people for a concert in the town; they had to return empty for not one person went' (25.1.50); 'I addressed five meetings today. We simply cannot get the people away and meetings will continue until tomorrow morning. People are here from every parish in

Lewis and Harris' (8.3.50); 'So deep is the interest that during my visit to a certain district all work was stopped, and the day regarded as a Sabbath; meetings were held during the day and at night. Yesterday, buses brought the people a certain distance, others came by boats, but most came over the hill and moor on foot' (24.5.50).

In Stornoway he says: 'On Sunday night every available seat in the Town Hall was occupied' (7.6.50); of Harris he says: 'I never in my life witnessed such crowds in the Highlands. The people came from all over Harris' (26.11.50); 'Every bit of standing room was taken up last night, with the pulpit steps filled. I am addressing two and sometimes three meetings each night, with a final meeting in some home to help the anxious' (13.12.50); 'People are walking over snow-covered roads, many of them a distance of three miles, and walking back home in the early hours of the morning' (20.12.50); 'Meetings have been held in churches, halls, schools and on one night in a shooting lodge; the meetings in the latter place went on until 3.00 o'clock in the morning' (28.2.51); 'So eager were they a few nights ago, that on hearing we were to be in a certain church at 11.00 o'clock at night, they secured buses and arrived an hour before the service, filling the church, so that the people of the district had to remain outside for two hours' (14.3.51); 'On the last two nights, the church was crowded three times, between 7.00 o'clock and 2.00 in the morning' (28.3.51); from Bernera he wrote:'We had a praise meeting this morning at 1.30 a.m.' (15.8.51); 'At 4.00 o'clock this morning we were assembled on the shore singing the songs of Zion as the boats carried them across the sound to the main island' (22.8.51); From Berneray, Harris, he writes: 'One of the elders assured me last night that every person on the island who could be out was in the church' (30.4.52); 'I preached three times between 5.00 and 9.00 p.m. to a crowded church' (1.11.52); 'One church was so crowded that chairs had to be brought in from nearby houses, and even then crowds were outside. A late meeting was arranged for those who were not able to get into the first meeting' (19.11.52); 'Yesterday I had four phone calls from ministers asking for missions' (8.11.52); 'Between midday and 11.00 at night, I addressed five meetings' (13.5.53).

Preaching

Norman Campbell says: 'Duncan Campbell was a fiery preacher and he preached a full gospel. At the first he preached the law with its judgments, but then he would turn to Jesus as the Saviour and Lord. He was utterly sincere and you could see that he meant every word he said. He preached and he loved to preach the glorious truths of the Bible. Even the young people could see his love for the Lord and for the unconverted.'

Mary says: 'Every night now I walked to the church to hear this preacher thunder forth the judgements of God. He stormed up and down the pulpit expounding Scripture and preaching damnation to the lost and salvation to those who repented and savingly believed. I knew one thing – this man was sincere.'

Chirsty Maggie remembers: 'The preaching had been searching, but the night that revival broke out in Arnol it was simply overpowering. The Holy Spirit was applying the Word to many hearts as we listened to the intense presentation of the gospel. The text rang out time and again: "And thou Capernaum, who are lifted up to heaven will be cast down to hell." The preacher, Rev. Duncan Campbell, applied the Word personally: "You are here tonight and you have turned your back on God. Once, twice or even three times you have said, and are continuing to say, 'I don't want to know Christ.' You have been lifted up to heaven, but you will be cast down to hell!" The power of the Holy Spirit was overwhelming, the sense of the presence of God bowed all our hearts.

'Duncan Campbell was inspired. He was fiery, and his penetrating words spoke to the heart. He thundered forth the message in great power, and held our attention throughout his sermon. He preached with tremendous "grip" and boldness and we realized that he was utterly sincere in his proclamation of the truth. He preached to the heart. He was certainly God's chosen instrument at that time.'

Jack MacArthur remembers: 'If you had seen Duncan Campbell at the end of the meetings you would know that he put everything into it! He was wet through!'

John Murdo Smith says: 'Mr. Campbell would preach with great power, preceded by one of the prayer warriors engaging in mighty prayer. One could feel the power of God coming down, and then Mr Campbell was ready to preach. Further invitations came, and wherever he went, people were converted. The amazing thing was that most of them were in the eighteen to forty age group.'

Kenny Ban says: 'Mr. Campbell was undoubtedly God's instrument on Bernera.'

So much of the preaching in the island then was good theologically and biblically but was not always specifically applied to daily living. Duncan was not giving staid theological lectures. He was preaching from his heart, and that preaching was practical, plain, personal, passionate, penetrating, powerful. He spoke to the heart with tremendous authority and boldness, and he thundered forth the message with the utmost sincerity, quoting numerous biblical texts and passages as he went. You certainly knew where you stood before a holy God at the end of those meetings.

Andrew Woolsey writes: 'There was nothing complicated about Duncan's preaching. It was fearless and uncompromising. He exposed sin in its ugliness and dwelt at length on the consequences of living and dying without Christ.'[4]

Mr. Campbell's messages were written on papers of various sizes. Some on mere scraps of paper. They were not written out in detail at all. He would simply write a word to remind him of a particular illustration, so nobody but he would understand the scribbles which were his messages. They were in Gaelic.

Mary had mercy upon him and took his scraps of paper, sorting out the material as best she could, and, with his help and comments, printed them out clearly in an exercise book; all in Gaelic. They are preserved in this book which we have. Each sermon would take up but a page or two of A5 paper. It would consist of three or four headings with a few explanatory notes under each head. At the side of the sermon would be the dates and places at which it was preached. We have thus preserved a record – not complete by any means – of the sermons preached in the various places in which he ministered during the revival.

In our careful perusal of these messages we are again amazed at their sheer simplicity. There is nothing complicated or difficult to understand. There are no Greek verbs explained, no theological concepts unravelled, no detailed analyses of biblical passages. It was very simple exegesis backed up as he spoke, with numerous texts quoted from the Scriptures and applied with enormous power by the Holy Spirit in an atmosphere of the presence of God. It was God's method of reaching the hearts of the people at that specific time, and was greatly used to this end.

Theology

Mary says: 'He preached on an eternity without God, on the doom of the sinner, on the wrath of God, on the power of the Cross, on the glory of the redeemed, on the wonders of heaven. Oh, the gospel rang forth. It was terrible in the ears of sinners but thrilling to those who had responded and yielded to the Saviour. It was no easy believism. We understood very well that there was a hell to shun and a heaven to gain.'

---

4. Andrew Woolsey (1974), *Channel of Revival*, The Faith Mission, p. 127.

It was a theology which was personally applied. This is evident in the testimony of Chirsty Maggie when she speaks of the strong words which Duncan spoke to the hearers personally, applying the Scriptures to their specific conditions and needs. It is also seen in the testimony of Norman MacLean who speaks of the minister seeming to know all about his whole life, and preaching so forcefully on the subject of sin.

He spoke clearly on the *depravity of the heart*. The people knew this doctrine having heard it from the pulpits, yet he applied it to their hearts and they had nowhere to hide. Sin's wickedness had ruined their lives and distorted their nature. Their lives were corrupt. Their understanding was darkened, their hearts deceitful and desperately wicked. They were carnal and defiled. Their entire nature was perverted and depraved. 'All have sinned and come short of the glory of God.' Man was utterly unable to save himself.

He spoke on the inevitable *judgment of God* on the sinner. He is doomed and damned. He cannot work his way back to God and he cannot will his way back to God. He is bound by Satan and cannot free himself from bondage. He is defiled and cannot cleanse himself from sin. He is without hope and without God in this world. He is under the terrible wrath of an Almighty God.

In Lewis, a stronghold of Calvinism, the doctrine of *the sovereignty of God* takes a prominent place. Duncan often said: 'I believe in the sovereignty of God, but I do not believe in a sovereignty that nullifies man's responsibility.' He not only emphasised the sovereignty of God, but also the responsibility of man, securing a balanced approach. In Lewis no appeals for salvation are ever made in the churches lest they encourage superficial professions. He followed this tradition and never made an appeal, believing that God would bring those who were seeking Him through to salvation. He never actually led people to the Lord, but often cleared a room after a house meeting where he would meet those who were seeking God, to pray with them and to encourage and guide them in their search for salvation, giving them Scriptures as he did so. This was his normal method of operation. His practice did not disturb the island methodology.

He emphasised the subject of *holiness*. This key subject was at the heart of the revelation of the God of revival. When God reveals Himself in the community it is as the Holy One, for that is His essential nature: 'God is holy.' In the revelation of Himself, He can do no other than to show man who and what He is. Before His holiness man sees his sin and repents of that sin so that the relationship can be restored and a Holy God can dwell in the man whom He has cleansed from his sin. God calls man to Himself and therefore to holiness. It is His will that man should be holy; He commands man to be holy; He promises that He will cleanse man from his sin; He provides the means by which man can be holy, even the precious blood of the Lord Jesus Christ.

He emphasised *prayer*. This was always to the fore. Prayer was at the heart of the whole movement. The Barvas area was, in that telling phrase of Margaret MacLeod, 'a community at prayer,' meaning of course, the Christian community. It was not only the two old ladies and the men who prayed in the thatched house (which Duncan mistakenly thought was a barn); no! every Christian was absorbed with the possibility of God coming in revival power. He himself spent many hours in prayer, alone and with those who met with him for the purpose of storming the battlements of heaven. He called on men who knew how to pray to come and help him in the fight at one campaign after another.

On one occasion he was with Rev. Angus MacFarlane (Mary's cousin) for meetings in his church. Mr. MacFarlane told us that he was out on the croft when Duncan came to him from the manse, waving his arms and calling to him, 'Revival is coming; it's coming. I have been in prayer and have got through to God. Revival is on its way.' That night revival broke out in the meetings.

The After Meeting

Duncan Campbell never actually led people to the Lord in the revival. He did not sit down with them and point them to the Scriptures in which they could place their trust. He did not take them through step by step, Scripture by Scripture. He explained the Scriptures and exhorted them to trust in the Word and in the Lord, leaving them to actually commit themselves to God.

He arranged after meetings to which he invited those who were concerned. Sometimes in the church he would invite them into the vestry and sometimes just in an area at the front of the church. At times the Christian folk remained to be with the seekers, and at times the seekers were alone with him or together as well with any minister who was present.

In the homes he would sometimes ask for a room to be cleared, for every room in the house would normally be filled, and then invite the concerned to go into that room where he would accompany them and pray with them. He would sometimes ask someone to pray before he spoke to them, or he would pray himself and then give a brief exhortation before praying for them all, sometimes individually.

In these after meetings he would be so tender and compassionate, so kind and concerned, so encouraging and reassuring. It was in these intimate sessions that he spoke so tenderly, often on John 10:27: 'My sheep hear my voice. I know them and they follow me, and I give unto them eternal life.' The storming prophet had become the gentle counsellor. People sometimes came to faith right there in the after meeting, and sometimes, like Mary, it was the beginning of a search which led them to a radical experience of Christ.

Of these after meetings Rev. James MacKay says: 'Mr. Campbell would preach for fifteen minutes on the simplicity of the way of salvation from such texts as: Isaiah 1:18; Isaiah 55:6; John 10:27. He would shed light on the fact that seekers should be sincere in this solemn and personal matter – that they must believe the Word of the Lord and be obedient to it.' He speaks of some coming to faith immediately and of some being healed as they went, just like the lepers whom Jesus healed.

Chirsty Maggie recalls: 'The thundering prophet became the tender shepherd when he spoke to seekers in this gathering. He used to read from John 10: 'My sheep hear my voice...' and gave such gentle and compassionate advice before praying with them. He never went through the biblical points or steps to God, but he would let them seek the Lord on their own.... In the pulpit he was dynamic, but when he spoke to seekers in the after meeting, he was as gentle as a lamb. "I will say a few words on the simplicity of the way of salvation," he would say. He was like a different man altogether, explaining and helping – and the people loved him. Why, we must never move away from the simplicity that is in Christ Jesus.'

Phenomena

Mary says of these phenomena: 'We saw physical phenomena. They did happen, but they were not central. The awareness of the presence of God was central; the phenomena were peripheral. The physical phenomena were not distracting, because it was all happening in an atmosphere of God.'

Trances (or Faintings). Margaret MacDonald testifies to this phenomenon: 'People fell unconscious through the fullness of the revelation they received through the Word and their faces were radiant as they reflected the heavenly visions which they beheld. I have seen this on a number of occasions. No-one understands these experiences except those who were thus moved.'

Roderick MacKay says: 'Some Christians felt the presence of the Lord so strongly that they were completely overcome and fainted or went into a trance.'

This was the most common physical phenomenon of the revival. It was much more prevalent in the 1939 revival than the 1949 revival. It happened in several places but in others, e.g. Ness, there was very little of this, or any other extraordinary physical manifestation. The work, however, was just as deep. John Murdo Smith remembers the 1939 revival: 'Most of the meetings were held in the homes of the people, though there were many in the churches. I remember being in some house meetings where there were physical manifestations – perhaps prostrations, people raising their arms, crying to God. In some of the meetings, while someone was praying, one of the converts would stand up and pray loudly. Now, these things happened in the first revival I experienced in 1939.'

In speaking of the 1939 revival, Sandy Mor says: 'The next revival in our parish was known as the revival of manifestations, for many at that time fell into trance-like states and other manifestations like prostrations. These were common.... Many elders, members and even ministers looked on these manifestations as being a delusion. They said that the people were hysterical, but that was not true. This was the way that the Spirit of the Lord was handling people – people who, without doubt, were genuine children of God.'

He tells of his own experience in the 1939 revival: 'The first time I ever fainted in a meeting was on one occasion when I was last to pray. As I prayed, I was suddenly made aware of the state of the lost in our district. A great burden fell upon me as I interceded on their behalf. Eternity seemed to open up to my view and I felt my strength leaving me. I simply passed out. The intensity of that burden has left me but I have never forgotten those moments.'

Donald John Smith says: 'By the standards of the 1939 revival, the 1949 revival was very quiet.'

Norman Campbell says: 'There were many trances in the '39 revival, but not so many in the '49 revival.'

Kenny Ban says of 1949: 'On some occasions some fell into a trance for the duration of the meeting. They would not be a disturbance at all but would sit silently with hands upraised. When they came round at the end of the meeting, their words seemed to have the scent of heaven. We were awed at times and at other times they simply left the meeting with us all, having met with God personally in this unusual way. It was no hindrance, and the folk regarded it as something which was a characteristic of the workings of the Spirit.'

House Shaking. Sandy Mor tells of another great event: 'There we sat, waiting on the Lord when suddenly the house shook! It shook! There are witnesses still alive who will confirm this. The six girls on the bench fell to the floor. The daughter of the home called out to her parents who were in bed, "Get up, get up, the house is falling!" ' This took place in the 1939 revival but a similar event happened in Arnol in the 1949 revival.

Heavenly Music. Sandy Mor tells of an event in the 1957 revival in Point: 'Four of us heard this phenomenon on two occasions. We could not understand the words but it was like the singing of a congregation, but singing as I have never heard singing! I will never forget it as long as I live! It was awesome! It seemed to be travelling overhead and then downwards over the manse. We stopped in our tracks and listened, not knowing at that moment how to react to the phenomenon. We were filled with amazement.'

Annie MacKinnon (Harris) says, 'One day before the revival in 1945, I walked to the tweed shop which was just below my aunt's home. As I climbed up the hill to her house, I heard beautiful singing. On my arrival, I said to her, "You are surely in great form today." "Why?" she asked. "Because I heard you singing and your singing was simply wonderful," I replied. "No, my dear," she said, "I haven't been singing." Amazingly, I was privileged to hear this heavenly singing before I knew the Lord as my Saviour, and furthermore, before the movement of the Spirit in that area. Perhaps it could be described as a moment of joyful heavenly anticipation.'

Of a cottage meeting in Arnol, Chirsty Maggie says: 'My brother and I were sitting near the bottom of the stairs when a wonderful thing happened. It was near the end of the meeting. My brother and I heard heavenly music as if it came out from the closet under the stairs. It seemed that a heavenly choir was passing through! It was somehow not like voices, but like an orchestra, yet more wonderful. It was simply a marvellous sound. It was heavenly! It wafted through from under the stairs and moved slowly across the foyer and out through the front door. We looked at each other. I leaned across and whispered, "Calum, did you hear that?" He nodded. Mrs MacFarlane, the minister's wife, was sitting in the doorway. She heard it too. She looked at us and saw that we were amazed for we had heard the heavenly music. She rose, tip-toed across to us, and said, "Did you hear that too?" Not everybody heard it, but to those who did, it brought a sense of awe and reverence. Wonderful moments!'

Catherine MacAulay remembers that as about twelve people sat around the table in the manse she heard something very wonderful. She says: 'Having filled their cups with tea I walked from the dining-room to the kitchen and between the doors I heard wonderful singing. I stood in the doorway and said, "Where is that singing coming from?" It seemed to be like heavenly singing. I had never heard anything like it. Another of the ladies heard it as well and said, "I heard it when you were in the dining-room filling the cups." '

Light. Margaret MacDonald speaks of the phenomenon of light in the 1939 revival: 'A bright light came through the door and passed between twins sitting in front of us. Then it seemed to pass through my brother. We could not speak of this experience but later when my brother was killed in the war I looked back on the occasion and wondered!

'A group of us converts were walking together with linked arms. Ruaridh Alex was talking and I did not want to disturb him. I saw a light at my feet and at last I said, "What is this light I see on the ground?" We looked behind us and the light was there. We looked upward and it seemed as if the sky was split open and we were encircled in this light. Everyone in the group saw it.'

Norman Campbell speaks graphically in his testimony of the wonderful vision of Christ which he had the night that he was converted: 'Suddenly a light like the brightness of the sun, on this dark night, shone around us. I looked up to see where the light was coming from and I saw the face of Christ. That was where the light was coming from – His face! I shall never forget it! It was like the sun, just like the sun! And the joy on that face; and the love reflected from that face! I cannot explain nor describe it. Then He said, "I love you," and the "you" was in the plural, meaning "all of you". The vision lasted only a few seconds but it seemed that it was a few minutes. I was simply flooded with inexpressible joy and seemed to be afloat in an ocean of love.'

Visions and Dreams. William MacLeod says: 'God amazingly spoke to some in dreams. Some women in Barvas had dreams about the awakening. On looking back they realized that these dreams had come true and that the Lord had been communicating with them in this manner.'

Annie MacKinnon recalls of the 1939 revival: 'Some people had such visions of hell and a lost eternity that they were even collapsing on the dance floors! These were never seen on the dance floor again!' She says again, 'There were prayer meetings every night in the home of one of my relatives during that revival. She said that a godly man had a significant dream before the revival commenced. He saw an angel passing over the villages, and the villages where the angel tarried were the villages where revival came and the ones the angel by-passed were not visited.'

No Age Gap

Kenny Ban records: 'There was a wonderful sense of unity and oneness in the Lord Jesus. There was no generation gap; there was no difference between young and old. The old became young! There was simply a blending of spirit and a oneness of desire, of longing, of waiting on God, of seeking His face. The unity was tangible. We loved one another.'

John Murdo Smith says, 'The young converts desired to be in the company of the older Christians whenever they could. We learned so much from them; we gained so much.'

Sandy Mor tells of the 1957 revival, but this could be said of any of the Lewis revivals: 'Someone said that if the young lambs came to the elderly it was because the elderly had something to give them.'

Mary says: 'We gathered in many homes, but there was one which drew us like a magnet, the home of a little hunch-back man named John. He had never gone to school, and all that he had learned he had taught himself. When, as young converts, we used to visit him, the first thing he would do would be to put away the clock, and say, "Now youngsters, forget about the time." That little hunch-back man would sit back on his seat and begin to speak to us about Calvary. His face was as the face of an angel. After singing and praying and listening to this man of God, we would come creeping home in the early hours of the morning.'

Alistair MacDonald adds, 'For the young converts, older Christians were there to encourage them in their spiritual life – and how we loved these old saints!'

Witnessing

William MacLeod said: 'Another result of the revival was the boldness which we all had; boldness to witness, boldness to rejoice, boldness and such freedom to tell to whoever was listening that we had given our lives to Christ. This was part and parcel of the revival. We were so full of it that we could not help but talk about it!

Margaret MacLeod said: 'We spoke to everyone about the Lord – and it was so easy! Words just flowed so naturally whether we were speaking to old or young, converted or unconverted.'

Song Writing

Catherine Campbell recalls: 'My brother John met me in the doorway of our house and quoted to me a verse of a hymn which he had just composed. He was newly converted and was the first convert to begin composing hymns.'

Chirsty Maggie from Arnol says: 'My sister Margaret wrote thirty Gaelic hymns. She had no such gift before the revival and her songs have gone on tape to Gaels all over the world. In fact five people in this village received the gift of poetry and wrote spiritual songs. That was just part of the revival.'

It was reported in the *Keswick Week*, 1952, that Duncan Campbell said that eighty-three hymns were written in the revival, and despite the fact that the message in the revival was one of severity, they were all on the love of God.

Continuance

Margaret MacLeod said: 'When we came to Uig we found that many of the office-bearers in the church had been saved in the revival. Not only were they converted but they continued steadfastly to follow the Lord, and became stable pillars in the church.'

John Murdo Smith says, 'So many of those who were converted were young, so many of them are still office bearers in the churches in Lewis. From that revival there were at least eight ministers, many lay missionaries, many office-bearers and members.'

Annie MacKinnon speaks of the 1939 revival: 'There was an element among the people who doubted the genuineness of the work but the fruit of the revival remained.' And again: 'Those who are saved in revival never seem to lose the glow.'

After a tour of several places in Lewis, Mr. Campbell says (28.5.52): 'It was a great joy to find the converts going on so well. Two-and-a-half years have now passed, and there has been practically no backsliding; only four of the hundreds who professed. For this we praise our God.' From Leverburgh he writes (28.10.52): 'Several days have been spent visiting districts touched by the revival, and in every place we saw much to encourage and praise God for; the converts are going on well and growing in grace.'

On 26.8.53 he writes: 'I, along with several ministers from the south, visited Uig, Bernera, Barvas and Arnol, and met with the converts of the movement. We were greatly cheered and encouraged to find them all going on and growing in grace, and to God's glory we can report that no-one in the districts mentioned has gone back.'

Rev. James Murray MacKay says this of the converts after the 1949 Barvas mission: 'There are over 100 in this district who have come to saving faith since the beginning of the awakening, God is keeping them all; not one of them has gone back.'

Chapter 10

Incidents in the Revival

The Beginnings

Much has been said of the two old ladies and their praying. Peggy and Christine Smith lived in a small cottage next to the garage on the Stornoway side of Barvas. Their home has been demolished. Duncan Campbell highlighted them on several occasions in his messages. Although both were over eighty years of age, infirm and arthritic, they were effective prayer warriors and knew God in a special way. (In fact Christina was still attending church in 1949, but Peggy was blind.)

But they were not the only ones. 'It was a community at prayer,' said Margaret MacLeod. What a statement! Others agree; the Christians were praying.

In 1949 everyone who was truly longing for God was seeking the Lord for an outpouring of the Holy Ghost. The Christians were praying! When Duncan Campbell found it impossible to come to Barvas, the two old ladies declared that God would bring him, but many other people who were walking with the Lord and who had that same burden for revival on their hearts said the same thing. There was huge expectancy in the air and people were not going to take 'no' for an answer. Prayer was spontaneous. As people visited one another in their homes, they would pray and then continue on until they felt that they had got through to God. The community was already seeing God at work in the salvation of souls before Mr. Campbell set foot on Lewis. That he declined the invitation to Barvas, saying that his programme was full, only added fuel to the fire and they prayed all the more fervently that God would overrule and bring this man to them. A huge volume of prayer ascended from Christian folk all over the Barvas area for revival. The place was soaked in prayer. It became a way of life – to seek the Lord for His mercy.

God gave promises; to the aged sisters: 'I will pour water on him that is thirsty, and floods upon the dry ground' (Isa. 44:3); to others He gave many other promises as they sought the Lord.

Some of the church officers met, on occasions, in the thatched cottage of Kenneth MacDonald (Coinneach Beag). There were only a few of these thatched cottages or 'black houses' left. People had built attractive homes and were using these cottages for storage until they succumbed to the weather. To make a distinction between the normal homes and the old style, low, thick-walled thatched cottages, Duncan Campbell described the place where they met as a barn, perhaps thinking that it was actually used as a barn.

Kenneth MacDonald, John Smith the blacksmith, Ruiridh (Roderick) Alex MacLeod and Donald Saunders Snr., were some of the great prayer warriors at that time and they, together with others of the church council, were at the heart of those burdened for revival. They were converted or were deeply blessed in the 1939 revival, so they knew what they were asking for and they continued to plead the promises of God. They normally prayed twice a week into the night while the Smith sisters prayed at the same time in their cottage on the south side of the village, and others prayed in their homes as well. This continued for months.

One must not forget that many were burdened and were also praying and seeking God for a move of the Spirit just as earnestly as the sisters and the elders and deacons. The Spirit of supplication was being poured upon the community.

One night when they were waiting on God in the 'barn', Kenneth MacDonald rose, opened his Bible to Psalm 24 and read, 'Who shall ascend into the hill of the Lord? Or who shall stand in His holy place? He that hath clean hands and a pure heart.' He then said, 'It seems to be worthless to be gathered here night after night seeking God as we are doing, if our hands are not clean and our hearts are not pure. O God, are my hands clean? Is my heart pure?' At that moment the presence of God flooded the place and several of the men fainted or fell into a trance, with the overwhelming awareness of the Eternal. God had come to them in this wonderful and humbling manifestation. John Smith said that at that moment they all became aware that the holiness of God and revival were inextricably linked. God came, and when He came it was in a revelation of His holiness.

While Mr. Campbell highlighted this story, it is interesting to note that no-one to whom we spoke knew anything about that meeting, for so many mighty prayer meetings were being held at that time. God came to meeting after meeting in the district. As Duncan himself said, 'Revival was already there before I came to Lewis.' The fact that some of the men in that meeting fell into a trance was not particularly significant as that was the case in other prayer meetings as well. The people still had vivid memories of the 1939 revival when this phenomenon was widespread. Donald Saunders Snr. often fell into a trance in prayer. So while that meeting was significant, it was one of many other meetings which were equally significant as the praying people of the community of Barvas sought God in importunate prayer. Others were getting through to God in other homes and they were soon to see what God could do as this community waited before Him.

The House that Shook

It happened in Arnol, just two miles south of Barvas. The meetings were hard at the beginning, so increased prayer was required and the praying men of the district rallied round. They gathered in a large home in Arnol for an extended period of prayer. It was the home of Donald and Bella Smith (no. 10A Arnol). The meeting was making heavy weather and prayers were not flowing freely. It was a hard battle as one after another attempted to break through in prayer.

Some time after midnight, Duncan Campbell asked John Smith, the blacksmith, to pray. He had not prayed all night. He rose and prayed for some time and then said: 'Lord, I do not know how Mr. Campbell or any of these other men stand with you, but if I know my own heart, I know that I am thirsty. You have promised to pour water on him that is thirsty. If You don't do it, how can I ever believe You again. Your honour is at stake. You are a covenant–keeping God. Fulfil Your covenant engagement.' It was a prayer from a man who was walking with God.

At that moment the house shook. Someone next to Mr. Campbell said to him, 'Mr. Campbell, an earthquake.' The next day they were to discover that no other house shook.

It was a mighty moment that Donald MacPhail remembers, for he was sitting on the crowded stairs beside two unsaved neighbours, Christina Campbell (no.33) and Donald MacLeod (no.31). They had been dozing, but in a moment they were wide awake under deep conviction of sin. They began to cry for mercy. In fact Christina wept and cried aloud for help. Both were saved that very night.

Campbell pronounced the benediction, and they left the house to discover that at that hour the people were moving to the meeting hall. Some were carrying chairs wondering if there would be enough room for them. Torch lights shone in the darkness as the folk moved towards the hall. God had stepped in to a scene that seemed so hard and difficult. The move of the Spirit in Arnol had begun.

Berneray, Harris

Mr. Campbell had on many occasions received invitations to minister on the small island of Berneray with its population of about 500, but had been booked elsewhere on each occasion and was unable to go. This Berneray is called Berneray, Harris, but is closer to North Uist and was normally approached by a ferry from there, or by ferry from Harris. Today there is a splendid causeway connecting North Uist and Berneray.

Duncan Campbell was one of the speakers at the large Faith Mission Easter Convention in Bangor, N.Ireland. On the platform at Bangor, he felt an overwhelming urge to go immediately to Berneray, Harris, and told the chairman of the convention that he must leave immediately despite the fact that he was to speak the next night. He felt that he had no choice but to obey God.

Leaving Bangor he undertook the wearisome journey over land and sea and eventually stepped off the boat on to the island of Berneray. He saw a small boy and asked him to tell the minister that 'Duncan Campbell was on the island'. The boy replied that there was no minister on the island, and Duncan asked him to tell the leading elder the news. The boy soon returned with the news that he was expected and that he was to stay with the elder's brother.

Later it transpired that the elder, Hector MacKinnon, the postman, had been wrestling with the Lord in the barn the previous day, saying, 'Lord, I don't know where he is, but, Lord, You know. Please send him to us.' That was the time in Bangor that Duncan sensed that he had to go to Berneray.

During the meetings which followed, the Holy Spirit was poured out in a similar way to that which they had experienced in Lewis, and numbers of people were saved. The central fact again was the sense of the presence of God.

Hector wrote many spiritual songs and hymns, some of which, Mary has sung on the BBC Gaelic Radio programmes.

The Dance at Carloway

This is a wonderful story which has been told many times. It concerns Rev. Murdo MacLennan who, in the small hours of the morning, walked onto the dance floor in Carloway. It was the night that the pipers were saved and when Alan Ian MacArthur, the Master of Ceremonies at the dance, also came to the Lord.

This story has been told by Alan Ian's brother, Jack, in his testimony elsewhere in the book, so will not be repeated here.

Praying at the Roadside

Sitting on the platform of the YMCA in Bayhead, Stornoway, at the Annual Faith Mision Convention in Lewis in 1964, Duncan Campbell leant over to Colin and said, 'See that lady coming in the door? She's the one who prayed at the road side.'

He was referring to an incident during the revival when he was driving along a road on his motor bike at 5.00 a.m. He saw a young woman seemingly in distress of soul near the road. He went to her, told her who he was and asked whether he could be of any help. She told him that she was greatly burdened for the nearby village in which she lived and that she was looking to the Lord to send revival to them. She and others had been praying for the village for some months, but they had not yet seen anything which would encourage them.

Although it was not exactly the done thing for a Presbyterian minister to be praying with a young lady at the road side, he felt that they should do so. They knelt at the road side and poured out their hearts to the Lord for a couple of hours crying to Him to come and visit them.

Fourteen young men in the village were deciding how much drink to bring in for the weekend. One said, 'I think that we had better bring in more than normal for this may well be the last time that we bring drink into the village.' Another said, 'You don't mean that the revival will come here, do you?' In a little while those men were under deep conviction and they were converted – every one of them. There was no preacher to enlighten them, no special gospel event, no charged atmosphere; just the power of God working by the Spirit in their hearts. Led by the Spirit they trusted Jesus Christ as their Saviour.

Years later they were still following the Lord and many of them became elders and deacons. God works in amazing ways His wonders to perform.

Chapter 11

Opposition to the Revival

One of the painful experiences at this time was the opposition to the revival. It is sad to speak of these things, but to gain a picture of the whole, this subject needs to be mentioned. We do not want to cause any grief to anyone on the island or to those who may be related in any way with these events. We trust that all that is recorded here is as accurate as it is possible to be. There is no vindictive spirit at all in the recording of these matters, but it is told with the hope that lessons may be learned and that such unwelcome events will not be repeated in any future movement of the Spirit.

The opposition came mainly from the pulpits. All the Church of Scotland pulpits were open to Mr. Campbell and he was eagerly awaited and gladly welcomed from one church to another. He came to the island at the invitation of the Church of Scotland.

The small Free Presbyterian denomination was strong in its opposition. They urged their people 'to have nothing to do with the so-called revival activities of the present day'.[1] They were altogether outside of the revival zone.

The Free Church, dominant on the island, was rigid in its opposition. To understand this, it is necessary to grasp something of the history of religion in Scotland.

Historical Divisions
The great Disruption of 1843 was an enormously emotional event when families and communities were torn asunder. It was virtually the evangelicals who came out of the National Church to form the Free Church.

In 1900 when the Free Church joined the United Presbyterians to form the United Free Church, most of Lewis was against the union and remained in the Free Church to keep their biblical and Calvinistic distinctives. There

---

1. *Stornoway Gazette*, 22 June 1951.

were those in Lewis who nevertheless joined the United Free Church. Only one minister, Hector Cameron of Back, remained in the Free Church; the others went into the union (another minister, Hector Kennedy of Park, changed his mind after a few months and returned to the Free Church). Nevertheless the vast majority of the people did not follow their ministers into the new denomination. Rev. Alistair MacDonald, who was the Church of Scotland minister in Ness, relates the events of those turbulent days in the Ness congregation: 'This was a very boisterous time to say the least, for Rev. Donald MacDonald of Ness decided to go into the Union. Stones were thrown through his windows, corn stacks of those who stood with him were burnt, and peats and stones were hurled at those who sided with the Union. In fact a force of policemen from Dingwall landed at the Port-of-Ness to keep the peace, standing on the roads and at the church to allow those who wished to worship to do so in peace!' *The situation described by Alistair MacDonald was that of a congregation prevented from using its property because their former minister had joined another denomination. While this does not excuse the behaviour of some, it does explain the strong feelings.* He continues, 'The case of the ownership of the church property eventually went to the House of Lords which ruled that the majority should have it, which of course was the Free Church. Finally in 1908 a building was erected which is now the Church of Scotland in Ness.' Naturally these strong feelings were passed down from one generation to another, lessening with the passing of time.

In 1929 when the majority of the United Free Church merged with the Church of Scotland, again the Free Church remained a separate body. It is worth noting that Duncan Campbell also remained outside this union, but became a minister of the minority who had continued as the United Free Church. These changes merely strengthened the resolve of the Free Church not to yield to liberalizing tendencies but to remain separate. They would not give an inch to the liberal views of those who were joining together to create a large and broad national church. They would remain a biblical and Calvinistic community. Their people would not worship or associate on a religious level with those of the Church of Scotland lest they be tainted by liberal views. These attitudes strongly persisted in 1929.

The widespread 1939 revival was only ten years later and these attitudes were still very prevalent then. When Christians from both the Church of Scotland and the Free Church rejoiced together in the Free Church in Barvas in the 1939 revival, the minister, Rev MacLeod, was having none of it and locked the church, refusing to allow them to meet there again.

Margaret MacDonald says that one of his elders, 'Sandy Alex's father, cried out, "I built this church with my own hands and now it is locked to me!" ' There was deep hurt at the insensitive handling of this and other incidents. The people had found one another to a large extent, but the ministers guarded over their flocks in lesser and greater degrees, not wanting them to be contaminated by possible liberal views emanating from the Church of Scotland. The ministers then had great power and what they said was virtually law. The fact of the matter was, however, that all the Church of Scotland ministers on the island at that time were thoroughly evangelical, and preached the Word clearly. It mattered not — they were of the broad national church which was then largely liberal.

Rev Kenneth MacRae was the minister of the largest and most influential church on the island, the Free Church in Stornoway, from 1931 to 1964. He was the spokesman for all kinds of issues and was well respected in the island. He felt very strongly that the Free Church should not lose the Reformed doctrines upon which it stood and was outspoken about these issues. He took a decided stand at Church assemblies and caused some discomfort among his own colleagues in the ministry. He wrote a booklet called *The Resurgence of Arminianism* in which he takes a stand against anything which he regarded as not being Reformed. 'In MacRae's mind one of the greatest hindrances to evangelism in Scotland was the inculcation of unbelief by the Church of Scotland.'[2] Generally the Free Church ministers were very sceptical about the Church of Scotland and looked on it with grave suspicion.

The 1939 Revival

There were several reasons why the Free Church leadership were concerned about the 1939 revival. Firstly, from the Free Church point of view, the 1939 revival was questionable because it was a layman's revival happening mainly in the Free Church. No minister took a leading role. Godly elders felt the burden to pray and gathered the people in prayer meetings where God's presence was such a powerful reality that many found the Saviour all over the island. On occasions when a minister was present, he was asked to preach, but generally the meetings were held in homes, halls and, sometimes, churches, led by elders and deacons. Various ministers felt differently about the movement, and to some its progress was acceptable although they may have felt somewhat uncomfortable as to the physical manifestations.

---

2. *Diary of Kenneth MacRae*, edited by Ian Murray (1980), The Banner of Truth, p. 447.

Secondly, it was questionable for some in the Free Church because their people mingled freely in these wonderful prayer meetings with the Christians from the Church of Scotland, and that opened the door for future problems! Most churches at that time had missionaries who assisted the ministers, and on occasions these Free Church missionaries worked closely together with the Church of Scotland missionaries. Some ministers in the Free Church wanted nothing to do with a church which, although preaching the gospel on the island, was linked with what they saw as apostasy on the mainland. Yet their own members and sometimes their missionaries were thrilled to be enjoying the presence of God together in homes and halls without a thought of the distinction between the churches.

Thirdly, it was questionable because of the manifestations. Some thought that they had just gone too far and regarded it all with suspicion. Many have testified to the fact that the 1939 revival was a revival in which there were many manifestations. There were, in places, loud shoutings in some of the prayer times and there were faintings and trances. There was unusual excitement, and all this was regarded with unease by some of the Free Church ministers, despite the fact that most of this revival occurred in the Free Church. Some looked upon the manifestations as delusions and avoided the meetings.

Kenneth MacRae believed that all these phenomena could be explained as 'mass hysteria'.[3] When his own congregation showed signs of that which was taking place elsewhere, he noted on 16th May 1940, in his Diary, 'There has been no "swooning". I think that matter has been effectively scotched in this congregation. I shall be surprised if it gives us any more trouble.'[4]

In Point, where the Free Church minister, Rev. William Campbell, had experienced revival in his own church, there was no opposition. Both Kenina MacLeod and Norman Campbell remember that 'the two churches were as one'. The unity was such that if the one church service ended before the other they would wait for one another and walk home together.

It largely depended on the minister of the church as to how strong the opposition was to the movement, or in fact, whether he actually felt an affinity with the movement and was able to rejoice with those who were involved.

The 1939 revival, however, certainly did not have the same bitter criticism as the 1949 revival, but the movement slowly diminished in intensity as the war encroached on all of society in the years that followed.

---

3. *Diary of Kenneth MacRae*, p. 442.
4. *Diary of Kenneth MacRae*, p. 371.

The 1949 Revival

After all this mistrust of the Church of Scotland and after the interlude of the war, the revival began again but with significant differences. It centred now in the Church of Scotland and a minister from the mainland of Scotland led the movement.

It is obvious, given the history of the two churches, that it would be very difficult for the Free Church ministers to believe that any good thing could come out of 'Nazareth'. Why, they were not part of the broad church, and surely God would not send His blessing to that which, to them, seemed to be tainted and liberal.

Many of the Free Church people joined spontaneously with the Church of Scotland Christians and rejoiced together with them in all that the Lord was doing, but the Free Church ministers stood askance and would have nothing to do with that which emanated from so questionable a source. No Free Church minister ever attended even one of the meetings of the 1949 revival, but they all, except one, stood aloof from it and criticised it with varying degrees of intensity.

This revival was taking place in the Church of Scotland but many of the members of the Free Church attended and joined the band of worshipping and rejoicing Christians. Amongst the laity there was no distinction. It did not matter what church you belonged to. The blessing of the Lord was enjoyed by all who knew Him. There was no distinction in the meetings. They loved one another in the wave of mighty blessing that enveloped them all, whether they were of the Free Church or the Church of Scotland.

This mingling was not acceptable to the Free Church ministers of the day. Some set up rival meetings to keep their flock from straying into forbidden territory. They spoke out against the movement in strong and unequivocal language. Some even stated that the devil had sent Mr. Campbell to the island to create as much havoc in the church as possible, or that he had come to steal members from the Free Church for the Church of Scotland. Unfortunately they did not investigate sufficiently concerning what Mr. Campbell was actually saying and their zeal for purity of doctrine carried them along a line of action which did not advance the work of the Spirit. The opposition was vicious at times and resulted in confusion and bitterness. Some who had come to the Lord in the revival were not accepted at the Lord's table, and sadly turned away to find fellowship in other churches. Some of the Free Church Christians were divided and did not know what to do. On the one hand they knew that the mighty blessing was from God and they rejoiced with those of whatever church connection they happened to be, and on the other hand their minister was opposing the work with strong conviction. Some withdrew from the meetings. Some were saddened and silenced and others took the minister's part and became bitter opponents of the revival. In places the Christian community was divided with rifts which took years to heal. People who had been great Christian friends before the revival were now barely on speaking terms because of the criticism which had split their community.

Most ministers of the Free Church would have no association with the Church of Scotland. The fact that Rev. William Campbell of the Free Church in Point worked so well with the Rev Harry MacKinnon of the Church of Scotland in the revivals which took place there, was incomprehensible and unacceptable to Kenneth MacRae. How could a Free Church minister do that!

Further they had problems with the very man whom God was using in the revival. They called him an Arminian, and that was the crux of the matter. Their criticism emanated from history and culminated in theology. They had assumed Mr. Campbell's theological position but had not verified it for none of them had heard him. On this misinformed assumption their criticism rested and with ardent zeal they fought for the purity of their Calvinistic cause seeking to protect their flocks from the damage which they thought would occur if the people absorbed any of Duncan Campbell's teaching.

Mr. Campbell was not a trained theologian. In fact he did not have any fixed theological position. He was not a five-point Calvinist, and in this they were altogether correct, but he was not a rank Arminian either and in this they were completely wrong. There are degrees of both Calvinism and Arminianism. Mr. Campbell preached a biblical message. No-one who ever heard him doubted that! It was not couched in theological terms but was full of biblical substance. He was a Bible preacher and he quoted extensively as he preached. He was also a simple preacher, ruthlessly exposing sin and pronouncing God's judgment on that sin. That was the message of the revival – a message of judgment and yet of God's great mercy.

Many Free Church people who heard him were thrilled with the substance and theology which he presented. On some occasions he was invited by Free Church people to hold meetings in their Free Church area in spite of the opposition of the ministers. Donald MacAulay tells how that he was encouraged by the elders both of the Free Church and of the Church of Scotland to go and hear Mr. Campbell. In 1954 Mr. Campbell held a mission in Lemreway, Lochs, at the invitation of the Free Church people themselves. What Duncan Campbell came in was not acceptable. In fact some even denied that there was any revival at all! In the midst of salvation blessing, they would not acknowledge that which was evidently happening all around them. Donald John Smith says of the 1949 revival, 'The break between the churches was very sad, and damaged the spirit of the revival.'

Duncan Campbell had a definite message on the fullness of the Holy Spirit and it has been assumed by a recent writer that this was the cause of the opposition, but this had nothing to do with it, for the message of the revival was one of severity, of judgment, of mercy and of holiness. Issues of the deeper Christian life were not to the fore as the preacher dealt almost exclusively with sin, judgment and initial salvation. Others have supposed that the main reason for the opposition was jealousy, and, we would probably be naive if we were to exclude this from the sources of opposition, as well as the fear that their own folk would leave their church in the flush of spiritual blessing.

It is a matter of great regret that the movement of the Spirit on the island was handled in this way by those in positions of authority. The men did not appreciate the worth of that which was taking place and opposed it, sometimes very harshly, because they thought they were acting in the best interests of what they felt was the pure gospel. Sadly they were mistaken.

Today there is a very different picture. The Church of Scotland denomination, even though it has declined enormously in numbers, has had a return of evangelicals to its ministerial ranks, and keen Bible-believing, gospel-preaching born again men of God occupy many of the pulpits in the land. On the other hand a far greater openness and ability to communicate with other believers has come to the Free Church. The situation which pertained in 1949 would not be repeated today, and it is difficult to think oneself back into the harsh events of those days. We trust that lessons will have been learned in the realm of spiritual sensitivity and out-poured blessing.

The Free Church has men of spirituality, stability and standing, of scriptural knowledge and clear evangelical exposition. We hold them in high regard and appreciate their desire to maintain a church based on biblical truth. There is a spiritual depth in the Free Church that is not found in many places in Britain today. We have very good friends in the Free Church and we cherish their friendship in the Lord.

Chapter 12

God's Choice - Lewis

Prayer - Soul Travail

God used a rod in the hand of Moses to part the Red Sea, the jaw-bone of an ass in the hand of Samson to win a decisive battle. God used but 300 men under Gideon to rout the Midianite hordes. God chose young David to defeat the mighty Goliath, and David used five small stones in his victorious conflict. God chose not the king's palace for His Son's birth, but the lowly stable. Jesus chose, not the wise and great men of Jerusalem, but simple fishermen to build His church. He used a little boy's lunch to feed a multitude. He did not ride into Jerusalem on a prancing charger, but on a lowly donkey.

'But God hath chosen the foolish things of the world to confound the wise; and God has chosen the weak things of the world to confound the things which are mighty; and base things of the world, and things which are despised, hath God chosen, yea, and things which are not, to bring to nought things that are; that no flesh should glory in His presence' (I Cor. 1:27-29).

The remote Hebridean islands, in 1949, were a seven hours boat journey away from the north-westerly shores of Scotland, far away from industry and the progressive life-style of the big cities.

Barvas finds itself in a treeless, flat countryside surrounded by peat bogs. And God comes to this island which faces the brunt of the savage Atlantic gales, and to Barvas. Rev David Searle wrote after a visit to the island: 'Barvas (no intended insult to its gracious and lovely Christian people) is one of the most desolate spots on God's earth. Surrounded by monotonous peat moors and bogs, saturated by brine-soaked winds straight off the Atlantic, and with as inhospitable a climate as you'll find in the United Kingdom, this scattered community with its straggling houses along miles of lonely road, was chosen by God. For some reason which we will never fathom, God set His love upon the place, and purposed that it should become the seat of His Shekinah glory. I believe that in the Divine Operations Room, where the map is up on the wall marked with forward battalions in that divine conflict with the powers for evil, Barvas is a golden star, one of the choice companies engaging for the battle for the kingdom. Yet Barvas has no organ, no guitars, no orchestra, no choir, no hymnal even.'[1]

We could add that there are no organizations, no coffee mornings, no Awana programmes as many American churches have for their young people, no boys' organizations, no girls' organizations, no church staff, no seminars, no highly prized programmes. Apart from the Sunday services it has the weekly prayer meeting and other spontaneous prayer meetings which occur here and there. That's all!

Perhaps we should learn some basic spiritual principles. In churches with different needs in modern city life, various organizations will, of course, be needed, but the emphasis in Lewis is so obviously that of prayer; an activity and objective that supersedes all else. All that which we deem to be so very necessary for success, in God's eyes, may not be so necessary after all. In fact these issues might well get in the way of better things. They could well be hindrances and not the necessities which we thought them to be. We can be so occupied with the trappings when God is waiting for the worship and adoration of our hearts. He is waiting for us to get to the place where He can put within us something of the burden which He bears for a lost humanity, which will then in turn drive us to our knees to intercede mightily in the power of the Holy Spirit.

But we have our programmes; yes sir, we have our programmes! our activities; our essential organizations; our games evenings; our study groups; our musicians; our practices and rehearsals. Many of these activities are wholly legitimate and wonderfully used in the service of the Master. We are busy, busy, busy in the Lord's work. And Lewis prays!

We have perhaps forgotten that the church in the New Testament prayed mightily and 'turned the world upside down!' We have perhaps forgotten that the apostles said, 'We will give ourselves continually to prayer, and to the ministry of the Word' (Acts 6:4). Prayer was first and ministry next. We have perhaps forgotten that God calls us primarily to humble ourselves, to pray, to seek His face and to turn from our wicked ways of barren busyness, of prayerless service, of scant acknowledgement of divine help, of

---

1. Searle, David C. (1987), *Lewis Land of Revival, Thiry-five Years After*, Christian Irishman, p. 2.

engineering our own plans, assuming that God will bless that which we, in our cleverness, have forged and established. Yes, we have our programmes; necessary, necessary programmes! And Lewis prays!

We have our outings too, our parties; and some even have their barn dances, their ceilidhs. And Barvas prays!

Jesus said, 'My house shall be called the house of prayer' (Matt. 21:13). But it's not just Barvas!

Since the 1820s when Lewis was totally transformed in that mighty movement originating in Uig under Alexander MacLeod, all over Lewis these principles of prayer and of waiting upon God for His blessings are well-established principles. Again and again, there have been outbreaks of the working of the Spirit on this favoured island. Uig has seen the mighty working of the Lord; Carloway has been so mightily blessed of God; and Ness; and Point; and many smaller places on the island. Over the years they have been privileged to see the outpouring of the Spirit of the Lord.

Why have these places been so favoured? Why has the Lord been pleased to shower His blessings and reveal His presence in these remote parts? Why? Because they prayed! They prayed expectantly; they prayed persistently; they prayed whole-heartedly; they prayed believingly. They learned to pray as they prayed. The Holy Spirit has taught them in their praying. They have come to learn the secret of pressing through into the courtroom of heaven and of touching the throne. They have waited upon God! As Margaret MacLeod so strikingly said of the Christians in the Barvas area, 'It was a community at prayer.'

Because they have come to know the secret of humility, of seeking the Lord, of depending on Him to work, of importunately laying hold of Him, of passionately pleading with Him, God heard from heaven and came to them, forgiving their sin and healing their land.

They had known revival and they knew how it came. It came, not by organizing, by programmes, by games evenings, but by prayer – and they prayed; it came by soul travail – and they travailed.

Of course, God is sovereign in revival. He comes to us in His own time and as He wills. But He has given us principles, He has left instructions for us to follow. He said: 'Pray!' He said: 'I will build the ruined places and plant that that was desolate: I the LORD have spoken it, and I will do it. Thus saith the Lord GOD; I will yet for this be inquired of by the house of Israel, to do it for them' (Ezek. 36:36-37).

In 2 Chronicles 7:14 we have the classic verse where we are exhorted to humble ourselves, pray, seek God's face, turn from our wicked ways, and

He will forgive us and heal our land. In Isaiah 64:1 we read, 'Oh that Thou wouldest rend the heavens, that Thou wouldest come down, that the mountains might flow down at Thy presence.' The Psalmist prays: 'Wilt Thou not revive us again, that Thy people may rejoice in Thee?' (85:6). We read: 'Break up your fallow ground; for it is time to seek the LORD, till He come and rain righteousness upon you' (Hos 10:12). 'O LORD, revive Thy work in the midst of the years, in the midst of the years make known, in wrath remember mercy' (Hab. 3:2). 'Ask, and ye shall receive, that your joy may be full,' says Jesus (John 16:24), and again, 'If ye shall ask anything in My name, I will do it' (John 14:14). We are to pray! These are God's specific, unalterable instructions.

Yet it is not an easy thing to pray. There is a price to be paid, a price of curbed freedom, of resolute concentration, of agonizing supplication. Prayer is the acid test of devotion. To stay in the presence of God and to wait upon Him, baring your soul to His searching gaze, costs everything. The one who prays must be transformed. Prayer must make him holier, purer, more Christ-like. Prayer is a purifying medium. In prayer we get to know God, and 'the people that do know their God shall be strong, and do exploits' (Dan 11:32). From the place of prayer Samuel Chadwick's great words ring out, 'Men ablaze are invincible. Hell trembles when men kindle.'

We have the supreme example of the Lord Jesus as One who prayed. He prayed in the night (Mark 1:35) so that He might have undisturbed communion. He prayed before His public ministry (Luke 3:21,22), before an evangelistic tour (Mark 1:35, 38), before choosing His twelve disciples (Luke 6:12, 13), before the great revelation of His death (Luke 9:18, 21, 22), after the great achievement of feeding the five thousand (John 6:15), before the simplest affairs of life (Matt. 14:19), when He was busy (Luke 5:15, 16), when He was weary (Mark 6:45, 46), and in the last moments of His life (Luke 23:34). The life of Jesus was a life of prayer. If Jesus needed to pray, how much more do we!

Jesus withdrew into the solitary places to pray. He needed the fenced spaces of silence. We too need habitual times of quiet waiting upon God where we enjoy sweet communion with Him and where we are revived by His presence. We must force ourselves to be alone to pray! Let no excuse hinder your prayer time, for your real effectiveness depends on your communion with God. Become familiar with the courts of heaven. Prayer lifts the soul into heaven, it brings us into contact with eternity, it gives us vision of the invisible, it brings fragrance to the life, beauty to the face, heaven to the earth. 'Those who look to Him are radiant' (Ps. 34:5, NIV).

Agnes Morrison

Catherine MacAuley

Foursome - Mary's parents and the Campbells
Alex Morrison, Mrs Campbell, Mrs Morrison, Rev Campbell

Donald John Smith

Donald MacPhail

Catherine Campbell

Fay Hay

Mary's scooter
Mary Morrison (Peckham)

Margaret McDougall

Mary and Colin

Norman Campbell

Rev Duncan Campbell

Norman Maclean

Rev James M MacKay

Rev JM Smith - Shader

Rev Kenneth MacDonald
(Kenny Ban)

Rev Murdo Maclennan

Rev W MacLeod

Young Mary
Mary Morrison (Peckham)

John Smith's anvil where he prayed daily
before work in the 'Smithy'

Barvas Church of Scotland

Cottage where two elderly sisters, who prayed for the
revival, lived – Barvas. Now demolished

Mrs Annie MacKinnon – Kintyre

The Memorial Hall which Duncan Campbell
entered the night he came to Christ

Duncan Campbell with a piper in
the Highlands of Scotland

The house that shook – Anrol. Now uninhabited

The thatched cottage where the elders met for
prayer before revival – Barvas area

Peat cut from the fields – drying before
being brought to the homes

Peat stacks – fuel for the homes

Prayer is a transforming exercise. Here is the secret of the burning heart and the shining face.

Get through the barriers of wandering thoughts and weary bodies and press on into the presence of God. This takes time, but time must be made! Don't imagine that dreaming or dozing is praying. Prayer demands every faculty of mind and heart, but the treasures it yields are always worth the price that it demands. Wait on God! This is the open secret of spiritual vitality, growth and effective intercession.

Many of us pray just enough to ease the conscience but not enough to win any decided victory. We are playing at praying. We have put very little into it and therefore have received very little from it. Prayer has not been a mighty force but merely a harmless conventionality.

There is such a thing as the *burden of intercession*. There is a cross at the heart of true intercessory prayer, a burden, a passion, an agony. Ezekiel tells of the city given over to defilement but speaks of those upon whose foreheads God had set a mark. They are favoured and spared in the divine judgment for they 'sigh...and cry for all the abominations' that take place there (Ezek. 9:4). Hannah, one of the most profound intercessors, had no language. 'Her lips moved but her voice was not heard' (I Sam. 1:13). Her heart was so full of grief that she could only groan. Rachel in an agony of distress cries, 'Give me children, or else I die' (Gen. 30:1). It was this cry which John Knox was to take up and apply to Scotland in his famous prayer, 'Give me Scotland or I die!' The psalmist cried, 'It is time for Thee, LORD, to work; for they have made void Thy law' (Ps. 119:126), and again, "Rivers of waters run down mine eyes, because they keep not Thy law' (Ps. 119:136).

I set out this burden in a poem which expressed my own heart-cry:

> Barren altars! What reproach!
> Empty cribs! The church forlorn.
> Hear we ne'er God's grand approach?
> Blessed cry of babes new-born?
>
> Havoc wrought midst Zion's sons,
> Dimly burns the feeble flame.
> Few the faithful, burdened ones,
> Vision, passion – but a name!
>
> Bloodless prayers can never bless,
> God forgive! Oft these are mine.

Give, O Christ, Thy brokenness,
Pain-filled fellowship divine.

Christ dwells in the broken heart,
This enshrines Gethsemane,
O, dear Lord, give me this part,
Sacrificial ministry.

Servants of His passion we,
Dazed and aching for the lost,
Marked the sighing forehead see,
One with Christ at life-blood cost.

Supplicate in bloody sweat,
Intercede in agony.
Plead for souls with faces wet,
Passion learned at Calvary.

Souls! My heart breaks with the cry,
What counts else! What matters more!
Give me souls or else I die!
Violence storms at heaven's door.

Sobbing in the secret place,
Broken-hearted anguish know,
Children will be born in grace,
God's transforming blessing flow.

Earnest spirit's fervency,
Flaming breath ascends, avails,
Prayer transcends vocab'lary,
Spirit unctioned prayer prevails.

Heav'ns shall rend and mountains flow,
Fiends of hell in terror flee,
Christ shall reign above, below!
His the glorious Victory!

Moses knew intense agony as he lamented, 'Oh, this people have sinned a great sin…yet now, if Thou wilt forgive their sin; – and if not, blot me, I pray Thee, out of Thy book' (Exod. 32:31-32). In the same vein Paul with 'great heaviness and continual sorrow' of heart wrote, 'For I could wish that myself were accursed from Christ for my brethren' (Rom. 9:3). This attitude is again revealed in his prayer for the Galatians: 'My little children, of whom I travail in birth again until Christ be formed in you' (Gal. 4:19). The Lord Jesus 'offered up prayers and supplications with strong crying and tears' (Heb. 5:7). Paul longs to know 'the fellowship of Christ's sufferings' (Phil. 3:10). The Spirit of God 'maketh intercession for us with groanings which cannot be uttered' (Rom. 8:26).

The gospel of a broken heart demands the ministry of bleeding hearts. True intercession is sacrifice. When we cease to bleed we cease to bless.

F.W.H. Myers in his great poem *St Paul* says:

> Desperate tides of the whole great world's anguish
> Forced through the channels of a single heart.

And again:

> How have I knelt with the arms of my aspiring
> Lifted all night in irresponsive air;
> Dazed and amazed with overmuch desiring
> Blank with the utter agony of prayer.

Because of the demands and price of intercessory prayer, many do not enter its portals and consequently do not gain its benefits. But this is absolutely necessary if revival is to be expected and experienced. If the preacher knows little of this great subject, what will be the results?

Should we not begin to give heed to His command to pray? Should we not call a halt to some of our activities and begin to seek the Lord? Has prayer been on the back-burner in your fellowship? Does it take a prominent place or is it just something we do because we feel that as Christians we have to? Do you know anything of the heart-cry for revival? of soul-travail? When last did you shed tears for the state of our country or for the lost? When last did you feel the pain-filled fellowship of the pierced hand? Do you know what it really means to pray? Or do you just say your prayers? What kind of prayer-life do you have? Shall we not learn the lesson, the biblical lesson, and begin to call upon God?

It is a costly business and few will respond to the call to pray – but this is the way, the only way. Time has not changed God's pattern. As we pray God deals with us. We can never be the same after having had a mighty and glorious encounter with the living God. When in communion with

Him we cannot cling to sin or anything that displeases Him, for we stand before Him in His pure shining glory. Prayer is a purifying medium. He leads us to Calvary – always! And there we come to understand a little of what it cost Him; a little of God's heart-beat for a lost humanity. It is there that He imparts His burden. It is there that we learn of soul travail. It is there that we recognize that we are insufficient for the task of winning lost men and women, and can only be utterly dependent on Him to work and to bring in the lost.

He then sees our dependence upon Him, our acknowledgement that He alone can meet the need; He hears our desperate cry to Him, and then He hears the prayers of the destitute.

There is also the *blessedness of intercession*. Not only is there the passionate plea but also the prevailing power of intercessory prayer. There is the grief and the groaning but also the glory; the agony and sorrow, but also the bliss and ecstasy. 'As soon as Zion travailed she brought forth her children' (Isa. 66:8). 'He that goeth forth and weepeth, bearing precious seed, shall doubtless come again with rejoicing bringing his sheaves with him' (Ps. 126:6).

Abraham pled for Sodom (Gen. 18:23-33), Jacob wrestled in the night (Gen. 32), Moses stood in the breach for the nation of Israel (Exod. 32), Elijah prayed on Mt. Carmel (I Kings 18:36), Daniel prayed in the lions' den (Dan. 6), and they prevailed! Jesus tells the parable of the importunate friend who asked for bread at midnight and whose request was granted because he persevered (Luke 11:5-10). He also tells the parable of the unjust judge who responded to the widow's persistent plea for help (Luke 18:1-8). What power there is in prevailing prayer! Pray on! Pray on!

As we pray God teaches us to pray. No book on the subject, no sermons, no advice can substitute for the Spirit as a teacher in prayer. It is in prayer that the Spirit cries out within us for souls to be won. We may sometimes have to pray through a period of unbelief. Don't lose heart in the battle. Sometimes God will give you a promise upon which to stand as you determinedly pray through to victory.

Our prayers should be Spirit-taught and definite (Rom. 8:26); they should be persevering (Luke 11:9,10; 18:1); they should be believing (Heb. 11:6; Jas. 1:6,7).

Let us use this great weapon of prayer which God has given to us! By spending time in prayer we do not decrease our activity but we increase our productivity and accomplish vastly more. Wesley said, 'God does nothing but by prayer, and everything with it.' Jonathan Edwards said,

'There is no way that Christians, in a private capacity, can do so much to promote the work of God and advance the Kingdom of Christ as by prayer.'

Then let us pray!

Barvas and Lewis, you are teaching us an enormous lesson. Please God, let us learn it, and learn it well!

*Testimonies of those who
experienced the Revivals*

I

MARY PECKHAM
(nee Morrison)
Port-of-Ness, Lewis

Tring...tring...tring!
'It's for you, Mary.'
That phone-call which I received in Glasgow, changed my life.
'You're needed at home in Lewis, Mary. Both your parents are ill and they need you to care for them.'

Back to Lewis

Up to then I had no intention of returning to Lewis. There was far too much religion there for my liking especially as recent disturbing reports reaching me told of another revival in the district where young people of my own age were coming to Christ and attending all the church meetings. No, I was not for going back to Lewis!

I had left the restrictions of my island home to see and experience the big wide world. There were many churches in Glasgow but I had not attended one. My grandmother had placed a Bible in my case when I left home, but it lay there unopened. I enjoyed the free and easy life in Glasgow. There were places of entertainment on every corner. I went to dances and the cinema, and I took part in and thoroughly enjoyed the ceilidhs, the happy, singing gatherings of the Highland folk in Glasgow.

At heart and in mind I was a Highlander and I joined in the Highland activities in the big city with a will. As a child I had been introduced to the concert platform and I was taking part in Gaelic singing competitions. I read avidly but all the wrong books; the gangster stories and the love stories, and I imbibed all their cheap vulgarity. I was learning the worldly ways of all my new-found friends. I never descended into gross immorality, for the teaching of the Bible in school restrained me, but I was far from God. The job which I had held but briefly, was coming to an end and I intended to go down the coast to Ayr and look for another. Now this! I had no option – I would have to go back.

I took the train from Glasgow, the seven-hour boat journey from Kyle to Stornoway, and then the bus to the end of the road at Port-of-Ness. Our home is called *Cliff House* and it overlooks the harbour, the sands where I had spent so many happy days as a child, and the beautiful bay with its imposing headland thrusting majestically into the wide open sea.

I expected my parents to be wrapped up in bed, but my mother met me when I alighted from the bus! I was angry, but I never discovered whether they had contrived to bring me home so that I would be brought under the influence of that which was happening in the district, or whether they were genuinely sick and had made a remarkably quick recovery. Even though they did not know the Lord at that time they knew that this rebellious teenage daughter who had left home for the lights and pleasures of Glasgow needed what they were hearing in the church night after night.

You can take a horse to the water but you can't make it drink. I refused to attend the meetings. Long, long ago my grandmother had taken me to church. I had felt much better for that, but when I attended a Sunday School meeting and the elder prayed for twenty minutes, that was the end of church for me. I never went back! I suppose that I could count on one hand the number of times that I attended church before I was seventeen.

The Influence of the Scriptures

But we could not escape the influence of Scripture, for successive revivals in the island, beginning with the great revival in Uig in the 1820s, had brought the Scriptures into prominence in the schools. There children were taught to honour the Word of God and to memorize many psalms as well as whole chapters of Scripture in both English and Gaelic. They were taught and tested by the ministers of the island to see if they knew the basics of religion and the Westminster Shorter Catechism.

As a child I would go home to repeat that *God is a Spirit, infinite, eternal and unchangeable in His being, wisdom, power, holiness, justice, goodness and truth.* And again that *Repentance is a saving grace whereby a sinner out of a true sense of his sin and apprehension of the mercy of God in Christ, doth with grief and hatred of his sin, turn from it to God with full purpose of, and endeavour after, new obedience.* Quite a mouthful for a primary school child! We were immersed in Bible teaching and theology. We knew right from wrong. We knew the Ten Commandments! In fact it is recorded in the June 1947 issue of *The Instructor*, the Free

Church of Scotland's youth magazine, that I was one of the prize-winners of the denomination's Bible knowledge exams.

At that time, family worship was held, both morning and evening, in each home. Whether the people knew the Lord or not, the Bible was brought out and read and someone prayed. The island was religious and the people knew theology. They drank it in with their mother's milk! Children were nurtured in the fear and admonition of the Lord. Sunday was respected as the Lord's Day and no secular activities took place. In our own home my unsaved father would conduct family worship each night. The Bible had a special place in the home and it was revered as the Word of God.

It was from all this that I had fled, and now here I was, trapped once again in this religious atmosphere. No, I would not go to these church meetings! Outwardly I was bold and brazen in my attitude against all this religion, but inwardly I was afraid. I did not know that the Son of Man had come to seek and to save that which was lost and He had engineered circumstances for me to hear that which I did not want to hear.

The revival was the talk of the place. Go where you would, they would be talking about what had happened the night before, or the night before that, when so-and-so had come to the Lord. 'Did you hear, Mr. X who has been such a drunkard, is now praying in the prayer meetings?' And so it would go on.

One night, when I was in a house where they were talking freely about the work of God in the hearts of people, I suddenly felt such a warmth towards the whole subject that I took fright and exclaimed, 'I'm getting out of here in case I get converted,' and fled!

I had a godly grandmother who suffered from arthritis, and she provided a wonderful excuse for me. Never before had I been concerned about Grandma's needs, but now she was the ideal cover. 'Grandma's dishes have to be washed, and I cannot attend the meetings!' Oh, she was well cared for in those days – until mother put her foot down. My mother was a very determined woman; in fact, my brother declared that the only reason that Rome wasn't built in a day was because Mother was not there!

'Mary, if you are not going, then we are not going.'

'But, Mother, I have no clothes.'

'They are all laid out for you on the bed.'

'I don't know when to stand and when to sit.'

'Just do what the rest do. You just come with us, for we are not leaving you here to make this place a synagogue of Satan.' (When they went off to the meetings I would settle back with a book and turn up the Scottish dance music on the radio. That was mother's idea of the synagogue of Satan!)

Thus it was – Mary went to her first meeting.

The influence of the Revival

There were very few cars then, so we walked the two-and–a half miles to the church. I pretended to be in a towering rage and stormed up the road. As we approached the church, there seemed to be an aura around the whole area. Conversation died and people eased themselves into their seats in silence. The church was packed with young and old. When the people sang, oh, the shivers chased themselves up and down my spine. I had never heard singing like this. They sang the psalms from their hearts. The words rose to heaven in a power that could only be sensed but not described. The singing was fire! It went right through you.

All eyes were on the pulpit and people listened intently to every word that was uttered. There was a tremendous sense of what I later knew to be the presence of God. On my return, as I walked into the house, my father said, 'Well, Mary, how did you like the meeting?' 'I did not,' I replied in a faked rage and stormed up to bed without my supper. The next night no-one had to ask me to attend. My head was telling me that I should not go but my feet were taking me! I never missed a meeting after that for I was being drawn by an inexplicable power. God was at work in me.

Every night I walked to the church to hear the preacher thunder forth the judgements of God. He stormed up and down the pulpit, expounding Scripture and preaching damnation to the lost and salvation to those who repented and savingly believed. I knew one thing – this man was sincere. He preached on an eternity without God, on the doom of the sinner, on the wrath of God, on the power of the Cross, on the glory of the redeemed, on the wonders of heaven. Oh, the gospel rang forth. It was terrible in the ears of sinners but thrilling to those who had responded and yielded to the Saviour. It was no easy believism. We understood very well that there was a hell to shun and a heaven to gain. I knew that these things were true, for I had believed them as the truth of God's Word from my earliest days, but I also knew that I needed salvation and that I was not on my way to heaven. Everywhere I went this strange awareness of eternal things followed me. There seemed to be a canopy of God-consciousness over the whole area and I could not escape it. Not only did I sense the presence of God in the church, but everywhere I went I was conscious of Him.

Scriptures which I had learned at school came flooding back. Whole chapters would course through my mind. Isaiah 53 with its pathos and pictures of the dying Saviour, Isaiah 55 with its great invitation to take freely of the waters of life, I Corinthians 13 with its great emphasis on love, the Beatitudes with their high and holy teaching, Exodus 20 – the ten commandments. These passages, as well as others, returned to haunt me as I daily pondered all these issues before God.

One day, when I was walking down the village street, these words came to me suddenly: 'Put off thy shoes from off thy feet for the place whereon thou standest is holy ground.' I stepped off the grass onto the road for I didn't know what to do. Again the words came to me with such clarity. I stepped back onto the verge. It seemed as if the whole of creation was holy and I alone was unholy.

God was speaking through every little incident. I watched the lark flying overhead and heard it sing so beautifully, high above me. It reminded me of the One who made it. I went out in the boat with my father and there watched the fish swimming beneath me. God made them. The imprint of His hand was everywhere.

But enough of this! I would go to the pictures. These came but twice a month and were shown in the nearby hall. I determinedly marched into the hall to rid myself of all these strange feelings and convictions. There were very few people there, for most were at the church meetings. The first film came onto the screen with the title *The Wonders of the Deep!* God was probing into my heart right there in the hall.

One Sunday, with a cousin of mine, I went upstairs into my room. 'Catherine, let's read the Bible,' I said. We were getting hungry. We each picked up a Bible and began to read. But since we did not want to be found out, we also took a magazine of serial and love stories called *The People's Friend*, so should there be but the slightest sound on the stairs, the Bibles would disappear and we would be found reading *The People's Friend*. Soon afterwards we were sitting together in the church, when the preacher pointed right down at us and said, 'You've got *The People's Friend* in one hand and the Bible in the other.' We gulped in amazement and in anxiety.

One night five of us girls hurried to the church in Kinloch. We were late and would have to find places to squeeze into when we entered the church. As we approached, I looked at the girls and said, 'There are five of us and we are late. You'll see, he will be preaching on the five foolish virgins tonight.' When the preacher announced his text we looked at each other in amazement, for he said, 'Tonight we will turn to Matthew 25 and consider together the story of the five foolish virgins.'

It would be all right if this conversion business did not come to our home. It was good for some but, please, not too near us. There was a fear in my heart lest any of our family became concerned for their soul. One night in the meeting I kept my eye on my mother who was sitting down at the front. To my consternation, I saw her take out her white handkerchief and wipe the tears from her eyes. She buried her face in her handkerchief. A tremendously solemn sense of God came over my soul.

When we came home that night we hardly knew how to speak to Mother or what to do. We trod softly and moved quietly. She was under conviction but it was some time before she found peace with God. A sense of awe came into our home. Here was a situation which we could not handle. The solemnity in our home seemed to be everywhere.

I remember standing outside my parents' room one day when I heard my father, who was a big strong seaman, weeping his heart out as he cried, 'Oh, God, be merciful to me a sinner!' He told us later that he used to go down to the harbour, and there behind the boats he would weep brokenly as he sought God for salvation. One night he was leading the nightly family worship in our home, and in the midst of his prayer, a formal sort of prayer which he repeated so often, he suddenly realized the truth of a personal salvation – a salvation for him! The light broke through as he prayed. He knelt burdened and convicted because of his sin and he rose from his knees saved by grace. He said later that he wanted to go out into the street and tell everyone he could find that he was saved! The joy was irrepressible.

One night during the mission, my mother suggested that I buy a Bible. I did, and seeing other young people going to Rev Duncan Campbell and asking him to sign their Bibles and write in them, I thought that I would do the same. He did not know that I was unconverted and would surely autograph my Bible. On approaching him I found him to be so human, so nice, so approachable, so kind. I thought previously that ministers were away in their own important world, a world from which I was completely excluded, and I was sure that 'ne'er the twain shall meet'. But he was pleasant, so I decided to go and hear him at the cottage meeting which followed the church meeting.

These cottage meetings took place every night in different homes and people would flock in from the church to gather once again to hear the Word and to sing and pray together. This would go on until all hours of the night or early morning. The home would be filled with people, not only in the front room where the speaker was, but every room, with the stairs affording seating for many as well. At times others would be listening at the windows when they could not get in. A great deal of spiritual work was done in these cottage meetings, with their informality and friendliness. They were times of great rejoicing and also of great conviction when many sought the Lord. It did not matter to which denomination you belonged, you were always welcome in the cottage meetings. I can remember coming home on one occasion at six in the morning when the revival was in full flow.

With God's People, Yet Not Of Them

This was my first cottage meeting. People sang and prayed, the preacher preached, and there were those who obviously had been touched by the Word, for the meeting was full of the vibrant power of God. At the close, the preacher asked that a room be cleared and indicated that those who wanted to seek the Lord were to go there. My two friends were weeping and they made their way into the room. I did not know what this was all about, but thinking that it was yet another meeting I accompanied them into the room. The minister came in and closed the door behind him. Suddenly I realized that I was in the wrong place. They were weeping, but I did not feel as they did. I was disturbed about my condition before God, but not like them. I was trapped!

He approached the first girl and asked, 'Are you really in earnest about seeking Christ to be your Saviour?' She managed to squeeze out a 'yes' between her sobs. 'Horrors,' I thought, 'he is going to ask me that too. What shall I say? I can't say "No" to the good man.' So, when he came to me with the same question, I said, 'Yes,' and I felt the biggest hypocrite in the world. With but a few words of explanation he prayed for us. I thought that it was very nice to have someone pray for me like this, but I knew that if I were to be saved, it would have to be God who would save me. His prayers, although very much appreciated, would do nothing for me if God did not work in my heart to draw me to Himself.

We emerged from the room and were ushered outside to Christians who shook our hands. They were so thrilled, so happy. They beamed with joy. The more they shook our hands, the more miserable and convicted I felt. They assumed that I was part of the happy throng who had come to the Lord Jesus, but I was as miserable as sin. I did not belong here and felt like a fish out of water. The more they rejoiced, the sadder I became.

They stood outside the house and sang. It was two in the morning and the singing was simply out of this world. I had never heard anything like it.

Opposite me in the large circle of rejoicing Christians a young girl sang with the rest. The light of God was on her face and I saw there something that I had never seen before. I knew that she had something that I did not have and that I would never be at peace until I found it.

They sang, 'Take the world but give me Jesus.' 'Take the world?' My kilt was in the making for a large concert in Glasgow where I was to sing. This was my first big break in the world of entertainment. Suddenly it all crumbled into little bits. I wanted Jesus more than anything else. It was a night of decision and I decided to follow the Lord. I did not know Him but I knew that this was the right thing to do. The decision was not enough, for mere decisions are never enough. It would be a few months before I found His peace and assurance, but I was now on the right road.

At about three o'clock that morning I knelt in the kitchen of our home beside the old black stove and I prayed the prayer that my unsaved mother had taught me to pray as a child: 'Lord, be merciful to me, a sinner.'

I did not emerge early the next morning for I knew what would be said. The news had spread: 'Mary has been converted; have you heard?' I felt very unconvinced about it all, and there was nobody to whom I could turn for help.

All I wanted now was to go to the meetings and hear the Word of God. On to the cottage meetings after the church meetings and often I would be back home at five in the morning. I went everywhere to hear the Word, but I had no peace in my heart. The Word searched my heart and I was convicted and condemned. People came from all over to these meetings. They came singing and they left singing. Many came to the meetings and wept their way to the cross and then were filled with joy as they were swept into the kingdom. For so many it seemed to be so easy to come to Christ, but for me it seemed to be impossible. I would sing with them and join in all the glad fellowship of those blessed days, but when I got home I would break my heart, for I was empty. I was a stranger to the grace and reality which I saw all around me.

My house had been emptied, swept and garnished, but left unoccupied. I feared that I would slip away and become worse than at the beginning. My desires for the wonderful concert and all that would open for me fell away. I loathed the world now. I had seen the light of God upon not only the face of that young girl but upon many faces. The thought of going back to the world was altogether repugnant. I wanted God more than anything else but it seemed the more I wanted Him the more sinful I became in His sight and the more distant He appeared to be.

One night I was in a cottage meeting on the island of Bernera, off the coast of Lewis. Duncan Campbell was preaching in one of the rooms of the house. Every room was full. I was sitting near to the kitchen but could not hear the preacher for the strange noise that was coming from the kitchen which was crowded with teenagers. They were not hearing what the preacher was saying for they were sobbing. They were gripped with the impression of the presence of God and the fact of their sins. The Word which they had learned at school suddenly became alive and they knew that they stood guilty before the bar of God. These were days of great conviction and outpoured grace. Sometimes at the close of a meeting the preacher's voice could hardly be heard for the sobbing of the people.

That night on Bernera, a young man left the meeting determined not to yield to the Spirit. He went three times to the gate but every time he heard in his heart the Spirit speaking to him and saying, 'It is hard for thee to kick against the pricks.' He returned, closed the door and stood, leaning with his back against it. That night he made his peace with God.

In another house meeting on Bernera, the power of the Lord was so mighty that a number of girls sitting on a bed just bent towards one another and wept. Duncan Campbell passing looked at the weeping girls and said, 'What a beautiful nest!' They were weeping their way to the Cross.

Every night the preacher seemed to hold up a picture of me. How he knew my inward failings I could not tell, but I felt more miserable as the days passed. Sometimes in the presence of the people of God floods of joy and happiness came over me as I rejoiced in their company. I had left the old paths and was with such lovely people. I loved them and didn't want to let them down, nor be a disgrace to them, but I knew that I did not have what they so obviously had.

Lost

One thing of which I was becoming very certain was that I was lost, Lost, LOST! I read the Bible but it condemned me. I listened to the prayers and the sermons and they condemned me. There seemed to be no hope for me. One night coming home from a meeting I was breaking my heart, and to prevent my parents from hearing my sobs I stuffed my handkerchief into my mouth as I passed their door. I wept myself to sleep on many occasions because my attempts to find God seemed to be all in vain.

I was sitting outside in the sun one Sunday afternoon, when our neighbour, my mother's uncle, who did not know the Lord, wandered slowly up to me with his hands behind his back. He looked at me and must have sensed something of the battle within, for he said, 'It's no good trying to get peace by attempting to picture Jesus on the cross, Mary. God must reveal it to you.' That was all – and he walked away.

Lewis is strongly Calvinistic, affirming its emphasis on predestination and election. I began to persuade myself that God did not want me because I was not in the elect. I argued that it would not be right for God to give me eternal life as I had rejected Him. Why should I expect God to have mercy on me when I had lived without Him? One night, in a meeting where there was a large group of teenagers, a minister who opposed the revival said strongly: 'If you are in this meeting tonight and you are not in the elect, the sooner you stop praying the better, for it will do you no good.' Imagine it!

Five of us walked home after hearing this outburst and decided to go and ask Granny what we should do. We had great faith in my godly grandmother. She listened patiently to our sad story and then, without a comment on the theology of the statement, said, 'Don't you worry, you just go and hear Duncan Campbell.' Three of us obeyed and were all converted. One said, 'If I am to be converted, it will be through my own minister.' The minister is long gone to his reward, and there is no word of that man coming to the Saviour. The fifth, a young man, ceased to attend church.

But I was not in the elect! There was no hope for me. I deserved only hell, so there was not much point in my attempting to find God. I was destined for hell and that was my fate. From all eternity it was decreed that I would go to hell. I could not fight against God's decree. My fate was sealed. I therefore prayed a strange prayer and said to God: 'Lord, I love Your people. Please grant me the privilege of spending the rest of my life in their company, (I was only eighteen), and then You can send me to hell, for that is the only right thing for You to do and that is what I deserve.'

Saved

One night I sat in the prayer meeting which I always attended, having resigned myself to my miserable condition, knowing that I was not in the elect. I listened to the elders and others as they prayed. Then the minister closed in prayer, and in that prayer he quoted a verse of Scripture which I knew very well, and as he quoted it I was transported to the place called Calvary. The word he quoted was: *He was wounded for our transgressions, He was bruised for our iniquities; the chastisement of our peace was upon Him; and with His stripes we are healed.*

It suddenly fell on my ears as the sweetest sound I had ever heard. God applied it to my heart. As I gazed at the crucified Jesus, I heard the words, *With His stripes You Are Healed!* I felt the healing balm of Calvary go through my whole being. Nobody needed to tell me. The Spirit of God through the Word of God witnessed with my spirit that, miracle of miracles, I was a child of God! Oh, the thrill of it! What I had despaired of ever receiving was now mine as God applied the Scriptures to my heart. Yes, I was His, and His love and glory flooded my being.

Tears gushed down my face, and I knew – suddenly I knew – that by His stripes I was healed, I was forgiven, I was free. I didn't know the terminology, I didn't know how to put it into words, but I knew that it was done.

> 'Tis done! The great transaction's done!
> I am my Lord's and He is mine!

After that meeting, off we went to another about nine miles away. There the preacher preached on the marriage feast of the Lamb, and I thought that I would soon be there. It seemed as if heaven was bending down over my soul and that I would soon be taken up to be with the Lord. It was glorious! What an atmosphere!

We climbed aboard the coal lorry (truck), which was regularly washed down for the meetings, once again for the return journey, but when we reached the house we looked at each other and thought, 'What a shame to have to go to bed. Surely we should be praising the Lord. We don't want to go to bed.' It was only two in the morning and we were so bound together in spirit that we didn't want to part from one another.

'What shall we do?'

'Let's walk along the shore.'

It was a lovely moonlight night and this group of teenagers walked along the shore, saved by sovereign grace. We began to sing above the sound of the waves:

> Now none but Christ can satisfy,
> None other name for me.
> There's love and life and lasting joy,
> Lord Jesus, found in Thee.

Every one of us had been outsiders, but now we had come into the fold of God.

'Well, we had better go to bed. It's a waste of time, but we'd better go!'
'We'll pray first.'

None of us had ever prayed audibly before, but there we stood on the seashore, a little group of teenagers with bowed heads. Not a sound except the sound of the sea as we each in silence lifted up our hearts to God in gratitude for the salvation that had reached us and lifted us into the arms of Jesus and had imparted to us eternal life.

What a moment! I shall never forget it! Reluctantly we parted and went to our homes.

The next day I met my cousin Morag on the road. 'Morag,' I said, 'something wonderful happened to me last night.' Morag looked at me, burst into tears and fled. She too was under conviction and soon after that came to the Lord as well.

Yet I still could not put it all into words and could not tell what had actually happened to me until one night I listened to an elder praying. He said, 'We thank Thee that Thy Spirit beareth witness with our spirit that we are the children of God.' 'That's what has happened to me,' I thought and rejoiced all the more that I could now express the experience in words of Scripture. He had come to me, was indwelling me and was giving the inward knowledge and joy of that wonderful union with the living Christ. Oh, the thrill and unspeakable joy of those days.

The Burning Heart

But that was not all! I wanted to tell people about Jesus. Over the years I had stood dressed in my kilt on the concert platform in Stornoway and sung to the people, thrilling to the 'Encore! Encore!' Then, I had nothing to sing about – now, I had a message! 'Please God, give me the opportunity of singing to them about Jesus and of telling them about this great salvation;' yes, and later He did give me that opportunity, from that very platform.

I used to weave Harris tweed and I would go to my loom in the shed and would sing as I wove. I became conscious at times that neighbours would gather outside and listen. How I sang then! They must hear this wonderful story of Jesus and His love.

At times I would leave the loom, run upstairs and get down on my knees. I would pray for each house in the village and beyond as well. The burden of lost souls was coming upon me. I had no disciplined quiet time then; why it was just a case of an overflowing expression from the heart.

I had previously told a cousin in the village, how angry I was to be back in Lewis, and had said it in no uncertain way. One day he came into the loom-shed and I looked up at him and said, 'What a wonderful place this is, Angus! This is the most wonderful place in the world!'

'What,' he said, 'only recently you were saying that this was the most miserable place in the world!'

'Things have changed, Angus!'

God had gripped and arrested this life of mine, and I had become a new creature in Christ Jesus. Old things had passed away for ever and all things had become new.

We followed the meetings everywhere. One night we were returning in the back of a truck from a cottage meeting, expecting yet another meeting, but there was no further meeting that night. So we went to the Barvas manse and told the surprised and now awakened minister, Rev MacKay, that we were looking for a meeting. Mr. Campbell was there and rose from his sleep to minister to these hungry, thrilled, but unwise, young people! Some cheek!

We gathered in many homes, but there was one which drew us like a magnet, the home of a little hunchback man named John. He had never gone to school, and all that he had learned he had taught himself. When, as young converts, we used to visit him, the first thing he would do would be to put away the clock, and say, 'Now youngsters, forget about the time.' That little hunchback man would sit back on his seat and speak to us about Calvary. His face was as the face of an angel. After singing and praying and listening to this man of God, we would come creeping home in the early hours of the morning.

We followed the meetings from place to place. The power of God was everywhere. One night a young lad still in his teens was asked to pray in a meeting. Young Donald MacPhail rose and in all the simplicity of his soul, he clasped his hands together as he would do at school. I only heard one word and I was reduced to tears. He said 'Father,' and suddenly the realization of what that word meant dawned on my heart, and I was melted to tears.

Called

I watched the pattern unfold on my loom, and I began to wonder what pattern the Lord was weaving for my life. As the pattern unfolded before my eyes I knew that God had a plan for me. Often meetings closed with the singing of the words of Psalm 45:10: 'Hearken, O daughter, and consider, and incline thine ear; forget also thine own people, and thy father's house.'

What strange thoughts to have when they did not believe in women missionaries or preachers here on this island. There was not one single woman out preaching the gospel. And yet I seemed to be preaching perpetual sermons to sinners. It was a fire burning in my soul. I was at Granny's house one day and I picked up a tract which I found to be an explanation of the text, 'Forget thine own people and thy father's house.' I could not get away from it.

'Lord, I have never given my testimony in public, I have never prayed in public, I just would not know what to do or what to say. And as far as speaking in English, well, I know nothing about English religious language. It is impossible for me to go into Thy service. There are so many fine young men who have been saved in these days. Lord, send them into Thy service.' And He did. Sixteen known to me went out at the command of the Lord into His service.

But the call was persistent – 'Forget also thine own people, and thy father's house.' I argued and argued.

One night, as a group of teenagers stood outside the church before the meeting, Rev. Campbell called me out of the group and said, 'I would like a word with you after the meeting.' What did he want to say to me? When the meeting was over I slipped out of the church hoping to avoid the preacher. He left the church by a side door and came across to me. He did not know me, but must have sensed that God was working in my heart. 'Young lady,' he said, 'Is the Lord calling you into His service?' What a fright I got! More and more I was convinced that I was to go into the service of the Lord. It was burning in my soul. I did not know of anyone who was doing what the Faith Mission was doing, and I wanted to tell people about Jesus, so maybe the Lord was calling me into the Faith Mission.

We were at a communion on the island of Bernera. One message came so clearly to my heart with the story of the colt, 'The Lord hath need of him' (Luke 19:34). Another night at the church meeting Rev. Campbell lost his voice for he had been speaking so often. A house meeting was announced and the people crowded in. It was absolutely full. I found myself sitting on a polished table in a room far away from the speaker. How was he going to speak? He had lost his voice. It mattered little, for if there were no speaker, the meeting would be turned into a prayer meeting and we would be blessed in the fellowship of the Lord's people. His booming voice sounded down to where I was sitting. He announced his text and immediately lost his voice again. But it was enough for me, for the text was, 'Mary, the Master is come and calleth for thee'(John 11:28). He called me by my name. 'Lord, You don't need to call me from the house-tops, I'll go!' I said in my heart.

On the Monday morning of that communion weekend, Rev MacLennan from Carloway, Lewis, preached on 'I press toward the mark for the prize of the high calling of God in Christ Jesus' (Phil.3:14). That message spoke clearly to my heart, and I knew that I had to go. It was a momentous weekend.

How would I break the news to my Free Church parents? The Free Church as a body in Lewis had condemned the revival. Church allegiance was strong and the walls were high between the denominations. Mr. Campbell came at the invitation of the Church of Scotland and preached in its pulpits, but never in a pulpit of the Free Church even though both churches were Presbyterian in doctrine and church government. Because the Church of Scotland (the National Church) is a broad church with ministers of liberal theological persuasions in its ranks – though on Lewis they were all evangelical – the Free Church leaders in Lewis did not believe that revival could come in the Church of Scotland and either denied its existence or opposed it strongly. Their opposition also applied to the Faith Mission, and if I were to identify with the Faith Mission, I could be sure that my parents would suffer. Many Free Church people had been saved and deeply blessed in the movement but officially there was no warmth towards a work which did not originate in their denomination. Denominational prejudice was high.

One day at the meal table I dropped the bombshell. I said, 'I'm going into the Faith Mission.'

After a moment or two of shocked silence, my mother responded. 'Well, if there was anything strange that nobody else would do, you'd do it!'

The possibility of opposition from some quarters made my parents apprehensive and fearful. They did not encourage me to pursue this course of action. Years later my contrite mother said to me, 'Whatever the Lord tells you to do, Mary, do it. I have suffered much in my spirit for opposing you at the beginning, when you first wanted to go into the Faith Mission.'

Bible College

The big moon shone brightly on the water the night I left the island. There was no valedictory service. No-one accompanied me to the boat. It was incomprehensible that this young lady should be going off to an unknown Bible College in far off Edinburgh. I carried my suitcase alone. I suppose that those close to me felt somewhat ashamed of me and what I was doing. I was breaking the mould and it took a lot of courage. Today things have changed and there is an entirely different atmosphere, but I had to wait years for the change to come about. All I knew was that I was obeying God. It was a long and arduous journey, but at last I arrived in Edinburgh.

I came off the coach too soon and carried my case until my arms were nearly wrenched out of their sockets. Eventually I arrived at the imposing buildings and, after all the formalities, handed my £4.00 to the secretary, saying, 'That's all I've got but God has called me.' Two years later I left the College with all my fees paid and £8.00 in my pocket! How faithful is the Lord.

I discovered that some of my fees were paid by an old lady who kept sheep on her croft on the isle of Tiree. She heard that there was a Gaelic speaking girl in the College who would possibly be coming to minister in her island in the coming years. A few years later, my co-worker and I actually spent several winters on Tiree, and were privileged to see the hand of the Lord work in a remarkable way when many sought the Lord for salvation and blessing. Her investment in that young, inexperienced and shy country girl paid off and the Lord allowed her to see the results of what she had been moved to contribute to her training before He took her home to glory.

The College was very strange to me, for I had never been in an open prayer meeting before. I had never heard women pray, nor had I ever prayed in public. I thought that the students had been told who was to follow who in prayer, and every time I wanted to pray, some zealous Irish student would get in first. I would just weep. I thought that I was the Jonah in the College. Gradually I became used to the ways of the Christians on the mainland and fitted into the huge cultural differences.

Service

Training ended and I was out into the work. I was placed in the Highlands and Islands of Scotland. How we gave ourselves to that to which God had called us. There were difficult times and wonderful times. There were times when God drew very near and when the tears flowed freely, when people yielded themselves to God and when we were privileged to witness the wonder of lives transformed by the power of God.

Missions were held in Ardnamurchan, Sanna, Kilmory, Appin, Connell, Skye, Tiree, North Uist, Glencoe and in other places too. Two of us ladies would go to the various places and work in the villages. Praying and preparing in the morning, visiting in the afternoon and speaking in the evening was our normal routine. This programme just went on and on and we were thrilled to be in the service of the King. I also spent two summers working open-air campaigns in Stornoway with a team of Faith Mission lady workers. Conferences, conventions and special meetings were also part of our lives as we continued serving the Lord.

Singing

During this time I was asked to record some Gaelic singing for the BBC (British Broadcasting Corporation) in their Glasgow studios. In total they recorded twelve Gaelic hymns, all with a very definite gospel and spiritual message. This broke the mould, for in the Gaelic culture only the psalms had been used for religious services. Now here I was singing spiritual songs, some of which had been composed by those whom I knew in the revival. The BBC paid me £40.00 and I have never had a penny since!

Ever since then, on Sundays and Friday evening request programmes I have had the privilege of singing the gospel. Ministers, too, when they need a hymn to accompany their sermon over the air, have sometimes used some of these messages in song. It has been a wonderful extension of gospel ministry, for the last forty years, to have had the privilege of singing the gospel to the Gaelic people in Scotland. And this continues, praise the Lord!

One day after recording, as I was leaving the BBC studios, another artist came in. We were introduced. The producer said, 'This is Mary Morrison, and she is a dead loss to us.' He said it in a jocular fashion but he meant it, for they had wanted me to sing worldly songs for the broadcasts, but I had refused, as I only sang for the Lord. I walked down the street thrilling at the thought that I was a dead loss to the world. I had given my life to God and my voice would be used in His service. Over forty years have passed and many of those artists and singers of the worldly songs have long disappeared from the scene. But for forty years I have been privileged to sing the gospel to the Gaelic nation and even now, every three or four weeks, someone will request one of my songs to be sung. 'Him that honoureth Me I will honour.' I just thank the Lord for the continued witness and praise Him for giving me this wonderful opportunity.

Perhaps two places need special mention in the realm of ministry because it was here that we experienced the outpouring of the Spirit as in the days on Lewis. What a privilege to be able to observe the workings of the Holy Spirit.

Tiree

When Jean Wilson (now Blanshard) and I went to the Isle of Tiree in 1953, with its population of about 1,000 people, we arrived just before their annual church social. Neil MacDonald, a former worker in the Faith Mission, then retired, was one of the number who took part in that gathering. He said, 'Every ten years or so we have had a move of the Spirit on the island, and it is just about ten years since the last one took place. We are looking to the Lord for Him to move among us in mighty power in these days.'

We felt very insignificant and inadequate to meet the expectations of these praying people, but we were there and could only look to the Lord to do His own work in our midst.

Over the next two winters we held a number of missions in the different areas of the island, speaking every night in Ruaig, Cornaig, Balephuil, Balemartin, Hylipol, not one of them being less than four weeks in duration; Balemartin being nine weeks, 26th September to 24th November 1954. We visited every home on the island and shared the gospel and sang in most of them. God honoured His Word and blessed us in a wonderful way. Numbers were saved and added to the churches and we rejoiced in the mighty outpouring of the Spirit in so many of these meetings. As in Lewis we sensed the penetrating, humbling, glorious sense of the holy reality and tender nearness of His presence.

At Cornaig we laboured under great difficulties, for the tumbledown former United Free Church in which we were working had its shutters closed against the wind as it howled through the broken windows. There was a space under the door through which the wind swept with a force which would chill you to the marrow. The gales were blowing and we were battling against the elements.

Few people came to the meetings, and sometimes there was no-one. We would then hold a prayer meeting – just the two of us. One night there were two people there. Jean asked the one to pray, but he was deaf and started to sing for he thought that she had asked him to begin a song. This forlorn state of affairs continued for seven weeks. The mission seemed fruitless, but we knew that the Lord had sent us and we were determined to see victory in this place.

We were burdened for the souls of those amongst whom we were working, and would spend long hours in prayer for them. We visited them in their homes, shared the gospel and prayed with them. They were all very friendly and kind but they just did not turn up at the meetings. They gave us eggs to eat in our little cottage. Eggs! We had seven dozen of them! We had eggs for breakfast, for dinner, for tea, and we had them in every conceivable cooking concoction!

One day we had great freedom in our prayer-time together. We said, 'Lord, we did not come here to prove that You could supply our needs, nor for the honour of the Faith Mission; we came here that Your great Name should be glorified and exalted in the salvation of souls and in the sanctification and edification of Christians.' Jean had great liberty in prayer and the joy of victory was so marked that she laughed as she broke through in prayer. 'The devil's on the run!' she exclaimed. We prayed on with great joy and expectancy. The break in the atmosphere had come and we were soon to see what the Lord would do in our midst.

The next night we looked out on the dark, flat, treeless landscape, and wonder of wonders, we saw them coming. Lights were moving towards the church; lights of torches as the people converged on the meeting place. Suddenly there were about eighty people present! Some brought heaters which they placed in different parts of the hall, and this certainly made a difference! God was coming to our aid and the people were coming to hear the gospel. Soon the place was full of people and of the power of God, and we were conscious of His mighty working in so many hearts. God was in the meetings; God was moving everywhere! It was a wonderful time of mighty spiritual blessing. God was in the midst and drew forth from so many hearts that abandonment to Him and that trust in Him as Saviour and Lord. Many yielded to the Saviour and became staunch pillars in the churches on the island.

Recently when we were back on the island we observed that a goodly number of those who attended church on the Sunday were converts of those great days of the moving of the Spirit in the early 1950s. They had stood the test of time and were useful members in the church of Jesus Christ on the island.

One of those converts, together with his wife, attended the Faith Mission Annual Convention in Edinburgh this summer. As he left the convention, he turned, and said, with tears in his eyes, recalling not the convention just ended, but those times of such blessing almost fifty years ago, 'O Mary, those were great times! Great times, Mary!' Yes, he and I knew just what he meant. Great times indeed!

North Uist

The North Uist revival has now been documented and published by Rev. John Ferguson, Church of Scotland minister of Portree, who was a convert of that blessed time, in his book, *When God Came Down.*

Four young girls from the Faith Mission landed in Lochmaddy in April 1957, and made our way to the village of Claddach Carinish where we held our first meetings. We later moved on to Locheport but these, though demanding, were really exploratory and pioneering in nature.

In October 1957, we returned to Claddach Carinish, and then on to Lochmaddy, the main village on the island. I was the only Gaelic speaker of the group and so was constantly called upon to speak to the people in their own tongue. We prayed and prayed. That was the heart and soul of these missions. People began to realize that something was happening in the atmosphere of the place. As the mission progressed, it became obvious that the whole community was gripped by an awareness that something unusual was happening in the meetings. Even the most godless seemed to be restrained, for the lives of folk whom they knew were being transformed and they could not simply shrug that off. People were being saved and the community knew it!

We sent for Rev. Duncan Campbell to come and help us at a few of these missions and he stayed for a few days on each occasion. On one visit the dear man became sick and we had to look after him instead of his being an inspiration to us in the meetings!

In all these missions we normally had two messages each evening, sometimes both in English but often one in English and one in Gaelic. The meetings would last at least two hours. After the meetings we would return to our lodgings and the folk would crowd in. We would hold what was called evening worship with them, and prayer and singing would be part of this time together. The people just could not get enough of the Word and we had to keep pouring out that which the Lord gave us.

From Lochmaddy to Sollas we went. The headmaster granted us the local school but told us that very few would come to hear us. Like a flash God spoke a thrilling word to my heart, 'I will work and who shall hinder it?' And work He certainly did.

The schoolroom as well as the side room were filled. Something was going on that we could not contain, something much bigger than our efforts. The hard work of visitation in inclement weather was all forgotten in the joy of seeing the lost being saved and of seeking God for others. The local Church of Scotland missionary, Alastair MacMillan, threw his whole weight in with us and held after-meetings in his home for the converts until the small hours of the morning. A bus coming from Bayhead to the Sollas meetings on one occasion, carried so many people that its springs broke!

The movement probably reached its height at Tigharry when, in that very rural setting, the first meeting began with 111 people full of expectancy. Kate-Ann Shirran remembers that the talk in the playground at the school centred on those who had been saved the night before. She also remembers the power of the singing in the meetings. 'Revival singing is anointed singing,' she said. 'It is like a fire that goes through one's whole being.' The children would sometimes hold their own meetings at school, modelling them on the evening meetings which so many of them were attending.

Eventually the papers got hold of the story. On 12th February 1958, a report in the *Daily Record* announced, 'Girl Preachers Rock an Island.' Sales at the local bar plummeted and the *Sunday Express* came to get the story of all that was happening during those remarkable days.

Daphne Parker, who later went to the Far East with the Overseas Missionary Fellowship, was normally occupied with the children when the main meetings took place, particularly in Tigharry. She led Kate-Ann Shirran to the Lord as a little girl and Kate-Ann is now serving the Lord very ably and acceptably as a cook in the Faith Mission Bible College. After Daphne had returned from her life's work, she said, 'I went to the Far East and served in the Philippines for about twenty-five years but never again saw the Lord work in the same way. I just thank Him that He allowed me to be there.'

The memory of those days is that of a deep awareness of God and a deep reverence for His Word and work. Each service was different for God was in control. Mr. Dale of the Faith Mission and Rev Duncan Campbell visited us at the close of this memorable period and Mr. Campbell gave the closing message. 'The atmosphere was charged with the power of God,' reports Rev. John Ferguson, 'and in my youthful Christian enthusiasm, I expected every unsaved soul in the place to be converted.'

As I look back over the years, I can only thank God for the privilege of being in Tiree and in Uist at a time when His favour was so remarkably demonstrated. Often we felt that we were no more than spectators of what God Himself was doing.

Elsewhere

Jean and I were later assigned to the Midlands of England, and we laboured largely in the Leicester area until Jean left me to be married.

Invitations were coming in for me to minister here and there and I was released by the Faith Mission to accept these invitations. Meetings followed all over the country. I was given a Vespa scooter and I went everywhere on that little vehicle. On so many of the busy roads in the Midlands, the areas in and around Birmingham and Leicester, that tiny little imp carried me, weaving through the forest of huge trucks, whizzing cars and everything in between. I am sure that my protecting angels – and there must have been quite a few! - were working overtime!

All the 400 miles from Leicester to Edinburgh – it was very cold in the winter with the snow on both sides of the road – and all the way from Edinburgh to Stornoway, over all the mountains and through the isolated Highland glens to my home in Port-of-Ness, right in the very north, that little Vespa carried me at the breakneck top speed of 30 mph! Imagine it, travelling with the icy wind blasting its worst and with the traffic roaring around me; those were some days! God wonderfully protected me as I chugged from one assignment to another. They were days, nevertheless, of great joy and fulfilment in the service of the Lord. Later I graduated from the Vespa to the slightly larger Lambretta scooter and later still to a brand new Volkswagen Beetle which a fisherman from the North gave me to continue the ministry.

Invitations to Canada, to South Africa and to Rhodesia (Zimbabwe) followed. My third visit to South Africa ended in marriage to a preacher, and we spent fourteen years in ministry together in South Africa, twelve of these in a Bible College in Cape Town, during which time God gave us three children. Eventually we returned to Britain for my husband to take up the principalship of the Faith Mission College.

Having retired, we are still very active in the service of the Lord, and are travelling much in this and other countries preaching the Word of God. We look to Him for yet another movement of the Spirit before He comes or calls.

2

ALEXANDER MACLEOD
'Sandy Mor' (Big Sandy)

A Testimony to Four Revivals – Point

Not many people today can testify to having been through a period of revival but the following pages, which Mary translated from a Gaelic audio tape, were recorded by one known locally in the district of Point in Lewis as Sandy Mor (Big Sandy), an elder of the Free Church of Scotland. He testifies to having been through four revivals in his lifetime. This is the first time that this testimony is published in English.

There is something so sacred about these times of divine visitation that it is difficult to put into words what it was like. Sandy, in his opening remarks expresses this: 'These times were so blessed that it is not easy to talk about them.' We are so grateful, however, to Sandy for this vital contribution to the history of revivals. His motive in recording these events was that in days to come when old age would take the edge off his memory, he and his wife Catherine would play it over again and be encouraged and revived. No doubt this would be his desire for others who read this moving story.

We had four seasons of revival here in the district of Point, Lewis. Our minister in the Free Church at the time was Rev. William Campbell who was there from 1926 to 1962.

1934
The first outpouring of the Spirit in which I was involved was in 1934. There was much spiritual darkness at the time. The first awareness we had of a change in ourselves and in others was when we met together in the prayer meetings. There was a oneness of spirit as we engaged in prayer and an increased burden as we interceded for an outpouring of the Spirit in the community.

This led us, as the Lord's people, to have more gatherings together. There seemed to be a compulsion to pray, and we all felt it.

At that time there were plans afoot to build a community hall in the district in order to provide a place for concerts, dances and the like. The church opposed these plans and most of the homes added their signatures to a petition against this building project. The Land Court, however, did not honour this petition. The plans went ahead and preparations were made to build.

Then the 1934 revival broke out. Souls were saved and people from all over the district streamed to the church. Plans for the building were set aside and the hall was never built. It was mostly young people who were saved, young people who, in later life, in every congregation forwarded the cause of Christ.

I recall that at that time our minister Rev. William Campbell, of such blessed memory, preached on Ezekiel 37, that is, the account of Ezekiel's experience in the valley of dry bones. Half-way through his sermon he stopped preaching and began to pray. I have never known this to happen before. The Spirit was outpoured among us and I don't think there was a dry eye in the congregation. The power of the Spirit was evident in a wonderful manner.

I have a vivid recollection of that time. As we came from the meeting we came across young men and women on the road weeping and praying that the Lord would have mercy upon them. Oh! That we would see such days again!

The amazing thing was that there were those who spoke against the awakening – ministers, elders and deacons and others. I recall William Campbell making a statement from the pulpit in Sheshader, Point, about those who opposed the work of the Spirit of God.

'I will say this to you,' he said, 'that the children of God have never done anything more offensive to the Lord than to go against the work of the Spirit of the Lord among His people; inevitable consequences will follow. It will be the judgment of the hardening of the heart. You will be fortunate; indeed it will be a miracle, if this judgment does not overcome you until the day of your death. You may salvage your soul but you cannot escape the judgment of God.'

We saw this happening before our eyes where some were never moved again by the gospel until the day that they died.

1939

The next revival in our parish was known as the revival of manifestations, for many at that time fell into trance-like states and other manifestations like prostrations. These were common.

Many of the great preachers of the past testified of these strange happenings under the power of the preaching of the Word of God, including George Whitefield, John Wesley, Jonathan Edwards and others, and in many of the revivals recorded in history these manifestations were present.

Many elders, members and even ministers looked on these manifestations as being a delusion. They said that the people were hysterical, but that was not true. This was the way that the Spirit of the Lord was handling people – people who, without doubt, were genuine children of God. We ourselves recall going into trance-like states, and this we are certain of, that it was the Spirit of God who was handling us. How we long for such experiences again!

The first time I ever fainted in a meeting was on one occasion when I was last to pray. As I prayed, I was suddenly made aware of the state of the lost in our district. A great burden fell upon me as I interceded on their behalf. Eternity seemed to open up to my view and I felt my strength leaving me. I simply passed out. The intensity of that burden has left me but I have never forgotten those moments.

Many were saved at that time. We held services in our own village at 10.00 p.m. after the prayer meeting on Sunday nights. These were house prayer meetings. We also held these meetings every Tuesday and every Friday until the houses proved too small for the number of people attending.

I recall one night being in a house prayer meeting and being burdened for a particular young man. I went to his home just before the meeting and discovered that he was really troubled in his mind. He really wanted to come to the service for he was concerned about his condition. I did not ask him if he was coming to the meeting, but his mother informed me that he wasn't and that I could go on without him. I replied that I hadn't asked him if he was going. At that, the young man asked for his coat and his mother held it for him as he put it on. His mother then turned to me and said, 'You had better go down by the beach road so that you will not be seen.'

The young man then turned angrily to his mother and said, 'What does it matter to me who sees me? That is not the way Christ came to save me – a lost soul!'

We then left together. We didn't speak on our journey, for I knew that the Spirit of God was striving with him and that it wasn't necessary for me to say anything. All he said was, 'I am going to hell.'

The minister had unusual liberty that evening and six or seven came to the Lord. The elder asked another man to lead the singing of three verses

of a psalm but he declined, asking the elder to do so himself. The elder
did so, but instead of singing three verses, he led the congregation for
seven verses. We felt as if we did not ever want to stop. The singing was
beautiful!

The young man and I set off on our way home and as we walked we
came across a number of people by the side of the road crying.

'We didn't get anything!' they said. 'This one and that one is saved, but
we didn't get anything! What must we do?'

We went on a little further and we heard singing and then further along
the road another group were crying and asking the Lord to have mercy on
them. What a wonderful night that was!

I accompanied the young man to his home and as I returned I saw a
light in one of the homes. It was between midnight and 1.00 a.m. I thought
that I should go into the house in case there were people there who were
seeking the Lord. I glanced through the window and, yes, there were people
inside, so I entered. Six young girls sat on a bench by the window.

The lady of the house requested that I should conduct the worship, but
I was rather shy and did not wish to take the lead in front of so many
people, so I declined. She then said that we should pray for someone to
come who would lead us. Fifteen minutes later the door opened and our
prayers were answered. A relative of mine had gone home after the prayer
meeting and was drinking a cup of tea when suddenly he felt a burden
coming upon him. He set down his cup and stood up. His mother said to him,
'You mustn't go out any more tonight,' to which he replied, 'I won't be long.'

He felt that he should go to Lower Bayble to the first house where the
light was still on. And so it was that he came, in answer to our silent
prayers.

There we sat, waiting on the Lord when suddenly the house shook! It
shook! There are witnesses still alive who will confirm this. The six girls
on the bench fell to the floor. The daughter of the home called out to her
parents who were in bed, 'Get up, get up, the house is falling!'

An unsaved man who was in the meeting began to cry to the Lord for
mercy. 'O God,' he cried, 'have mercy on me,' and then he added in unbelief,
having come to the conclusion that he was not of the elect, 'You won't!'
His sister who was saved, cried out to him, 'O Calum love, He will! He
will! Don't stop until you find Him!' He repeated his cry and his sister
encouraged him to seek the Lord. I will never forget that night as long as
I live; and yet there were Christians at that time who did not believe that
this work was genuine.

It was spring time, the time of year when folk were busy out on the moors, cutting peat from the bogs for fuel. Sometimes, because of the meetings, we did not go to bed at all, yet we did not feel tired. We would arrive home from the meetings at 3.00 a.m. or even 5.00 a.m. We used to sing as we worked out on the moor, and the singing could be heard a mile away. It was wonderful!

Usually when the postman called he would bring all the local news, of sickness, or trouble, or glad tidings of any kind, but at that time the question asked would be, 'Have you heard if anyone was converted last night?' This was the focus of conversation at that time.

1949

On 13th November 1949, our minister, Rev. William Campbell, announced that the Lord was about to do a great work in our midst and that he was going to conduct services, one week in each part of the parish. 'Come out,' he exhorted the people, 'and seek Christ as your Saviour. I am acting,' he said, 'on the authority of the Word of God and I am sure that the Lord will honour His Word.'

The Word on which he was acting was 2 Samuel 5:24: 'And let it be, when thou hearest the sound of a going in the tops of the mulberry trees, that then thou shalt bestir thyself; for then shall the Lord go out before thee, to smite the hosts of the Philistines.'

For five weeks he preached and there were converts every night in all the churches. The district was as one church. There was no word of denominations. People whom I had never seen at church came. On one occasion people sat on every window ledge in the church as the minister preached.

Rev. William Campbell, on one occasion, asked the precentor to lead the congregation in the singing of a psalm and only to stop when he signalled to him to do so. He sang six or seven verses. Each line of the psalm, according to the custom, was sung twice.

The minister then announced that there were many people outside the church and he asked the local missionary to lead them to 'tigh Mhurchaidh a Bhac', a local house. This he did, but many remained as it was a lovely night. Numbers were saved that night. The minister would normally preach until 9.00 p.m. and then he would go to the manse for a cup of tea. From there he would go to the cottage meeting until midnight or 1.00 a.m. every night. On one such occasion Catherine and I went to Alex's house where we found a seat beside a man who was under deep conviction. He was very agitated and later that night he sought and found the Saviour.

The minister announced that the manse would be open every Sunday night for a prayer meeting and that one of the elders would take charge. Some people felt that he shouldn't do this. Whether this was out of concern for his health or simply for some other reason, they objected. It was clear that Rev. Campbell had a deep concern for his parishioners and was willing, despite ill-health, to go to all lengths to see them saved.

What joy to see God's salvation manifested in a row of four homes where, in each one souls were saved. A man and his wife in one; next door, a man, his wife and his sister; a man and his wife in another; and a mother and her son in the last house.

Some time later when it seemed as if the period of conversions was over, but yet the power of God's presence was still felt, three of us went to the first home and we conducted worship. My companions were the minister and an elder named Donald (Domhull an Thangaidh). There were only a few people in the house.

After we left, we proceeded to the next house and we saw that there was a lantern at the gate. 'This is an invitation,' said the minister, so we entered and after greeting the household we conducted worship there. On proceeding further, we saw that the next house also had a lantern at the gate!

'This is another invitation,' said the minister, and in we went! We again conducted worship, and then on we went to the next house which also displayed a lantern at the gate!

It was now 1.00 a.m. or even later. We had unusual liberty in conducting worship in this home, but the minister's wife was restless and I felt unhappy about this. She could no longer contain herself, and turning to her husband she blurted out, 'Don't you remember that the cow calved this morning and she has not been milked yet! She will have fallen in the stall!'

'Oh, woman,' replied the minister, 'the Lord created the cow and gave her to have milk. Surely He can look after her until we get back.'

Donald turned to the minister's wife and said, 'Christina, be quiet!'

They arrived home at 2.00 a.m. to find that all was well with the cow!

Many were converted in the awakening. If I sat down for weeks I could not relate all the wonderful things I saw during this time, and not only saw but felt. All these wonderful happenings enriched and blessed us wonderfully. The memory of it is still doing me good! I believe that those who experienced the power of God and the overpowering of the Spirit at that time, and still live in the memory of what they saw and heard, cannot but pray, 'Lord Jesus, come again and save us!'

1957

The next awakening that we had was in 1957. Quite a number were saved then and some of the converts went into the ministry. We had meetings which continued into the night.

I was with the minister in his study in the manse one night when his wife came in with tea. At that moment we were laughing heartily together. She turned in the door and rebuked us saying, 'How can you laugh when you see the state of the district? Young people without a thought for their souls, even here in this house! What is wrong with you?'

'Oh,' said the minister, 'you just exercise a little patience.'

'Patience?' she ejaculated!

'Yes,' I added, 'have patience.'

'You are no better than he!' she retorted.

'You must be patient and leave it to the Lord,' said the minister.

Two weeks after that I was in the same study and again the minister's wife came in with tea.

I said to her, 'You are so different tonight from what you were the last time I called.' Some of the family had, since then, come to the Lord.

'Oh,' she said, 'now I have reason to be happy!'

The minister added, 'I told her then that she must be patient! She had been looking at the dark side, but I saw the promises of God dispersing the darkness and I knew that this would happen shortly in reality. That was what I held on to and hence my exhortation to her to be patient.'

'You were right after all,' said Christina.

As people crowded into the manse, it was often full despite the fact that it was snowing at the time. There was no tarmac on the road and this meant that the people arrived with muddy shoes. I advised the minister to lift the rugs in the manse in case they would be destroyed.

'What does it matter if the rugs are destroyed as long as one soul comes to Christ!' said Christina.

That attitude would be rare today!

The people of God were wonderfully united in those days. The power of the gospel was reaching the majority of the people. Nobody knew exactly how many were being saved as so many were moved under the preaching of the Word.

One of the favourite psalms during the revival was Psalm 24, particularly the last few verses. How we sang!

Ye gates, lift up your heads on high;
Ye doors that last for aye,
Be lifted up that so the King
of Glory enter may.

But who of glory is the King?
The mighty God is this;
E'en that same Lord, that great in might
and strong in battle is.

Ye gates, lift up your heads; ye doors,
Doors that do last for aye,
Be lifted up that so the King
of glory enter may.

But who is He that is the King
of glory? Who is this?
The Lord of hosts, and none but He,
The King of glory is.

I recall one memorable night when Rev. Harry MacKinnon of the Church of Scotland was taking the service. He called on an elder to pray, and when he stood he quoted Psalm 133, 'Behold, how good and how pleasant it is for brethren to dwell together in unity!'

The windows of heaven opened and the Spirit of God descended. Many were saved that night. Some of the unconverted young people were assembled in the vestibule and I was called upon to pray. I was so burdened for these young people at the door that I moved in among them.

There were some amazing things that happened in this awakening. My father-in-law was in full sympathy with what was taking place in the revival. If there was a meeting anywhere, he would be there. It was impossible to keep him in the house. He was known locally as Murchadh Dhonnachaidh. The young people loved him and he loved them in turn. Someone said that if the young lambs came to the elderly it was because the elderly had something to give them.

Many of those who were converted in the 1957 movement have been called Home and those who remain are the ones who are upholding and forwarding the work of God in our midst. Among these are, one missionary, one minister, four elders and two deacons besides faithful members of the church. They were but youngsters in 1957, some only in their teens.

It is a sad thing to record that in the four revivals which I was privileged to experience, there were in each one some professing Christians throughout the island who denied that these revivals were the work of God.

One night we were visiting a friend when we suddenly became aware of some people crying, but we at the same time heard singing. The lady of the house, who had gone to bed, came out of the door in her night clothes and she cried aloud, 'Something is wrong! I was getting into bed when suddenly I heard crying and singing.' We told her that we had also heard it.

Four of us heard this phenomenon on two occasions. We could not understand the words but it was like the singing of a congregation, but singing as I have never heard singing! I will never forget it as long as I live! It was awesome! It seemed to be travelling overhead and then downwards over the manse. We stopped in our tracks and listened, not knowing at that moment how to react to the phenomenon. We were filled with amazement. After some time the minister joined us and said, 'Why are you not coming in?' We told him about the singing. 'Well,' he said, you ought not to be surprised at this. Is the Spirit of God not amongst us? This is nothing but the singing of the angels, singing and seeing Christ exalted and sinners repenting of their sins!' This was surely the case.

These were indeed wonderful and blessed days in the presence of the Lord. I am grateful to Him for allowing me to be there on those occasions when He poured out His Spirit.

* * * * *

It was in this 1957 revival that Rev. Neil Shaw of the Free Church of Scotland was converted as a young man. He reports:

About fifty were genuinely converted in the small community of Knock at that time. So great was the change in the lifestyle of many, that the bus company running the Saturday night bus run to the town of Stornoway had to cancel that run, in that they only had one passenger using the bus, as compared with a bus-load before the revival.

We met for prayer and fellowship two or three times each evening, going home in the small hours of the morning yet quite able to meet with the demands of work the following day.

A period of struggling and heart-searching lasted for three months before his conversion, and then, (when he eventually broke through to God) he says:

There was now a joy unspeakable and full of glory filling my heart and life. Love for God and His people, and lost souls became my life.

3

MRS. MARGARET MACDONALD
Shader & Ness

1939

I was brought up by my grandparents and at that time I cared for my grandma. I had a godly aunt who was dying when the revival came. I was sixteen then and could not attend the church due to the home circumstances. My aunt knew that revival was coming and told the missionary so. She spoke very naturally of those who would be saved.

'What about this fair-haired one?' asked the missionary, pointing at me.

'She will be one of the first,' she replied, and I left the room very quickly!

I respected the things of God and the people of God. As I could not go to the church I paid careful attention to the family worship and, as Auntie had said, I was one of the first converts!

There was a concert convened in the school hall on the Friday night of the communions in Ness. I was only seventeen at the time and was asked by a local boy to accompany him to the concert. I could not even think of such a thing. My brother went but came home early.

Revival began in Lemreway. People fell unconscious through the fullness of the revelation they received through the Word and their faces were radiant as they reflected the heavenly visions which they beheld. I have seen this on a number of occasions. No-one understands these experiences except those who were thus moved. People will not believe if you tell them. The people would weep. Some of the elders did not understand. Some did. The spirit of prayer would come upon them.

The revival broke out on the third night of the Point communion. The night the revival broke out in Point, a man from Lochs saw angels going across the moor towards Point. In fact he saw them two nights running. During this time there was heavenly singing. I heard it myself the night I was converted.

There were some people from Shader at the Point communion and the presence of the Lord continued with them on the bus home. My brother came under deep conviction on the bus. John Smith convened cottage meetings straightaway and that very night revival came to Shader. The homes were too small and they used the local Free Church which soon became packed out. Eight were saved on the first night. The minister was not pleased that people from both churches were mingling freely in the Free Church and he came and locked it! One elder, Sandy Alex's father from Shader, stood outside and wept saying, 'I built this church with my own hands and now it is locked to me!'

One night I went with my brother to the meeting. I was afraid that he would be killed in the war. We sat on the steps of the stairs to the balcony as the church was so full. A bright light came through the door and passed between twins sitting in front of us. Then it seemed to pass through my brother. We could not speak of this experience but later when my brother was killed in the war I looked back on the occasion and wondered!

A group of us converts were walking together with linked arms. Ruaridh Alex was talking and I did not want to disturb him. I saw a light at my feet and at last I said, 'What is this light I see on the ground?' We looked behind us and the light was there. We looked upward and it seemed as if the sky was split open and we were encircled in this light. Everyone in the group saw it. I have never spoken of this experience and have never understood its significance. One cannot explain these things but there was something personal in it. That was how it was in revival. Some people were so overcome with the presence of God that they fell to the ground. A group of people returning from a prayer meeting fell to the ground without warning. The presence of God was everywhere. At family worship one night, the atmosphere was so charged with the presence of God that one felt one could reach out and grasp that which surrounded us. Along with this came a sense of unspeakable joy.

One lady, Barbara, spent much time in prayer and seemed to be often in a trance. A man, Colin MacLeod, fled to the bar in the town to drown the convictions which so disturbed him, but he did not stay long. He took a lift home and came off near his house. Barbara knew that he had gone to the town and to the pub and came out to meet him. When he saw her he got down on his knees on the road and called on the Lord to have mercy on him.

One cannot understand these things. I have not felt free to speak of these things before as they seem to be too sacred to tell.

1949

The presence of the Lord was the same in the 1949 revival. God was in the midst – everywhere. Often when Duncan Campbell was in the pulpit his face shone. I was reminded of Moses' face shining when he came down from the mount. The glory of the Lord was in so many of the meetings.

The 1949 revival, as is wellknown, was opposed by some ministers of the Free Church, and converts in several Free churches were not allowed to come to the Lord's table. (Some left the Free Church and joined other churches.) They would not believe that it was of God. It was so distressing and hurtful.

People who have never been in revival do not understand the intensity of it all. God is real, eternity is real, people come to Christ in an atmosphere of God. There is no flippancy or light-heartedness. You are dealing with eternal things. I thank the Lord that I was privileged to be there.

One is reminded of what John Wesley wrote in his Journal (1.1.1739): 'Messrs Hall, Kitchin, Ingham, Whitefield, Hutchins and my brother Charles, were present at our love-feast in Fetter Lane with about sixty of our brethren. About 3.00 a.m., as we continued instant in prayer, the power of God came mightily upon us, insomuch that many cried out for exceeding joy, and many fell to the ground. As soon as we were recovered a little from that awe and amazement at the presence of His Majesty, we broke out with one voice, "We praise Thee, O God, we acknowledge Thee to be the Lord."

4

AGNES MORRISON
Shader

*Whilst it was evident that the Lord was at work, the real breakthrough
came a few days into the mission, on Sunday, 11th December 1949. The
first meeting of the evening was held on that occasion in the church in
Shader. After the service a young woman, Catherine Smith, broke down
outside the church. It was evident that the Lord was at work! Rev MacKay
and Rev Campbell went on to Barvas for the next meeting, but some of
the congregation gathered spontaneously at the home of the Morrisons in
Shader – a home of happy memories during the revival. This meeting was
unannounced but, amazingly, others who were not at the church but were
in attendance at a wake in the village also came to the house.*

*There was an awareness of God abroad and eternal realities were
foremost in the thoughts of the people. One young girl was so taken up
with her own personal needs that she put the kettle on the fire but put no
water in it!*

*Agnes, the young daughter of the Morrison household, who did not
attend the meeting at the church relates the events of that night:*

The Morrison Home

I was in the kitchen and the prayer meeting was in progress. I was crying
and I was swept into the kingdom. Six young people were converted that
night! (Cathie Ann, John Murdo, Chirsty Ann Martin, Dolag – my sister,
Maggie Mary and me). One of the six was John Murdo Smith who later
became a minister in the Church of Scotland. This was the beginning of
the great harvest in the revival, and could be regarded as the firstfruits of
the 1949 revival.

My mother came into the kitchen and finding me in tears, asked, 'Is
your toothache worse?'

'No,' I replied.

'What else is wrong?' she said.

'I want to come with you to the meeting,' I answered.

I then followed her and joined in the worship. It was a wonderful night!

Three other young people had come to the Lord before this outbreak of revival and another young girl came at the beginning of James Murray MacKay's ministry in April – so the Lord was already at work.

The 12th December was another wonderful night. We all went to the church in Barvas for the first meeting and afterwards we returned to our house for the late meeting. I will never forget how one of the converts of the previous night, John Murdo Smith, thumped the polished table and said with the utmost conviction: 'Who shall separate us from the love of Christ?' That very night John Murdo testified that he heard the call of God to preach, and he is still preaching with great acceptance over fifty years later!

Forty years after this incident, we were together with him and others in that very room. He recalled the incident tenderly, ran his hand over the table and said with a smile, 'I think that this table should be placed in the manse!' It had been a moment of intense power which all who were present will never forget.

I cannot recall how many meetings were held in our home or how many were converted there. We had planks as pews and we just left them in place. We did not even bother to remove them to brush the floor!

Mary recalls: 'I well recall being in meetings there and sitting on these planks. Such was the sense of the fear of God that I held the plank where I was sitting to keep me from trembling. I also recall a lady crying out in distress and being gently removed from the room by some of the men. A deep silence seemed to fall on us when we eventually left the house and made our way home taking with us an awareness of God too sacred to express and a conviction that we did not leave Him behind us in the meeting, for He was everywhere. The prayers we heard on that night will always be indelibly written on our minds. I can still picture the elder with uplifted hands and tears coursing down his cheeks supplicating the Throne on behalf of us young people – travailing in soul as he described us 'on the slippery paths of darkness.' His petitions were as the arrows of the Almighty in our souls. What a privilege to have been there!'

Before the revival on one occasion, whilst my father was in bed downstairs with heart trouble and the rest of the family had gone to bed, my mother and I went to the bedroom to join my father for family worship. Suddenly we heard an awful screech – oh! It was terrible! My mother and

I jumped up off our knees. We rushed upstairs to check on the rest of the family but they were all asleep. My father said, 'It is the devil,' so we started praying again. When the revival broke out, my father said, 'Yes, it was the devil. He knew that something good was afoot and the screech was one of anger.'

We were not at the prayer meetings before the revival but we knew there were many meetings where folk gathered to pray. There were some godly people in the district and they held prayer meetings. They were always getting together and praying in the house meetings.

I was only fifteen and still at Lionel school when I was saved. My two school chums said, 'Oh! We will soon have you out with us again' (meaning out at their worldly pleasures), but they too were converted!

It seemed that everybody went to church. They could not stay away. It was a wonderful time!

Whatever we were doing and wherever we were, we were conscious of the presence of God. We had no desire to go to sleep. Even though we had so little sleep we were not tired.

I recall one night when a few of our friends came to our house and on their leaving we accompanied them to the main road. Such was the bond between us that we did not want to part with them. We were not dressed for the weather and on our return my mother said, 'My goodness, you are soaking wet!' But we were not even aware of the rain!

Singing

In the small hours of the morning, on returning from a meeting, we stood on the street, loathe to part company, and we would sing and sing and sing! (*This is how they got their name – 'The Shader Singers'.*)

We recalled a visit by Mr. Reid and Mr. Bell of the Faith Mission some years before. They were staying in a home next door to us and they taught us hymns from 'Songs of Victory,' the Faith Mission Song Book. That is how we were able to sing English Hymns. One of the hymns frequently sung in the '49 revival was:

> There is a fountain filled with blood
> drawn from Emmanuel's veins
> and sinners plunged beneath that flood
> lose all their guilty stains.

Who will ever forget the strains of this hymn as young voices joined in, spontaneously giving expression to their new-found faith?

Another favourite often sung was,

I have decided to follow Jesus,
No turning back, no turning back.

How we sang these hymns with fervour and conviction! We also had the book of Gaelic Hymns from the Highland Mission in Glasgow. This mission no longer exists, but the 'little red book' as we called it, lives on.

Only the psalms were used in the church and the organized cottage meetings but on less formal occasions hymns were sung. Three of my sisters, as well as myself, were saved in this revival. When my sisters returned from that first meeting in the Shader church I knew that there was something different about them. The change was so obvious, and on the following morning when I woke up I was aware that something wonderful had happened to me. The assurance of salvation flooded my soul! A number of people were also saved in the Free Church.

At that time the church was packed, so much so that some had to sit on the window ledges and at times some could not get into the church. Almost every night people were saved in our home – some very notable cases – and so it was at that time in all the house meetings.

The results were not always visible in the church, but the very fact that they would follow on to the house meetings indicated that they were truly seeking the Lord. The less formal atmosphere of the house meetings encouraged them to 'nail their colours to the mast'. People were praying, and that was the secret of the whole movement. We were young at the time and we did not understand it all, but looking back we can see it now. Prayer was at the heart of the movement. We are following their example and are even now meeting weekly to pray for revival.

The words from E.M.Bounds come to mind: 'What the church needs today is not more machinery or better; not new organizations or more and more novel methods, but men whom the Holy Ghost can use – men of prayer, men mighty in prayer. The Holy Ghost does not flow through methods, but through men. He does not come through machinery but on men. He does not anoint plans, but men – men of prayer.'

The Walk

A group of us young ones went from Barvas and Shader to the small island of Bernera for the communion services. We had a great time of blessing and on Monday after the final morning meeting, Donald MacAulay took six of us in his boat to Breasclete, on Lewis, a few miles from Carloway. At Breasclete we jumped on to the back of a lorry and off we rumbled on the road home.

The lorry passed through Carloway, and there we stopped the driver and jumped off. We wanted to see and have fellowship with the minister in Carloway, Rev. Murdo MacLennan. What blessing we had received from his ministry and we wanted to get more! We were welcomed into the manse and enjoyed a wonderful time of blessed fellowship together. Mrs. MacLennan promptly put on a pot of potatoes and we soon sat down to a tasty meal of salt herring and potatoes – the staple diet in those days.

Billy MacLeod decided to stay overnight at the manse for further fellowship. He walked home alone the next day. The rest of us started out on the long trek home. John Murdo Smith and Finlay MacRitchie, who later became an elder, were there with the three of us girls. Not many cars were around then but nevertheless we hoped for a lift. We were thrilled with the fellowship which we enjoyed with each other and with the Lord. There was such a bond of unity and love as we walked.

We quenched our thirst at a well near the road, for the salt herring made its demands! On reaching Bragar we knocked at the door of a relative of one of the group. The lady of the house was making pancakes at that very moment. Great! Amidst the happy chatter we had our fill of pancakes. 'Don't sit down,' said John Murdo, 'we'll get stiff and not be able to go on.' So we ate standing and were soon on the road again.

Amazingly, none of us had blisters. We arrived home at 11.00 p.m. having had a wonderful sixteen mile walk, made so light and easy by the warmth of true Christian fellowship. We will never forget the day when we walked with such joy from Carloway to Shader.

5

REV. KENNETH MACDONALD
'Kenny Ban' (Fair Kenny)

Point

I often thought about God – and God, no doubt, thought about me. But while I thought about God, I certainly did not walk in His ways; far, far from it. When God moved in revival power in our part of the island, I was twenty-nine years of age, but I had no taste for the things of the Spirit.

I had been in the war. What terrible scenes we witnessed! I once stood on the top of a trench when six shells landed at my feet and lifted me into the air. Thank God they did not explode or I would not be here to tell the tale. I dived back into the trench which had about a foot of water in it, and found my New Testament. It was covered with ants, and even as I turned its pages, the words came to me as if from God: 'Will you give Me your heart now?'

'No Lord,' I said, 'but if You will leave me till I am seventy, I'll come then.' I had every intention of coming, but no, no, not now! I was not going to miss out on life! Here I was, having survived that awesome incident when I could have been blown to bits, and yet I would not heed the warning. I had my own agenda and I would not yield. God was a vague, though awesome Entity, far-off, yet continually penetrating my armour and bringing discomfort and unhappiness to my soul. I would not recognize His holiness and majesty.

In November 1950, Duncan Campbell came to Garrabost, Point. I had been going to church, and because everyone seemed to be going to the meetings I also attended.

My parents had come to the Lord in the 1939 revival, which was a revival of prayer rather than preaching, and which had a great influence in many places. At that time, to attend the meetings, they would walk all the way from Garrabost to Shader, Point, and back, arriving home at 4 a.m. This they did many times but it had no ill effects on their health. They were thrilled to be involved in the glory of those days, and now here it was again. They revelled in the meetings and were so grateful that God had given them the privilege of seeing once again the gracious movings of the Spirit.

In spite of all this background, I was as wild as could be! The Pub was my joy and delight. Our hobby was drinking, and yet more drinking, to which was added the fun of playing darts and going to the cinema. Often we were so drunk that we could not even see the screen and had to be taken out for a while to sober up. Yet I was not happy! There was such deep dissatisfaction in my heart and whatever I did I could not fill the ever-increasing and yawning hole within me. I tried to be happy, oh, yes, I tried and tried; but the more strenuous my quest, the more distant my goal. I was miserable and could not lift myself from the despondency which enveloped me.

Every now and again, the word would come to me, as from God, 'Kenny, will you give Me your heart?' I did not realize that the Lord Himself was speaking to me. And now the meetings were here – every night! I walked together with others to the meetings. They would be talking about the sermon, the singing, the blessing, the fellowship. I was engulfed in all this religious mania.

Remarkably, even as an unsaved man, I never swore, nor did I take the Lord's name in vain, but one night, coming from the meeting, I used a word that brought a strong reaction from some of my companions. 'Are you swearing, coming from the Lord's house?' they said, and I felt condemned.

Later on, there was a meeting in my aunt's house, and I went along. The place was packed. I went through the hallway and around the corner, for I was petrified that I would get converted. I had responded to the invitation to come to the meeting, but I did not want to listen. They sang – oh, how they sang! I will never forget the singing. It was so whole-hearted and so full of unction and power. Duncan Campbell was sitting on a seat in the kitchen before the service started, and when the service began, he got up and came directly to me.

'Will you please go and sit where I was,' he said, 'for I want to go from room to room with the message.' I did as requested, but throughout the service I was plagued with the thought, 'Why did he pick on me?' As I sat there, I had a conversation with myself:

'Kenny, how old are you?'
'I am twenty-nine.'

'Kenny, are you happy?'

'No!'

'What else can you do to make yourself happy?'

I thought of the celebrations at the end of the year and at the beginning of the next. I had ordered a bottle or two, but just the other day, after the Sunday service in the church, I had sneaked round the back of the church and had consumed almost a whole bottle in my attempts to drown the gnawing conviction. 'What could I do to make myself happy? What, oh, what could I do?'

All this time, while I was musing, Mr. Campbell was preaching. I was busy with my thoughts, when suddenly, in the midst of all this turmoil, a word penetrated my soul. It came from God – I knew that it came from God! In my innermost being I heard, 'I am the Way.' God spoke it to my heart. The service came to a close, and in my misery I wondered how to come to terms with all my conflicting emotions, and what to do with this insistent word: 'I am the Way.'

The preacher was still speaking. He said, 'A room will be cleared and all those who have come to the place where you feel that nothing in this world can satisfy your heart, please get up and make your way there. I cannot convert anyone, but God can, and He will fill the longings of your soul.'

The sheer horror of it. How could I get up and walk through these people so tightly packed? Everyone knew me. I looked upon a sea of heads. It seemed to me that there were so many people. Why, every one had a hundred heads! I could never get through. Suddenly I received unusual and amazing strength. I stood up and in my heart I said, 'Lord if You'll take me, I'll come now.' It was settled. In an instant my life was changed. It was as sudden as that. As I began to walk to the room, an elder took hold of me with such obvious delight. Suddenly, even as I walked, I was filled with unspeakable joy. My heart was absolutely free.

Duncan Campbell was in the room with some of the converts. He spoke a few words about the gospel and prayed. I was filled with glory. I knew that God had come to me and that I had met Him savingly in Christ.

As I emerged from the room, someone said to my mother, 'You'll not need to pray for Kenny any more,' to which she replied, 'It will be a different kind of prayer now.'

I never, ever, looked back. God saved me that night in the house and He will never hear the end of it! I will praise Him throughout eternity for His patience and grace with a sinner like me. I have never lost what He gave me that night. In addition to the joy of salvation, He gave me tears, and I have never lost the tears. What a sacred moment! One can never describe on paper the sacredness, the wonder, the glory, the inspiration, the thrill of that moment.

It was a revival; I have no doubt about that. It was God working in our midst. Numbers came to the Lord at that time. Wherever you went, you could not get away from the presence of God. This is the one thing that I will ever take with me, the abiding memory of that time – the presence of God. You were in God's presence wherever you went. It was just like a canopy over the whole island.

Sometimes that presence and power of God was almost overpowering. I remember being on the island of Berneray, Harris, for communion services before Mr. Campbell went there. The Spirit of God was working in an unusually powerful manner. In some of those meetings, if you wanted to say anything about the Lord, you would have to sit down, or you would fall. If you started to sing, you would have to sit, or you would fall. The singing was so powerful! This is quite unbelievable to anyone who has not experienced the immediate, awesome presence of God in this way. That was the situation on the island before Mr. Campbell went there. No-one came to the Lord then, but God prepared the hearts of the people so that when Mr. Campbell arrived they were all ready to receive the Word of God. Even before he came – and he was undoubtedly God's instrument on Berneray – it was just like heaven on earth. People were open, convicted, ready to receive and ripe to be plucked. God went before and prepared the ground.

In the district of Point, there was no harsh rejection of the revival, as in other parts of the island. Rev. William Campbell of the Free Church had himself experienced revival in his own church and knew what it was to have God move in the community. If the Free Church concluded its service earlier than we of the Church of Scotland, the people would wait until we caught up with them and we would walk down to Shader, Point, together.

There was a wonderful sense of unity and oneness in the Lord Jesus. There was no generation gap; there was no difference between young and old. The old became young! There was simply a blending of spirit and a oneness of desire, of longing, of waiting on God, of seeking His face. The unity was tangible. We loved one another.

A rather comical incident occurred one day. Norman Campbell's father called to ask my father to go to a meeting in Barvas. The centre of the revival was in Barvas, and Barvas kept it going! My father was in his working clothes having just come in from working on the croft. He always liked to be smartly dressed before he would go anywhere. 'O.K.,' he said, 'I'll just change my clothes.'

'No, no,' said Norman's father, 'there's no time to change; just come as you are.'

'Come on,' said my mother, 'the Lord doesn't mind.'

Off they went to Barvas and arrived just after the meeting had begun. The leaders in the meeting saw my father and asked him to pray. He stood up and prayed but had no liberty at all. Soon, however, the Spirit of the Lord came upon the meeting and the presence of God was sensed to a remarkable degree. My father stood again to pray and this time it was altogether different. There was such power and he was released in the Spirit with such a flow of language and with such glorious liberty that it contributed greatly to the atmosphere and power of the gathering. On the way home in the car, Norman's father said, 'What happened to you in your first prayer?'

'Oh, it was my trousers,' he replied. He was so conscious of his working clothes that he lost his liberty!

There was a Free Church elder in Garrabost, Point, and he was altogether opposed to the revival. He actually prayed for revival, but of course, it could not come through the Church of Scotland! At times there were mysterious happenings in the meetings. On some occasions some fell into a trance for the duration of the meeting. They would not be a disturbance at all but would sit silently with hands upraised. When they came round at the end of the meeting, their words seemed to have the scent of heaven. We were awed at times and at other times they simply left the meeting with us all, having met with God personally in this unusual way. It was no hindrance, and the folk regarded it as something which was a characteristic of the workings of the Spirit. He, however, opposed the work because of these happenings which he could not explain.

There was a Christian man from Shader, Point, who heard about these trances and thought that it was of the devil. He opposed the meetings, but then he heard of people whom he knew to be godless, who had attended these meetings and who had now begun to attend the church and the prayer meetings. This he could not understand. He could not believe that God would send these people whom he knew to church and to prayer meetings as a result of first attending these strange revival meetings. He was puzzled and troubled about it all, so much so that he sought God about it. One day God spoke to him, giving him the vision that He gave to

Peter: 'What God hath cleansed, that call not thou common or unclean' (Acts 10:15).

One night he stood in the middle of the road by his house, and as the people came, he directed them to his own house. They wondered what was happening and why he was inviting them to his home. The tears ran down his cheeks as he told them of his opposition to the work of God. That they knew full well! But he continued to relate God's dealings with him and told them that God had spoken clearly to him. He was so sorry for his blindness in this regard. From that time he identified himself with the revival and was fully involved in all the meetings and activities.

Communion seasons are an important part of religion in the islands, and the Lord's table is guarded jealously. Before you are allowed to participate in communion in other churches you must first of all have been accepted by and have taken communion in your own church.

I recall attending a communion service in Stornoway after I was converted. The familiar words of the communion rang out, 'This do in remembrance of me.' I was not eligible for I had not yet given an account of my conversion before the session of my own church to be accepted or rejected, and my heart nearly broke. I so wanted to participate! I cried to the Lord, 'Lord, please keep me alive until the next communion season in two months time in my own church.' In the two months I grew in strength and in the knowledge of the Lord Jesus and was thrilled to be part of the Christian scene in my home area. That which I had avoided I now fully embraced.

The communion season came round and after the first service of the week-end, I went in to appear before the kirk session. This was an awesome event. 'They will ask awkward questions and I will make a fool of myself. They will probably reject me, and even if they accept me, they will ask me to pray in public the next Sunday.' The battle raged within me. I felt that I would rather go and drown in the loch than face these authoritative, serious and solemn elders. What a turmoil was in my breast! But go to them I must, so I went around to the church hall to meet them.

I need not have feared, for when I took my seat the men began to weep. Some sobbed openly. To them it was so wonderful to see me in the church when they knew what I had been. One of them at last stuttered, 'The only sign we need of the reality of the work in his soul is to see Kenny Ban here before us.' They had observed the change and had rejoiced together in the wonderful work of God in my soul. I was accepted with great joy and gratitude to God for His grace towards me. Praise His wonderful Name!

6

NORMAN CAMPBELL
Point

How can I tell the story?!

I was under conviction nearly all my life but tried to shake it off by joining the boys at the pub. I tried to drink it all away. One day Rev. Lachie MacLeod put his hand on my head and said, 'This boy will yet be a good boy,' meaning that I would be a godly Christian. None of the other lads with me on that occasion, to the best of my knowledge, ever came to Christ. They are all gone now, except my brother. Mr. MacLeod's words were prophetic.

There had been a revival in 1939 – a revival in which prayer was the dominant factor. No preacher led the movement but people came to the Lord in the prayer meetings in the homes. There were many trances in the '39 revival, but not so many in the '49 revival. The work in the Point area was in the Free Church but it also embraced the Church of Scotland. Unfortunately it was opposed by some of the Free Church clergy and others who would not accept that it was of God despite it being in their own denomination. It began before the war and really went on for years, although not with the same intensity. A number of young men came to the Lord, went to the war and never came back. God took a harvest before the terrible carnage when so many lost their lives.

Meetings went on right through the war, and afterwards, but the revival did not continue all the time. The people who had been blessed in the revival kept the meetings going. It was a wonderful period.

After the war the young men returned, shattered, lost and disorientated, for they had seen and experienced so much tragedy. They turned to drink, parties and revelry. It was then that God sent Duncan Campbell to Lewis and it was then that the Lord gave another time of revival to this favoured island.

Duncan Campbell began his ministry in Barvas and it was only later that he came to Point. God blessed us in a wonderful way. One night during the movement of the Spirit in Point, both Rev. MacLennan and Rev. Campbell were in the pulpit together. Mr. MacLennan was deeply moved and his face was white as he challenged us with words which were applicable to so many of us. He said, 'You are here tonight, but there was a time when you were in the stern of a ship praying to the Lord and promising Him that if He would get you out of here alive, you would follow Him and serve Him. Have you kept your promise? What are you going to do tonight?'

I remembered that I had been on the *California*. It was a passenger boat at the time and we were put in the stern of the ship. There were about forty men from Lewis in the crew. Some of them prayed. One young fellow had his Bible and he would kneel to pray. It all came back to me at the close of that meeting when God spoke to many souls.

Mr Campbell then asked for those who wished to be prayed for, to join him in the church hall. I joined others who were seeking help. Mr. Campbell and I knelt together and he prayed. He then asked me to pray and ask the Lord for mercy. As soon as I stood to pray, my chains were loosed and I was set free. Old things passed away and all things became new. It happened in a moment. I was launched out on a sea of love. I felt that I was no longer in the flesh. I left the hall feeling as if I were swimming in a sea of love.

The minister's wife put out her hand and asked me where I was going. She took me into the bus that was going to the next meeting. I felt so disappointed that she had disturbed me for I felt as if I were in heaven, and to heaven I wanted to go! Half the passengers went to one house and the other half to another for their supper. We went into the kitchen where the table was prepared with food and tea, and there they were eating and drinking. How could they eat and drink when we were on our way to heaven? I couldn't conceive that such a thing could be possible! All I wanted to do was to go to heaven! I was thrilled with the presence of God.

After the meal we went to the bus, and just as we approached the vehicle, suddenly a light like the brightness of the sun, on this dark night, shone around us. I realized that Padruig, the elder, was by my side. I looked up to see where the light was coming from and I saw the face of Christ. That was where the light was coming from – His face! I shall never forget it! It was like the sun, just like the sun! And the joy on that face; and the love reflected from that face! I cannot explain nor describe it. Then He said, 'I love you,' and the 'you' was in the plural, meaning 'all of you.' I grabbed the elder's arm and said, 'I was there too,' for the light enveloped both of us, and I wanted to assure him that I also experienced that which

I now thought was the common experience of every Christian. But Padruig did not see the vision. The vision lasted only a few seconds but it seemed that it was a few minutes. I was simply flooded with inexpressible joy and seemed to be afloat in an ocean of love.

If this was a baptism of the Spirit, I know one thing, that the baptism of the Spirit is most certainly a baptism of love. That is the kind of baptism I experienced and in which I believe – a baptism of love. God has not changed and what I received from Him, He is still able to give. It wasn't something for which I asked; I did not deserve it, but He gave it to me freely.

'Why did they not tell me about this,' I thought. 'If they had, I would have become a Christian long ago.' I did not realize that I was experiencing something very special from the Lord. How I rejoiced and praised the Lord on that journey! My heart was filled with joy. I had not expected love and joy to be such a part of the Christian experience. I thought that if I became a Christian I would, like many around me, have to walk around with a long face – but this was joy!

Only later did the full significance of the vision dawn on me. I was kept humble by the fact that the Lord had said, 'I love you all.' It was in the plural. The Lord did not only love me but He loved all His people. It was not something for me to boast about. I received the vision but all were included in His great love. This still lives with me and I have never lost that love which He put in my heart that night.

The day after the vision, I asked the Lord to give me the same experience again, but nothing happened! I hadn't asked for it originally when God gave it to me. I had to learn that you cannot dictate to God. Duncan Campbell told us not to ask for certain experiences but only for what He chooses to give. What would have happened to me had God given me the vision again, I do not know. I would probably not have been able to bear it.

The outstanding feature of the 1949–52 revival was the presence of God. This was also the case with the 1939 revival. This did not occur so markedly in the smaller movements in between these two revivals, nor in smaller movements since then, but in both the '39 and the '49 revivals this was very definitely so. You could sense and feel the presence of God everywhere. Even the children sensed something. It was the power of God let loose! People went on their knees anywhere.

We would be out at the meetings at 7.00 p.m. and then go home at about 9.00 p.m., have something to eat, then off to the next meeting in

Aird or somewhere else until 11.00 p.m. or midnight. After that we would go to a house meeting until 4.00 or 5.00 a.m. This would go on night after night! Imagine Duncan Campbell going to all these meetings. He was not young! Amazingly, we kept going and did not get tired. The power and presence of God strengthened us. It was supernatural, for it could not have happened without the Lord strengthening us for the task.

Before the '39 revival, under the ministry of Rev. William Campbell in the Free Church in Garrabost, Point, there were local revivals. But during the '39 revival churches were filled with people crowding into every corner of the church and sitting even on the pulpit steps. Rev. William preached until the perspiration flowed down his face. His face seemed to change as the light of God shone through. When, however, the revival faded and that sense of the presence of God decreased, his preaching was not as dynamic. He spoke quietly, but when the Holy Spirit came upon him he was authoritative and dynamic. Souls came to know the Lord and lives were changed.

Duncan Campbell was a fiery preacher and he preached a full gospel. At the first he preached the law with its judgments, but then he would turn to Jesus as the Saviour and Lord. He was utterly sincere and you could see that he meant every word he said. He preached and he loved to preach the glorious truths of the Bible. Even the young people could see his love for the Lord and for the unconverted.

It is not the custom in the Highlands to speak easily about your personal experiences and consequently the young converts were sometimes, as it were, silenced or 'put on probation' for quite a while until the church, in which they worshipped, observed their behaviour and eventually accepted their experience. Duncan Campbell, on the other hand, encouraged immediate testimony and he rejoiced to hear it.

Let me illustrate this kind of thinking by relating a telling incident. There was a group of Christians in the home of an elderly man. They were enjoying fellowship and spiritual conversation while the old man of eighty was in his bed, sobbing his heart out with conviction of sin. He was left to mourn his state whilst the others ignored his distress, though no doubt, they rejoiced to see his concern. God must do His own work! They saw themselves as having no responsibility in this situation. They must not interfere! No doubt, God did His work and had mercy on the penitent sinner, but they could have, at least, prayed with him, taken him to the Scriptures, counselled him with guidance and encouragement, and showed him the biblical way to God. The teaching that man has no responsibility in the work of God was taken to an extreme, while the strong emphasis was upon the sovereignty of God. He will do His own work and we are not to do or say anything, lest it be man's work which will not last, giving seekers a sense of false security. Hardly anyone was ever counselled for salvation.

Duncan Campbell used to speak of the danger of putting a false pillow under the heads of enquirers and giving them texts to trust in when they were not ready to receive the Word, or when some counsellor may not be in touch with the Lord, but simply have a ready answer for every seeker.

How dangerous to put your trust even in the Scriptures, if they do not lead you to a living faith. I once visited a man on his deathbed and was told that he could quote reams of Scripture. When I arrived I found this to be true, but soon realized that many of these Scriptures had no relation to Christ. I testified to that which Christ had done for me. 'Oh,' said the man, 'I don't have that of which you speak. I don't have Christ.' I then went on to preach Christ to him, but he could not follow me. We were worlds apart even though he had such a knowledge of the Bible. Biblical knowledge must lead to living faith.

In the revivals with both William and Duncan Campbell (they were not related), knowledge of the Bible most certainly led many to a place of commitment, forgiveness and salvation. There was a movement of the Spirit in William's Free Church in Garrabost, Point, in November 1949, and Duncan came to Point in November 1950, in the Church of Scotland. God used them both and how grateful we are that God poured out His Spirit in our district at that time. There was a great deal of unity in the Point district among the people of God and folk from both churches were blessed in the presence of the Lord. We give Him all the glory. Amen and Amen!

7

RODERICK M. MACKAY
Carloway

For this testimony to be understood, one needs to know something of the church customs on the island of Lewis, for there are differences between the island ways and those of the church on the mainland.

At that time all the believers in the church attended the weekly prayer meeting every week. Unbelievers, even though they may attend the church regularly, knew that they were not converted and did not frequent the prayer meetings. This resulted in people fearing to go to the prayer meeting, for if they went there, they would immediately be seen to be identifying with the people of God, and would be regarded as Christians, or as those who were earnestly seeking God. If they, at any time in the future, did not attend the prayer meeting, they would be regarded as having backslidden. So going to the prayer meeting was a major step in a person's spiritual life and it was regarded as almost certainly the evidence of his or her conversion.

I was born in the little village of Tolsta Chaolais on the west side of the isle of Lewis in the district of Carloway. The Loch Roag was but a stone's throw from our door.

I was the third youngest of a family of seven, six boys and one girl. When I look back on my very young years I often wonder what anxious moments our parents must have had, bringing up a family of seven lively youngsters so close to the sea. Our parents were not Christians at the time and found it difficult to keep us all in order.

I left school at the age of fourteen at a time when work was scarce. Apart from work on our own croft and earning a few shillings a day helping others in the village with their spring work, I had no money at all.

When I was fifteen and a half I got my first job, from May to November keeping sheep away from the crofts in the village and driving them out on to the moor three times a day. My pay was £30.00 for six months work. I had two dogs and they hardly understood anything but swearwords.

Every hillock on that moor echoed with my cursing and swearing at the dogs and sheep, and I was not very nice to some of the men of the village either. An elder in the church heard me as he stood outside his house, and I was severely reprimanded. That incident pulled me up sharp, and as the days passed, it faded, but I did not altogether put it out of my mind. I sometimes thought that God would pour His judgments upon me for my wicked ways. Who knows to what depths I would have sunk had I continued on this pathway.

1936

The revival began at the beginning of 1936 on the Lochs side of the island around the village of Garyvard and it spread like wildfire to the west side. It made a big impression from Garynahine to Shawbost and across to Bernera.

I was just over eighteen years of age and with all this spiritual activity around me, my past began to trouble me. Satan attempted to divert me and lead me away from God. I knew that God's Spirit was striving with me and although I didn't know how to pray, and had never prayed in public before, I tried to ask God for forgiveness for all the cursing and swearing and the other sins that I had committed when I was shepherding sheep.

By the month of April we heard daily of somebody new going to the prayer meetings. Hardly a day passed without our hearing of someone being converted. I longed to come out on the Lord's side, for I was so troubled and disturbed about my spiritual condition, but I didn't have the courage to take my stand. The Lord was awakening me and calling me, but I was afraid to go to the prayer meeting, despite my strong desire to attend. Should I attend, that would be seen by all as the sign that I had begun to follow the Lord.

One Wednesday morning I bravely announced to my mother that I thought I would go to the prayer meeting that night. Her discouraging warning struck me deeply, my faint heart failed me and I did not attend, for she said, 'If you go, you will have to keep on going.'

My parents were adherents of the Church of Scotland, and I knew little or nothing about the church, but my desire to know more was growing by the day. There were numbers of Free Church people there, but only about half a dozen families belonging to the Church of Scotland in the village, and at that time none of them showed any interest in the things of God. There was only one meeting place in the village and both churches shared it. The Church of Scotland minister, Rev. Murdo MacLennan, had a service there once a month. He was a very good man and saw a great deal of blessing in his ministry.

I seemed to be the only teenager in our village and I felt lonely. There was no-one near at hand with whom I could share my burden. There were, however, a number of young folk in the surrounding villages of Breasclete, Callanish, Garrynahine and Carloway. The church was in Carloway.

The large majority of the people were in the Free Church and numbers were being converted. In some homes two or three from the same family were being dealt with by the Spirit of God at the same time.

There were not many households between Garrynahine and Carloway that the Spirit of God did not touch. Here I was with the deepest desire to be among them, feeling on my own in one sense and afraid to take the next step. I cried to the Lord, 'Lord, show me what to do. Please give me courage to go to the prayer meeting. It doesn't matter whether it is the Church of Scotland or the Free Church.'

The Lord heard my desperate cry when I could hold out no longer, for I finally plucked up courage to go to the Free Church prayer meeting on Wednesday night. It was a huge step, for this was an indication to all that I was seeking the Lord.

On my way to the prayer meeting, the devil tried to turn me back, telling me what a fool I was. Why, the Free Church elders at the door would ask me why I had come. What on earth would I say to them? But when I got to the door I was welcomed with open arms. The relief and the joy was wonderful.

After the prayer meeting I went with them for yet another meeting in the home of an elderly Christian. On entering he said abruptly, 'And what are you doing here?' I felt embarrassed and very insignificant. I did not know what to say, only that I had a strong desire to be with them. They soon put me at ease and I enjoyed the meeting in the home. In fact two or three older Christians from Doune who were there that night, prayed earnestly for the young fellow who was with them in the home. I was the only young person present. On my way home I felt as if a load had fallen from me, and although I still had many burdens, I was so glad to have been in the prayer meeting that night. I had begun to follow the Lord.

When I reached home I was met with a barrage of criticism from my brothers. I had gone to the prayer meeting because I had heard that others were being converted and I was a sham! Their strong words and my own doubts certainly did nothing to help me. The Lord, however, gave me strength to go on, and my desire to be found in Christ grew stronger as the days went by.

The following Sunday, I rose early and cycled to the Church of Scotland in Carloway. On my way I caught up with other young people with the same feelings, doubts and fears as I had. Words fail me to tell of the joy I experienced in church that day. I don't know how the minister and his wife got to know, but they spoke to me after the service and told me they had heard that I was converted. I did not know what to say but I felt that I was walking on air.

I can never explain or find words to tell of that glorious transformation that took place in my life for a full year after that. We were caught up in the spirit of revival as the Lord worked wonderfully on the island of Lewis at that time. I got to know people young and old in the surrounding villages, especially Breasclete and Callanish, by going to house meetings nearly every night of the week. It was the most glorious period of my life.

I even thought that there was something of the spirit of revival in the animals around me! We had two cows and a few sheep at the time. I also thought it was in the glorious weather! I was seeing God at work in everything.

Although we were in house meetings nearly every night we didn't seem to get tired at all. One night I was in a house meeting until 6.00 a.m., and, without having any sleep at all, I started on the croft work as soon as I got home.

I was strongly criticised by my brothers and reprimanded by my parents for coming home at all hours of the morning, but I continued to attend these wonderful meetings. When I thought of what Jesus had done for me, I wanted to serve Him every day.

The Lord was working wonders every day and great changes were taking place in so many lives. Young people were being transformed as were some hardened rough characters. God's Spirit softened them and there they were with the tears streaming down their faces as they repented of their sins. Some Christians felt the presence of the Lord so strongly that they were completely overcome and fainted or went into a trance.

It was glorious to be with them and to know that I was a part of this wonderful work of God. It is beyond words to describe.

The years of 1936, 1937 and 1938 were glorious years of spiritual awakening in Lewis, and quite a few who were converted in the revival became ministers of the gospel in both the Church of Scotland and the Free Church.

I have known God's presence on many occasions down the years since then, but that time was glorious and indescribably special to me and to many others like me.

When I look back on these days of revival, gratitude wells up within me for all that God has done for me and will yet do for me. Many of those who started off with me are now in glory, possessing the blessings of which there will be no end. Yes, He is able to save to the uttermost all those who put their trust in Him. To God be the glory!

8

REV. WILLIAM MACLEOD
Uig

I was only thirteen when the 1939 revival took place. Two of my cousins, aged about sixteen, were converted at that time, so I knew what it meant to be saved. The Lord spoke to me but I did not yield to Him then. I do remember, however, asking Him for something specific in the practical realm and He granted my request. This encouraged me to go on seeking Him and during the period between 1939 and 1947, the godly example and teaching in the home and influence of Christians in my neighbourhood affected my life. Yet I knew not the Lord in a saving way. But great things were to follow, and when they did, they were 'marvellous in our eyes'.

Before the 1949 revival there was a stirring among the Lord's people. There were several new communicants and a number of people came to Christ for salvation; some of them young people. This caused great anticipation. Interest in the things of God quickened and all around us folk were expecting great things from God. Everywhere they were praying, trusting and waiting on God to work.

Prior to the revival, I did not attend church regularly, but on occasions I turned up to show that I was part of the community. I felt that I was still in the morning of life and that there was much more to life than simply attending church.

In December 1949, shortly after the revival began, I began attending the meetings and was impressed with the powerful preaching of God's Word and with the clarity of the message. The atmosphere was stimulating, the singing was uplifting, and prayer was made for those who were still strangers to amazing grace. You were left in no doubt about the reality of sin, death and judgement, but the love of God in Jesus Christ was presented with equal fervour. I realized that I was a sinner in need of a Saviour. I continued to attend meetings, but did not make my innermost thoughts known.

Then, exactly one week before Christmas, it happened. God spoke to my heart and I surrendered my life to Him. At the close of a wonderful meeting in the church hall in Barvas, I went back in for prayer and counselling, with at least four others from our village who were also seeking the Saviour. At a meeting in Shader, that same night, another group of young people found the Lord. All went on to become faithful witnesses to Christ. How the praying people rejoiced! That night Rev. MacLennan was conducting the meeting in Barvas and Duncan Campbell was not expected to attend, but before the end of the meeting, the door opened and he and Rev. MacKay walked in. They had been in a house meeting in Shader but had felt compelled to leave and come to Barvas. They were sensitive to the leading of the Spirit.

When I woke up the next morning, I was at peace and everything was new to me. The whole world seemed new! I found myself pouring out my heart to God. I had always said my prayers, but now I was praying! Joy welled up within me – a joy that was beyond explanation. This was one of the unspeakable gifts which we as the Lord's people had at that time – this indescribable and overwhelming joy.

Another result of the revival was the boldness which we all had; boldness to witness, to rejoice, and with it freedom to tell whoever was listening that we had given our lives to Christ. This was part and parcel of the revival. We were so full of it that we could not help but talk about it! The fact that people listened to us was also part of the revival; there was an awareness of God in the community.

An atmosphere of expectancy prevailed and a certain hope possessed us as we watched the Spirit of the Lord breaking down barriers, bringing conviction and leading one after another to salvation.

Older Christians were radiant in their joy and despite demanding croft work they attended as many meetings as we did and their energy never flagged. My mother who had become a Christian in her teens said that when we came to know the Lord she felt as young as we were, for it seemed as if she had been converted all over again.

Crowds came out to the church meetings. Among them were folk whom I had never seen inside a church door, as well as many who had attended for years. They had heard of the movement and they came from all over the village and from much further afield. There was a hunger for God. One man, referring to Duncan Campbell, said, 'That man has something to say to us.' His reaction came as a result of the working of the Holy Spirit all around him. Even worldly men would acknowledge that they were impressed with what was being said. Young and old were open to the gospel and the power of God was present to save.

Quite a number in the Shader area were converted at the time that I came to Christ. Five or six came one night in a cottage meeting in the Morrison's house. When we were swept into the kingdom, our expectancy rose and we were looking for new converts and praying that more would come and join us in our joy. Who would be the next to be welcomed into the fold? An atmosphere of excited expectation and certain hope possessed us as we watched the Spirit of the Lord in the community breaking down barriers, bringing conviction and leading one and another to salvation.

Incidents abound. There was a godless old man in his eighties who had a godly wife and daughter. Revs. Campbell and MacKay called on him in the course of visitation. They spoke to him and he agreed to attend the meetings. During this time his neighbours had noticed that he used to leave the house at unusual times; they concluded that the Lord was at work in his life, and they were proved right, for soon after attending the meetings he was converted. God saved not only the young but also those who had neglected spiritual things all their lives and were on the brink of eternity.

The meetings went on for a month and the people did not want them to end. During the third week and afterwards, at the very height of the movement in Barvas, there were three or four meetings nightly spread over the parish; one in both Barvas and Shader churches at 7.00 p.m. and 9.00 p.m. respectively and then some house meetings going on until the early hours of the morning. I shall never forget the intensity and blessing of those days. They made a mark upon me that has never been erased and for which I shall thank God for ever.

It warms the heart to contemplate that the Almighty God who inhabits eternity drew near to island communities to make a people for Himself. As the Psalmist expressed it, 'This is the Lord's doing and it is marvellous in our eyes.' It was awesome. This is our God. Is He yours?

9

MRS. MARGARET MACLEOD
Barvas, Uig

We lived just opposite the Church of Scotland in Barvas, so we did not have far to go to our place of worship. That geographical position and the warm welcome that my parents gave to all the Lord's people, irrespective of denomination, meant that I was singularly privileged. From my earliest years I was well acquainted not only with the professing Christians in Barvas but also those in Shader and elsewhere. Every Sunday morning worshippers coming from Shader and Borve would come into our house for half an hour before the service. There was fellowship, discussion, gentle banter, and of course a cup of tea and a 'blessing'. This covered the years of revival in 1939 and right through the anxious war years (when my father, newly converted, served in the Navy) and into the glorious days of revival in 1949, and later. After the evening service we invariably had Christian friends from our own village in for a time of praise and prayer – and often a few other nights a week.

At communion time the house was full of visitors from all over Lewis and Harris, both Church of Scotland and Free Church people. As children and young people we loved their company, so there was never a time when I was not aware of Christian concern for the lost.

We were well taught in both Sunday schools that we attended: our own immediately after the morning service and the Free Church one at 3.00 p.m. The hymns we sang in the one and the psalms in the other are indelibly marked in my memory and have brought blessing over the years. I thank the Lord for the faithful people who taught us.

Another event that left an impression on my young life was a winter of evangelistic meetings held in the school when I was eleven years old. The singing of hymns like 'Be in time, be in time –" and 'Will you be ready our Lord to meet?' linger in my memory. The soloist had a beautiful tenor voice and I just loved listening to the gospel message in song.

Now through all this I cannot recall being much worried about my soul, other than having a very high moral standard and a desire to do what was right. As I grew into my teens, a pupil in the Nicolson Institute living in the hostel in Stornoway, I thoroughly enjoyed all the extra-curricular activities and especially dancing. On Sundays I was quite glad of the excuse to look after my two little sisters rather than attend church. I certainly expected to give my life to Christ some day, but not yet. Not until after I was married, as I wanted to be able to dance at my own wedding. In our culture at that time Christians did not dance. So I thought I had that neatly sorted out.

Just at the time when my school life in Stornoway all week and my home life in Barvas at the weekend were both so satisfying socially, I became ill and had to spend three months in hospital. The Lord had put up a STOP sign. All my plans for the coming year had to be abandoned and my parents' prayers on my behalf took on a new urgency. I heard from them years later how a Scripture verse that my mother received from the Lord at that time comforted but terrified her at the same time (Ps. 45:15,16). She took it to indicate my imminent death. As she struggled to come to terms with it she shared her deep concern with Neil MacDonald, a divinity student lodging with them that summer. After thought and prayer he suggested to them in his wise and gentle manner that there was another way of interpreting it. The verse could still be fulfilled if I lived.

As I was restored to health I adjusted well to the restrictions placed upon me, but in my heart I longed for the time when I could resume my normal social life. I did not express it in words, but my goal in life was simply to attend a dance. I was not looking any further than that. Sad, but true.

In March 1949, John MacNaughton, a divinity student whom we had not known previously, came to stay in our home. I was surprised to find myself really listening intently to his prayers at family worship. Most days he would speak to me personally about the things of the Lord and my soul's salvation. I was very non-committal, gave practically no answers and certainly no hint that I was remotely interested in what he was saying. I was startled when one day he chatted about the transience of worldly pleasures, mentioning that the thrill of the dance was over the next morning – you had nothing left. I was not at all sure that I agreed with him but I did not like to say so.

With my cousin and dear friend, Peggy MacIver, I started attending the evening services on a Sunday. The personal evangelism continued at home and inwardly I was receptive but outwardly was as silent as ever – no response. Only the Lord could have encouraged him to persevere and must have somehow revealed to him that there were possibilities in continuing to speak to me. I am thankful that he did. By this time I knew that my thoughts and outlook were different and I remember thinking, 'If this is the Lord working in my life, I will listen.' That is when the inward struggle began. Yes, the love of the Lord was drawing me and I wanted to be His; but not publicly. I got to the point where I was willing to let the dances go but not to replace them with the prayer meeting. What would my friends think? I bargained with God but that did not bring peace. Then the devil presented a further obstacle: 'And who are you to dare join the godly old ladies who attend the prayer meeting? Whatever will they think?' My daily prayer was Psalm 51 especially verse 7 onwards; verses we had memorised in school. John underlined Psalm 27:13,14 in my Bible and I really began to wait on the Lord as much as He enabled me to do. Finally, I cast myself on His mercy and, come what may, I resolved to be in the prayer meeting at noon the next day. What a welcome I received from the Lord's people; what love and support, not only then, but throughout the years that followed, until one by one the Lord called them home.

Peggy came the following week and we both professed our faith in Christ at the September Communion that same year. Following the communion our friend and cousin, Maggie Mary, was converted, so the three little girls who had played together as toddlers now rejoiced together as sixteen-year-olds in their Christian faith. We went to Communion services in Ness and Point, and everywhere we were embraced and welcomed lovingly as we had been in our own congregation.

Thus we became part of the Christian fellowship in Barvas that prayed for revival and were completely caught up in it and blessed by it when it came – an unforgettable experience for which we shall be forever grateful.

My cousin and I were converted in March 1949, during the brief ministry of Rev. MacNaughton. On our own we simply trusted the Lord to save us, for we knew the way of salvation very well, having attended church since we were very small children. During the previous winter a number had come to the Lord from both the Free Church and the Church of Scotland. In September another friend was converted. The movement had already begun.

The Lord's people were alive! They met often and would pray and sing in the homes. That is my abiding memory of that time; in fact I do not remember the children of the Lord behaving in any other way. All that time as a young person and into adulthood, I knew the Christians to have been in this wonderfully revived manner of living. *The Christian church was a community at prayer!* There was great expectancy and much prayer – always! A visit to a Christian home, where the conversation would invariably be on the things of God, ended in prayer. God was at work everywhere and the longing of the people for the Spirit to break through in the community was intense. I remember the emphasis on unity; 'Make us as one rod in Thy hand' was a recurring theme in public and private prayer.

During the long vacancy of about two years, the Lord's people took responsibility in the congregation. Now and then a minister would come for a month from the mainland, and they always had many meetings during the week. Homes opened and meetings were held in different parts of the parish.

In April 1949, Rev. James Murray MacKay accepted the call to Barvas. I had just been converted before he came. People had great expectations and prayer intensified in the community. Everyone was looking forward to his ministry and looking to the Lord to work mightily in great revival power. People were praying, singing, praising. Much prayer was made and great supplications ascended from home after home in the district. Much is made of the two old ladies in Barvas who prayed. Well, there were many old ladies, and younger ones too, as well as the men, who poured out their souls to God to visit Lewis again.

Mr. MacKay's influence was tremendous, and this, to a large extent, has been left out of the reports of the revival. He did not adopt an air of superior spirituality; nor did he maintain an exclusive distance. He was not 'stand-offish'. He went down amongst the people, visited them, talked to them and prayed with them. He was so 'alive' – a real evangelist.

At that time the Strathpeffer Convention was in the summer and he and John Mackenzie from Arnol went to the convention. At the convention he approached Rev. Tom Fitch and asked him to come for a mission in December. He could not come but recommended Rev. Duncan Campbell who did not have a congregation to which he would be bound, and who might be able to go to Barvas. When Mr. MacKay returned he discussed it with the Church Board and with the members in general. All encouraged him. He wrote to the leaders at the Faith Mission Headquarters, who replied that his programme was fully booked and he would not be able to go. We were all disappointed at the news.

It is said that the two old ladies declared that he would come nevertheless. As a matter of fact, lots of old ladies, and others as well, said the same thing! The people felt that God had directed their minister and that they would not take 'No' for an answer. They believed that he would come, they were convinced that he would come, and that's exactly what happened – he came! His other bookings fell through and he was able to respond to the invitation from Barvas. I can still recall the anticipation. I remember praying, 'Lord, You worked through this man in other places, work through him here as well!' We prayed mightily. We believed that the Lord would work – and He did!

It was the regular winter series of evangelistic services which are held in every church in Lewis, called *orduighean beaga*, only this time it was to be two weeks instead of the usual one week.

Duncan Campbell arrived on 7th December, and began the meetings in the church across the road from our home. People from both the Free Church and the Church of Scotland were present. That first meeting was a great meeting with a good crowd. At the close Mr. MacKay announced that there would be an after-meeting across the road in the MacDougalls' house. My mother was at home looking after my two baby sisters, so I rushed home and burst in excitedly with the announcement: 'We're having a meeting here tonight!' The people crowded in and that was the beginning of the ongoing and blessed meetings in the many homes in Lewis during this movement of the Spirit.

On Sunday night Mr. Campbell preached in Shader after which they gathered in a house for another meeting. That night five young people, including (Rev.) John Murdo Smith, were converted. That was the beginning of the harvest time in Lewis.

Monday night in the Barvas church was wonderful. Revival had come. For me it was an overflowing of the Spirit – being broken with joy. I couldn't stop crying, but I was crying for joy. There was an after-meeting every night and after the ice had been broken, people were being converted every night. I invited two of my school friends for a weekend. Joey and Katie Mary were both converted. What a blessed weekend that was.

At the end of the fortnight Duncan Campbell was supposed to leave. I was still at school and coming back home, I thought, 'This is the last night of the meetings!' I arrived home at 5.00 p.m. and Messrs Campbell and MacKay came to the door. I opened the door and Mr MacKay said, 'He's staying for another fortnight!' I was so thrilled I just flung my arms around Mr. MacKay's neck! He said, pointing to Duncan Campbell, 'Go and do that to him.' It was a spontaneous reaction. I had never done that before! Completely out of character.

The meetings continued. People flocked from both the Free Church and the Church of Scotland. Many of them were 'hardy annuals' who only appeared at the communion season. Because of the little ones my mother could not attend all the meetings. She used to say that she could never forget the sound of the footsteps each night between 9.00 p.m. and 10.00 p.m. – footsteps of those on the road making their way to the Lord's house for a second meeting.

After the month of meetings in the Barvas church, they decided to move the main meetings to Shader, five miles away. My father and the policeman were both deacons, and they protested, 'You cannot leave the Barvas church without a meeting. There are so many people hungry for the gospel. There has to be a meeting in Barvas!' Mr. MacKay phoned Rev MacLennan in Carloway and he came to preach in Barvas. The first meeting at 7.00 p.m. was held in Shader, followed by a house meeting at 9.00 p.m. The meeting in Barvas was at 9.00 p.m. Both churches were full.

The two ministers in Shader came across to the Barvas after-meeting at the close of the Shader meeting. That was the night that my future husband was saved.

The meetings continued in both places for a week, followed in both places by cottage meetings which were announced at the close of the church meetings.

The atmosphere was full of joy and expectancy, but we were praying all the time; praying, praying, praying! Sometimes we were burdened for specific individuals, and sometimes it was prayer for the whole community.

We spoke to everyone about the Lord – and it was so easy! Words just flowed so naturally whether we were speaking to old or young, converted or unconverted. The subject of the Lord and the working of the Lord in the last little while seemed to occupy everyone's attention. Even the unsaved in my class at school would ask, 'Were you at the meeting last night? Who was converted?' They wanted to know what was happening at the meetings.

And the singing! It was simply glorious. It was almost supernatural, full of joy and spiritual power. Probably only 50% could sing well, but everybody sang from their hearts. There was such rejoicing!

One lad from the Merchant Navy, home on leave, was converted the night before he returned to the ship. We were all concerned for his spiritual progress but the Lord cared for him in that environment. People were praying for loved ones away from home and numbers of these were saved at that time in Glasgow, London and elsewhere.

We didn't realize at the time how wonderful it was. Only later, after the revival, we looked back and realized that we had been in a remarkable move of the Spirit.

Duncan Campbell moved on to other places, Ness, Carloway, Shawbost, Arnol, etc., and the praying people and many of the young converts followed him. By 1953 it was tailing off, but what a harvest was taken and what an uplift and blessing it was to the whole church.

When my husband and I came to Uig we found that nearly all the office-bearers in the church had been saved in the revival! There was a wonderful movement here when whole families were converted. In one family in the Bays of Uig, the father, mother, two sons and a daughter were converted in ten days. In another village, Timisgarry, all the male members who were home at the time and who were unconverted came to Christ in a short space of time. Not only were they converted, but they continued steadfastly to follow the Lord, and became stable pillars in the church. About twenty joined the church on one Sunday.

The small island of Bernera was touched too. There was no bridge to the island, nor were there any roads for cars then, but people came to the church there from all over the island. We went to a communion weekend on Bernera. Donald MacAulay skippered the *Marie Dhonn*, and when we left the Kirkabost pier he couldn't take another soul on board. It was packed! There were two precentors on board and how we sang! I shall never forget the singing on that short voyage from Bernera. What a blessed communion we had!

The outstanding mark of the revival was the presence of God. We had such enormous liberty in prayer and testimony and this was the result of God's presence in the midst. Often it would be the singing of the psalms that would, as it were, bring the Lord's presence to the meeting. As we sang from our hearts often the atmosphere would change dramatically and it seemed that heaven itself was present.

We just thank the Lord that we were privileged to be there and to witness His mighty hand at work.

10

MRS. ANNIE MACKINNON (nee MacLeod)
Harris 1945

One day before the revival in 1945, I walked to the tweed shop which was just below my aunt's home. As I climbed up the hill to her house, I heard beautiful singing. On my arrival, I said to her, 'You are surely in great form today.'

'Why?' she asked.

'Because I heard you singing and your singing was simply wonderful,' I replied.

'No, my dear,' she said, 'I haven't been singing.'

Amazingly, I was privileged to hear this heavenly singing before I knew the Lord as my Saviour, and furthermore before the movement of the Spirit in that area. Perhaps it could be described as a moment of joyful heavenly anticipation.

Soon after this there was a movement in the bays of Harris and people began to seek the Lord in earnest, with some coming to know Him. There was great expectancy in the parish.

The communion weekend in September was upon us and the people came out to all the meetings with great hunger and longing that the Lord would come and visit us. The Lord's people were alive spiritually. The Spirit had been, as it were, following the people around from place to place and they were conscious of His working in their hearts wherever they went, and in the district at large.

The church in Scarista was well prepared with chairs in the aisles and in any open spaces. The people filled them all and sat up the pulpit steps as well. It was crowded to capacity for the duration of the whole communion weekend. They were in the habit of coming out on communion Sundays but not, as now, on the weeknights as well, and never in such large numbers. Was God going to come at this time?

One night something out of the ordinary happened. Rev. Murdo

MacLeod was preaching on the text, 'Remember Lot's wife.' There was great power in the meeting and everyone was listening intently when suddenly someone gave an awesome cry. Others cried out as well. Some fell into a trance, some fainted. The minister waited for calm and tranquillity to be restored and then continued. The meeting settled and eventually closed with the singing of a psalm. The unusual events certainly sobered people up and caused them to further seek the Lord, for the fear of God descended upon the place.

My father spoke enthusiastically of the services and of the fact that one of our relatives had gone forward for membership, in other words, had come to Christ and wished to be identified with the people of God. This made a deep impression on me and I wondered if I could go through this season of communion without revealing the fact that I was under deep conviction of sin. The Spirit of God had been striving with me for some time now and I was very concerned about the condition of my soul.

On Saturday night, as was our custom, we boarded the boat to go to the meeting on the island of Scalpay. It was a prayer meeting led by a missionary known as the St. Kildan, MacDonald by name. The Spirit of God was mightily in the midst. It was enough for me merely to hear the Word of God being read. But I held out and would not yield.

As we left the meeting Chirsty MacSween turned to me and said, 'And what about you? Why aren't you joining us?' That was enough for me. I just sobbed and sobbed. When we arrived at the house, I went into the closet (a small room) and began to pray. I didn't want to see anyone. I just wanted to be alone. Food had been prepared, however, so I had to go to the table.

I stayed the night at this house. What a wonderful spirit there was! That night was the night of nights for me, for it was there on the island of Scalpay that I found peace with God. As we travelled back in the boat on the next morning, the people began to sing the psalms while the precentor led. The singing was wonderful! The missionary from Uig, Donald MacDonald, turned to Chirsty MacSween and said, 'You may think that you are singing, but the real singing is coming from this one,' referring to me!

I was very shy and wondered what my people would say. Kirsty went before me and spread the news of my conversion. That night I went to the service and even though I was sitting beside an unconverted uncle, what a night I had in the presence of God! Rev. Lachie MacLeod was the preacher. Later we boarded the boat and sailed to Drinishader. I went to the house of an aunt who was a godly woman. Her daughter had been told of my conversion and we ended up in the same bedroom, talking well into the night.

We went to the service that night and Lachie MacLeod preached with tears. Five more souls were saved. The local minister called me the lamb of the flock because I was the first convert of this wonderful move of the Holy Spirit.

The services continued from village to village and we could hardly wait for the time of the meeting. Other ministers were called upon and they came and preached. People came from all over the island, gathering together at the church and later in the homes of the people for cottage meetings. In Drinishader these meetings continued for a week. People came, homes were opened and many stayed for the meetings. At an after meeting in my aunt's house, every room was full. It was very late when the service was over, but my uncle stood up as the people were leaving and said, 'Why are you leaving?' He felt that the meeting should just go on and on, and that no-one should leave!

The revival spread and many were saved, including Alistair Mor (Big Alistair) Campbell who became a leading figure in the church in that area. Sixteen people went forward at the next communion to join the church.

Even people far away from the island came under the influence of the revival. When they heard of the work of God in their home area and knew the people who were being saved, they too came under conviction and sought God. The news of the revival brought them to consider their own condition before God and they yielded their lives to Him where they were, in different parts of the country.

We treasure the memory of these moments in the presence of God and pray that we may again be the recipients of His outpoured love and mercy as He comes to us again in revival power.

11

MRS. CHIRSTY MAGGIE MACLEOD
(nee MacPhail)
Arnol

The preaching had been searching, but the night that revival broke out in Arnol, it was simply overpowering. The Holy Spirit was applying the Word to many hearts as we listened to the intense presentation of the gospel. The text rang out time and again, 'And thou Capernaum, who art lifted up to heaven will be cast down to hell.' The preacher, Rev. Duncan Campbell, applied the Word personally: 'You are here tonight and you have turned your back on God. Once, twice, or even three times you have said, and are continuing to say, 'I don't want to know Christ.' You have been lifted up to heaven, but you will be cast down to hell!'

The power of the Holy Spirit was overwhelming, the sense of the presence of God bowed all our hearts. Mr. Campbell asked those who were anxious to remain for prayer. Ten stayed. The thundering prophet became the tender shepherd when he spoke to seekers in this gathering. He used to read from John 10: 'My sheep hear my voice...' and gave such gentle and compassionate advice before praying with them. He never went through the biblical points or steps to God, but he would let them seek the Lord on their own. He would not, as it were, 'lead them to Christ', but would allow the Holy Spirit to do His own work in the hearts of those who were seeking the Lord.

Ten stayed, but I ran all the way home thinking, 'This has nothing to do with any man. This is something between God and me. I have got to get through to God myself.' I went to my room and closed the door – and then the battle raged! Satan did his utmost to prevent me from coming to the Lord. He cast up one argument after another. I knew I had to come, but how? The text, 'Whosoever cometh to Me I will in no wise cast out,' was God's wonderful encouragement to me as I wrestled. He won't cast me out; He will accept me; but how do I come?

It took hours. I did not want to come, but I knew I had to come. I knew that I was lost, and I knew that to be saved, I had to come to Christ. I wanted to be saved but I did not want to yield my all to Christ. I was afraid of the consequences. 'Oh, God, have mercy on me and show me the way!' What a battle it was.

At a point of desperation, something happened that I have never been able to explain. It seemed as if a cool breeze went through the room, and I heard a clear voice say, 'Jesus of Nazareth passeth by.' It was so real that I put out my hand to touch Him and said earnestly, 'Don't pass me,' – and He didn't! I, as it were, touched Him and He saved me in that instant. The presence of God in that room was so real. Joy welled up within me and I knew that I was His.

That was forty-eight years ago – there's a lot of living in forty-eight years – and I can recall it as if it were yesterday. The Spirit of God drew me so tenderly to my wonderful Saviour. I loved Him then and I love Him all the more now. I am a widow now but not alone, for He is with me and is so precious to me.

I wasn't at the meeting in the house that shook when they prayed, and both the people who lived there at that time have now passed on. Twenty-four people came to Christ in Arnol and none fell by the wayside; all continued to follow the Lord. We had prayer meetings here for years after the move of the Spirit.

My sister Margaret wrote thirty Gaelic hymns. She had no such gift before the revival and her songs have gone on tape to Gaels all over the world. In fact five people in this village received the gift of poetry and wrote spiritual songs. That was just part of the revival. I long for another revival before I go to heaven. Evangelistic campaigns are good and necessary, but they are not revival! Revival is when God comes down.

There was a man in the village who was very hard. He had been to Canada and had returned as hard as could be. My father worked with him and one day said to him, 'Will you do me a favour?'

'If I possibly can, I will,' he replied.

'There are meetings in the village. My children have attended them and have been saved. I want you to go to these meetings. Will you come with me tonight?' said my father.

The man answered, 'I don't need to go to the meetings to know that there is something supernatural going on in the village. I feel it in my own home.'

God was everywhere, in the very atmosphere. Whether they were godly or godless, people knew that God was there. The man never went to the meetings but years later on his deathbed he trusted the Lord to save him. What a pity he wasted his life.

It seemed that the only thing we spoke about was God and the things of God. We went through the day waiting for the evening meetings. The converts followed the meetings from village to village, gathering strength as they went on. It was a wonderful time. The amazing prayers of a newly converted sixteen-year-old boy in the meetings brought great blessing to the community. His parents were also saved at that time.

How do you describe the indescribable? You have to be there to know and sense the wonder of it all. A sermon was never too long. We stayed at the meetings until two or three in the morning and we were never tired. God was at work.

Duncan Campbell was inspired. He was fiery, and his penetrating words spoke to the heart. He thundered forth the message in great power, and held our attention throughout his sermon. He preached with tremendous 'grip' and boldness and we knew that he was utterly sincere in his proclamation of the truth. He preached to the heart. He was certainly God's chosen instrument at that time.

In the pulpit he was dynamic, but when he spoke to seekers in the after meeting, he was as gentle as a lamb. 'I will say a few words on the simplicity of the way of salvation,' he would say. He was like a different man altogether, explaining and helping – and the people loved him. Why, we must never move away from the simplicity that is in Christ Jesus. Our problem is that we make it all too complicated!

Unfortunately there was opposition to the work of God. There were sad tensions in the community. Those who opposed the work were doubtless Christians but sadly they became hard in their spirits toward those who were not in their church, and especially to those who spoke of revival blessing even if they were in their own church. There were nevertheless more people saved in the revival from the Free Church than from the Church of Scotland simply because the Free Church is a bigger denomination on the island and their people were more numerous. Although some Free Church people did not attend the church meetings, many went to the cottage meetings and found the Lord there, for the power of the Lord was evident in the cottage meetings to a remarkable degree.

In the midst of all this turmoil, my father was thrown into confusion. 'What if these people are correct and I and my children are deceived?' The only way to know this, he thought, was to ask God.

We were busy in the peat-bog cutting winter fuel, but my father was very quiet. Eventually I said, 'We're tired, let's go home.' 'No,' he said, 'you rest if you are tired, but we will stay. I have asked God a question and I am waiting here until I get my answer. The question is, 'Is this revival from You or not?' Please tell me.'

Some time passed when suddenly he said, 'Let's go home; I have my answer. God has spoken to me from Isaiah 43:11-13: 'I, even I am the Lord...I have declared and have saved, and I have shewed...therefore ye are My witnesses, saith the Lord...I will work and who shall let it?' '

On his way home he called on all the homes where there were converts and read these words to them. One said, 'I never doubted it!' We were consoled and strengthened by these words and continued to seek and to praise the Lord for all that He was doing in our midst.

The preaching was convicting and the singing brought the mighty presence of God into the meetings again and again. How could I ever forget Psalm 72:

> His Name forever shall endure
> last like the sun it shall
> Men shall be bless'd in Him, and bless'd
> all nations shall Him call.

Psalm 126 swelled out so often:

> When Zion's bondage God turned back,
> as men that dream'd were we.
> Then filled with laughter was our mouth,
> our tongues with melody.
>
> They 'mong the heathen said, the Lord
> great things for them hath wrought.
> The Lord hath done great things for us,
> Whence joy to us is brought.

I remember well the power of Psalm 132:

> I will not come within my house
> nor rest in bed at all;
> Nor shall my eyes take any sleep
> nor eyelids slumber shall;
> Till for the Lord a place I find
> where He may make abode;

A place of habitation
For Jacob's mighty God.

You could close your eyes, listen to the singing and with them all just float to heaven! As the meeting progressed in power, many times the singers would take over the precenting as well, so every line was sung not just once but twice by all. How I recall, as if it were yesterday, the singing of Psalm 102:

Thou shalt arise and mercy have
upon Thy Zion yet;
The time to favour her is come,
the time that Thou hast set....

So shall the heathen people fear
the Lord's most holy name;
And all the kings of earth shall dread
Thy glory and Thy fame.

When Zion by the mighty Lord
built up again shall be,
In glory then and majesty
to men appear shall He.

And the prayers! So many of the elders who prayed were so inspired of God that we were overwhelmed with the consciousness of the presence of God as they prayed. I remember Ruairidh Alex! He was powerful in prayer. One night he was sitting in the window and when he prayed he got really worked up and slapped me on the shoulder. Afterwards he said to me, 'Oh *ghraidh* (my love), did I hurt you?'

The cottage meetings were often filled with people. Upstairs and downstairs, every room was filled and the stairs formed benches for the folk to sit on. In one such meeting my brother and I were sitting near the bottom of the stairs when a wonderful thing happened.

It was near the end of the meeting. My brother and I heard heavenly music as if it came out from the closet under the stairs. It seemed that a heavenly choir was passing through! It was somehow not like voices but like an orchestra, yet more wonderful. It was simply a marvellous sound. It was heavenly! It wafted through from under the stairs and moved slowly across the foyer and out through the front door.

We looked at each other. I leaned across and whispered, 'Calum, did you hear that?' He nodded. Mrs MacFarlane, the minister's wife, was sitting in the doorway. She heard it too. She looked at us and saw that we were amazed for we had heard the heavenly music. She rose, tip-toed across to us, and said, 'Did you hear that too?' Not everybody heard it, but to those who did, it brought a sense of awe and reverence. Wonderful moments!

We loved everybody! It did not matter to which church anyone belonged. They were all enveloped in the wonderful love of God! We just loved them all. And we didn't think that sin would ever trouble us again! We were wrong.

On one occasion as we were boarding a bus to go to church, an elder with whom we had been friendly for years, for we had grown up with him in the village, passed us without a word. He walked on in an eloquent stony silence. One of the young converts standing there said, 'There you are, sin isn't dead yet!' The elder, who had visited our house for years, for we were friends, stopped doing so, as we were involved in a revival of which he did not approve. It did not come in his church. Had it done so, he would have been thrilled with the workings of the Spirit of God.

Oh, what would have happened had they all embraced the revival? I had to watch that I did not become bitter in the midst of the revival, for there were those who truly knew God, who did not open their hearts to God's workings, but rather opposed it all. I must not quench the Spirit in my own life. You could have wrong feelings towards those who opposed the work of God and grow cold in your own heart, ending up far from God, even though you had experienced such wonderful things from Him.

My prayer is to get to know Him more, to get closer to Him; that's my prayer! We are not yet at the place where we want to be, but as we continue to seek Him, He surely will lead us ever closer to Himself.

12

DONALD JOHN SMITH
Ballantrushal

Donald John Smith's father, John, one of the leading figures of both the 1939 and the 1949 revivals in the Barvas area, was respected on every hand for his godly life and spiritual leadership. He was the blacksmith of the village. Donald John and his wife now live in the family home opposite the old smithy. He is an elder in the Barvas Church of Scotland.

The first meeting of the 1939 revival in this district was in our home. There were no phones in those days but word got around and the people came. At that time, what is now a garden was wasteland and they put planks of wood on concrete blocks for seating for the overflow from the house, so all were able to enjoy the meeting, the doors and windows being wide open.

This was not so much a preaching revival but a praying one. Should there be a minister available, he was asked to preach, but normally it was led by the laity. There was great unity among the Lord's people. Denominations were forgotten and God's people joined together in fervent worship, intercession and praise.

We children were sent to bed upstairs but we didn't sleep. We would creep out of the bedroom, venture down a few steps of the stairs, and sit there to listen to what was going on in the meeting. Sometimes we would hear someone praying in one room and someone else in another room at the same time, for the Spirit was moving in a powerful way. We children were deeply affected by what we heard and saw. The cry of the penitent frightened us and we listened the following day to the older people as they spoke about those who were converted the previous night. Our upbringing was in the midst of revival, so when the 1949 revival came, it was not new to us. We had been through these things before and were able to accept it readily. One could say that the two revivals were connected, with the war in between, but the emotionalism in the 1939 revival was not apparent in the 1949 revival. By the standards of the 1939 revival, the 1949 revival was very quiet.

There were, however, those who opposed the work of God. A young man was converted in the revival a few weeks before he was called up to go to the war. He was in a meeting in the church one night when his father stormed in and tried to drag him out, for he did not want him to have anything to do with the revival. The young man left for the conflict in Europe and was soon killed in action. The attitude of his parents changed after the sad loss of their son.

In 1939, some girls were walking up from Borve, past the school. They were able to hear singing from the meeting hall. Under normal circumstances they could not have heard the singing for the hall was too far away, but this being revival, the people seemed to have an inspiration which gives the voice more power. It is spiritually rooted, and, as they sing, the reality of it seems to give the voice extra force. As you sing in revival you sense the Spirit's presence and know the reality of the subject of which you are singing, to the extent that you want to reach out and touch it. And of course we were singing the Word of God, for the psalms are the hymn-book of the church in the islands.

We used to hear, 'The Spirit touched me during the singing of such-and-such a psalm' or 'God spoke to me when so-and so prayed'. Sometimes God spoke clearly during the reading of the Scripture. Everything was alive with the presence of God. You don't hear remarks like that very much today.

Before the 1949 revival there was a prayer meeting held in Shader on Tuesday nights. On Friday nights a short prayer meeting was held in the Free Church which was attended by people from both denominations, but on Thursday each church had its own prayer meeting. There was a great spirit of prayer everywhere, and that was actually the beginning of the revival.

The 1949 revival had already started before Duncan Campbell came to Lewis, and young people were being saved. Sometimes people broke down in meetings, but that did not always mean that they were converted. It might be weeks or months later that they gave evidence of the fact that they were truly converted.

The outstanding characteristic of the 1949 revival was the presence of God. The presence of God was so powerful that you were constantly living in the expectation that something was about to happen. You would feel a sort of excitement inside yourself. You were afraid of saying anything wrong. You were afraid of saying or doing anything that would cause God to remove His presence. There was a subduing, an awe that was everywhere. And the joy! Even in the fields you felt an inward urge to sing. We were up until 3.00 or 4.00 a.m. at the meetings and then up again between 7.00 and 8.00 a.m. to go to work, and we were not tired!

If a bus was going to the meetings the people began to sing as soon as there were two or three people on the bus, and they sang all the way. I was one of the Shader pipers and we went to a meeting one night in Arnol. The place was packed and when we came through the door, our minister stood up and called, 'Would the Shader pipers please come down to the front. There is room for you here.' I wished that the floor would open and swallow me up but we walked to the front and took our seats.

Meetings had been conducted for some time before I came to Christ. My interest was aroused and when I was asked to go to the late night cottage meeting, I did not hesitate, for I had already sensed the Spirit moving in the preceding church meeting. I was converted in an old missionary's home in Barvas. There were numbers of us who stayed behind for counsel. We left the house in the small hours of the morning. A bus appeared from nowhere in the rain, picked us up and took us home. I was saved and I knew it!

On one occasion when the meeting was held in our home, and the house was bursting at the seams, as the door leading from the lounge was in the way, my father unscrewed it and took it away!

The memory of the singing, as one of the outstanding aspects of the revival, remains with me. It would seem sometimes that the singing would raise the roof of the church! It was powerful.

New converts, who had previously sat with their friends at the back of the church, would often, the following evening, deliberately go forward to sit near the front, thus separating themselves from their former worldly companions. This would have a sobering and salutary effect on their friends.

On one occasion during the revival we sat around the table and my father said the grace. Suddenly, at the beginning of the meal, he cried out, 'Oh!'

Startled, my mother said, 'What's wrong?'

'A lot of people are going to hell,' he replied.

He put his hands on the table and began to pray. Everyone ate their meal in silence for it affected us all greatly. It was such a shock. He was in touch with God and God probably revealed to him at that moment the state of souls around us.

In my teenage years we used to go to the shieling (summer hut on the moor) about three miles away. Very often I would go there to milk the cows in the evening and in the morning. I was expected afterwards at home to start the fire in the smithy where I would often find my father on his knees at the anvil. This was a common occurrence, but the first time I saw it I froze in the doorway and stood there until he finished praying. He must have known that I was there but he stayed on his knees and later rose and got on with his work.

I remember conducting family worship at our shieling out on the moor. There is a loch beside our shieling and on a quiet night the singing at the worship in our shieling seemed to echo across the loch. Singing from other shielings wafted through the silence. It seemed to spread far and wide.

Following all these experiences I fell into a backslidden state. I first went to the army, and was later in Glasgow for years as a motor mechanic and then as a driver of Greyhound buses. Through various incidents God spoke to me and eventually after a heart attack in Lewis I returned to the Lord in as great an experience as when I first trusted in Christ. It seemed as though it were a repeat experience of my conversion! God later sent us a wonderful time of revival.

13

MRS. CATHERINE CAMPBELL
Barvas; Sandwick, Stornoway

From childhood my memory is of godly conversation, prayer and the singing of psalms and hymns in the home. The 1939 revival was still fresh in the memories of my parents and their friends and they were very burdened for the lost – always! When we went to the barn to milk the cows, my mother took us to the hay-rack and we prayed there every day. Mother told me years later, that as a child I said to her on one occasion, 'Mummy, be sure to remember to pray even if I'm not there!' She was always burdened for souls. The 1939 revival was born in prayer and that spirit of prayer continued, eventually increasing until the 1949 revival broke out.

I knew the Spirit striving with me ever since I was a little girl, but it did not change my way of life. I knew that the Lord's people had something that I did not possess but strangely I felt quite comfortable in their presence. My Christian upbringing kept me from the vilest sins but I entered into the entertainments enjoyed by young people: concerts, dances, cinemas and the like. I used to envy my friends who could enjoy these pleasures without any qualms of conscience. The home in which I grew up spread its godly influence, but that was not enough to cause me to yield. I used to try and fight off conviction.

I began nursing training. One day I was out for a walk and the church bells began to ring. I occasionally attended church, and as I listened to the bells I thought, 'What if this were the last trumpet sound, and I was going in the opposite direction?'

Shortly afterwards I began to feel a great emptiness in my life. I was on night duty at the time and suddenly it began to dawn on me that it was Christ I needed. I began to weigh up the patients in the female ward in the hope that one of them was a Christian. I decided on one of the older ones who seemed quite approachable. I poured out my heart to her with the tears streaming down my cheeks, asking for advice for a poor sinner like me. She told me that she had not found Christ herself as yet, but that she had godly parents and that this is what we should aim at. In the morning I kept well clear of her bed as the experience of the night before had evaporated and I was feeling very embarrassed.

About this time Rev. Duncan Campbell had come to Barvas. Another patient informed me that revival had broken out and that my brother was one of the converts. I reacted very negatively, saying to her, 'Wait till I get home; I will soon reverse that!'

On my day off I made my way home with mixed feelings. My brother John *(later to be Rev John Murdo Smith)* met me in the doorway of our house and quoted to me a verse of a hymn which he had just composed. He was newly converted and was the first convert to begin composing hymns.

As I entered the house my mother was singing, 'The valley will be full of light when Jesus comes!' The power of God gripped me there and then and I rushed to the privacy of a room where I could weep without being seen. That night I went to the meeting, trying hard to look composed and uninterested, determined not to give in. I had been so rebellious. The meeting was mighty and I was overwhelmed with conviction although I do not remember what was said.

Duncan Campbell preached and in the course of his address he mentioned a verse which my mother used to quote to us as children. She was sitting right behind me. She touched my back, whether by accident or deliberately I don't know, but I could hold back no longer. When I got out of the church I fell on my knees oblivious to all that was happening around me. I didn't care who was around! My need was of God's mercy. This was now paramount in my thinking! I sought Him and found Him! That was the night that Billy MacLeod came to the Lord *(later to be Rev. William MacLeod)*.

I went home and testified to my father who was unwell and not able to be at the meeting on that evening. He cried like a baby for joy; yet another of his family in the fold!

My next step was to testify to my boyfriend. I wrote and told him what had happened; that I still cared for him but that I had to put Christ first in my life. He arranged to meet me but, being rather apprehensive, he went to the pub first and drank in the hope that this would give him courage. This upset me profoundly and no doubt my reaction affected him, but I was determined that there could now be no serious relationship between us, as the Scripture says in Amos 3:3, 'Can two walk together except they be agreed?' Some months afterwards, on attending the meetings, Norman was radically converted. Later on we were married and we spent many happy years together before the Lord called him Home.

When I was saved I thought that I was going to heaven right away. My whole outlook changed. I was now praying without ceasing for my fellow sinners, waiting for a cry for mercy here or there in the meetings. This was music to my ears. I could not stop telling all I met about the wonderful experience which could never be put into words! It was as if a river flowed out of me and I was never stuck for words. I was naturally shy and timid and would never be to the fore in company, but God loosened my tongue and made me bold for him. Oh, how I long to see revival again!

The presence of God was everywhere and the cry of the penitent was as sweet balm to my soul. Many tears were shed and these were commonplace amongst saved and unsaved alike.

We had a precious pastor in James Murray MacKay. He was caring and generous, presenting each convert in his congregation with a copy of the Scriptures.

Our hearts were so full of love that we could not keep it in. After the meetings we would make a circle on the street, holding hands and singing at the top of our voices. It was heaven on earth. Everything was made new! Why, we wouldn't even want to read a newspaper! Cowboy stories and comics went out of the window, or rather into the fire. At 9.00 p.m. on Saturday, all our normal pursuits ended; sewing and knitting was put away in preparation for the Lord's day.

My mother stood outside on the path one night and she called my father saying, 'Come and hear this!' They heard the voices of angels singing! They followed the sound of the heavenly harmony to a home two doors away and there they found two women crying in distress of soul. There will be joy in heaven over one soul who repents. There were numbers of occasions at that time when heavenly singing was heard. Everything was so real to the people then.

We had great liberty talking to our friends in the community, in the shops or at our place of work. The revival and the converts were the main topic of conversation everywhere – even at secular gatherings. This caused a desire in the hearts of many to come and hear for themselves, and many who did were soundly converted.

The abiding memory of the revival was that the presence of God was everywhere, not just in the meetings. We could not get away from the working of the Holy Spirit. God accompanied you everywhere. This was the outstanding feature of the revival.

14

REV. DONALD MACAULAY

Bernera, Lewis 1936
Donald Smith began speaking for the Lord shortly after his conversion at the age of eighteen. He was then illiterate, but the lady next door taught him to read one or two chapters of the Bible. Eventually he became a missionary in the islands and was greatly used.

One evening he had a meeting in a house in the nearby village of Haclete. A young bare-footed boy was in the meeting and he began to cry. Donald stopped preaching and led the boy to the Lord. That boy graduated from Glasgow University with M.A. and B.D. degrees and went to Toronto later, beginning a College there. His name was Angus MacIver. Many years later, a lady from Toronto was visiting on holiday. Donald met her and said to her, 'I wonder if you ever came across Rev. Angus MacIver?'

'Oh yes,' she said, 'I would call him my father in the Lord.'

'Then I am your grandfather,' said Donald.

He was in a house in Strond one evening during his ministry. He read very little else but Spurgeon's sermons. Another missionary, a Mr Matheson, was with him. Donald said to Mr Matheson, 'I have just heard some news – Spurgeon is dead.' Sure enough, when the newspapers arrived in the islands a few days later they reported that Spurgeon had died! Donald had heard from heaven.

He had a very fruitful ministry in the Uists and in Harris and had converts wherever he went. He was a kind of supernatural man, strong in faith and much used by God. It is regrettable how rare these people are. You get one in a generation.

When I was a boy we would walk the three miles to school. There would be a whole crowd of us, about twenty boys and twenty girls. There were no cars then and no proper roads. Sometimes Donald Smith would meet us on our way home and he would take off his hat and say, 'Come on now, boys and girls, let's have a word of prayer!' He would then pray with us as we stood quietly like a small congregation together, and when he finished, he would say, 'Off you go now; home to your dinner.' He was then elderly, a truly remarkable man.

He was semi-retired in 1936 and lived in a house in Crulavig, near Uig. There was then no bridge to Bernera. A young lad and his father came across from Bernera in a boat one day. The father knew Donald but the lad did not. Donald said, as he looked across to Bernera, 'I'm going across one day with a sledgehammer to break those hard stones over there!' The lad said to his father as they left, 'Who was that daft old man who said he was going over with a sledgehammer to break those hard stones?'

'Oh,' said his father, 'forget about it, you wouldn't understand.'

A fortnight later he went across and a great revival began. He knew before that a mighty revival was coming and that he would be involved. This was just before the war. At least four ministers came out of that revival and numbers of people were saved. Some of the converts were killed in the war.

Bernera, Lewis 1951

After I had done my National Service, I joined one of the Donaldson boats in Glasgow and went to South America and to the west coast of the U.S.A. for eighteen months. Before I left, I remember the boys from Kirkabost, now in the Nicholson Institute, the high school in Stornoway, telling us about the revival. They couldn't talk about anything else but the revival in Barvas and the people in the high school who had been converted. I remember saying to them the night before I left Stornoway, 'Never mind, they'll soon be back to normal.'

I returned home and found that in Bernera the young people did attend church. My father was an elder and my mother a member. There was nothing else to do on the island, so we went to church. When Duncan Campbell came we had no minister and Rev. MacLennan was the moderator. He had done his best to get Duncan Campbell to come to Bernera and at last succeeded.

There was an air of expectancy and a lot of prayer before he came. Some of the elders in the Free Church and in the Church of Scotland encouraged us to go and hear the man whom God so blessed elsewhere. He arrived a few days before the communion season and began having services in the church and in homes. I did not go to begin with, but everybody went and the talk everywhere was about Duncan Campbell, the meetings and the revival.

My parents tried to persuade me to go to hear him. Finally I went to the house where he was to hold the meeting that night. There he was in a tweed suit – how very unministerial, I thought! But there was something different about the meeting that night and I could not explain it. He said, at the end of the meeting, that God was working in our midst. This hit me like a sledgehammer and it made a deep impression on me.

Mr. Campbell only stayed for a short time, but in that period numbers were converted. Some of them made a real mark on the church and in their community later on.

Lemreway 1969

Early in 1950 Duncan Campbell prayed earnestly that he might be able to go to Lemreway, on the coast about sixteen miles south of Stornoway, for he felt that the Lord wanted him there. He was unable to do so then because of opposition. Twenty years later I was the parish minister in the village of Lemreway. One could almost say that Duncan Campbell came to Lemreway twenty years late. He preached in our church, the Church of Scotland, in answer to prayer after all those years, and the Lord poured out His Spirit in revival power in that village and in that community. Just before he came several of the people there, including my wife, had great expectations and were trusting the Lord for a move of the Spirit.

Duncan Campbell had been speaking at the communion and said strongly, 'This congregation is near to revival!' When the revival broke out the presence of the Lord was felt all around Lemreway. It seemed to be a circle around the village or a canopy over the area. Outside of this circle there was nothing; it was just so ordinary. When one went to Stornoway, one just longed to be back in the area of the Spirit's operation.

We had services in the church every night at 6.00 p.m. Nobody wanted to leave. We would go to the nearby manse, have a cup of tea and then return to the pulpit for another hour-and-a-half. The people still would not go home but gathered in the manse for yet more preaching, singing and fellowship. People left the manse for work in the morning before they went home.

People were drawn by the Spirit and they were united together by the same power. Among the number of folk who were converted were those who were middle-aged, and some of the converts were from the Free Church. One felt that everyone in the village was moved and so many were converted. All along the road where we met people, they would stop and talk about the revival. It was a wonderful time but it did not last very long nor did it spread any further than Lemreway.

15

MRS CATRIONA MACAULAY

I am from Port-of-Ness. The Lord was working in revival power in our area, but I was determined not to be converted for my school friends would hear and the news would get around.

The first meeting I attended was in Galson. Duncan Campbell was at the door shaking hands with the people at the close of the meeting. I don't know whether I was afraid of the man or whether I was afraid that if I touched him something would happen to me, so I dodged him and escaped! I didn't want him to speak to me!

To start with, we went with the flow. Everybody seemed to be going to the meetings, so we followed. Something seemed to carry us along. In the end we wanted to go! We walked two and a half miles to the church in Ness and we did it willingly.

It is difficult to pinpoint an actual date on which I came to Christ. One night in a cottage meeting, together with two other girls, one being my cousin and neighbour Mary Morrison, I was under deep conviction of sin. I felt that I deserved to go to hell, for these eternal things were so real. A room was cleared for seekers and the three of us went in. I gave myself again to God, and later in our own home I sought God with increased earnestness. The love of Christ drew me and broke me down. One night, however, in the church in Cross, Mr. Campbell was speaking on the text, '...born, not of blood, nor of the will of the flesh, nor of the will of man, but of God' (John 1:13). That word brought peace to my heart and I sensed that I too had been accepted by the Lord.

Shortly after we were in a meeting in Carloway and eventually at a very late hour the older folk said that they should be going home. We said to the unconverted bus driver, 'You take them home, we'll stay for more and then we'll walk home!' Walk home! Just a mere thirty miles! But that was the spirit which existed amongst us. Fortunately the bus driver had mercy on us. He took them home and then returned for us! Time and distance meant nothing to us and, amazingly, we were neither tired nor hungry. We could still work and not be sleepy. We just seemed to be filled with the Spirit of the Lord and desired only the things of God. It was a wonderful time of mighty blessing and I praise God that I had the privilege of experiencing this remarkable outpouring of the Spirit.

Years later, in the ministry, we were privileged to experience another period of great blessing in Lemreway. Mr. Campbell came to us, ministered in the church, and God once again poured out His Spirit in a wonderful way.

Just after this period of refreshing in Lemreway, there were about twelve people in the manse one night after a meeting. They were around the table, so united in spirit as they discussed the things of God, remembering in particular the saints who had departed from us. Having filled their cups with tea I walked from the dining-room to the kitchen and between the doors I heard wonderful singing. I stood in the doorway and said, 'Where is that singing coming from?' It seemed to be like heavenly singing. I had never heard anything like it. Another of the ladies heard it as well and said, 'I heard it when you were in the dining-room filling the cups.' Rev. MacRae from Tarbert was there and he said, 'Don't be afraid, the Lord is with us.' Amazing and unexpected things happen in revival. Oh that He would again come amongst us in power!

16

DONALD MACPHAIL
Arnol, later a missionary to the Yemen

Donald MacPhail was a native of the village of Arnol, a few miles west of Barvas. He was affectionately known as 'Domhnull Beag' or Little Donald, as his father's name was also Donald. When the revival began he was a tall, slender high school lad. He relates the following experience.

One day I was out in the field on the croft and questions arose in my mind as to the meaning of life. What was the point of it all? I did not realize that conviction was coming upon me, just as it came upon many long before we attended any meetings. There was something in the atmosphere that affected us quite apart from the meetings. We did not realize that God was moving in the community.

I recall walking on the moorland and I just sat down sobbing. I did not know why I was sobbing. I spoke to the sheep and said, 'I envy you, for you are not disturbed by the thoughts that are disturbing me!' Then I would think, 'I am heading for eternity, and I don't know what eternity holds for me!' I had no answer to this situation. 'I am lost until I find an answer to these questions that are affecting me.' I would sob and sob. I knew that I was lost, lost!

I was not alone in feeling like this. Others, too, were deeply impressed by the atmosphere that surrounded us, an atmosphere of the presence of God – a felt presence.

There was a solemnity that settled on the community and we were convicted whether we attended the meetings or not. Others in the village who did not attend were similarly impressed and some simply tried to shake it off so as not to be caught in the 'epidemic'!

I was only sixteen years of age when I heard about the meetings which were being held in March/April 1950. I later discovered that the move of the Spirit had begun the previous year.

At the secondary school in Shawbost, I listened to the young folk from Barvas discussing the meetings. They described Duncan Campbell as one who spoke with immense fervour, sometimes in a high pitched voice. At one meeting, they said excitedly, he hit the edge of the pulpit and broke the lectern as he preached. I thought that would be something worthwhile to see as well as to hear!

The meetings moved to Arnol and I was one of the first to occupy the back seat of the Mission Hall. The meetings went on for a week and then it was announced that they would continue day after day. From then on, two houses in Arnol were opened for after-meetings at II p.m. and I attended every one of them. I came to know the Lord in the second week. These meetings would close at I a.m. or later.

Peace

It was on the third night of the late house meetings at No. 28 Arnol that I found peace. I had hardly slept during these nights for I was wrestling with all that I was hearing, and was driven to pray constantly.

Very often as time goes on and as conviction builds up, folk come to faith in Christ in the second or third week of an evangelistic campaign. On the Thursday we had an after-meeting at II p.m. at No. 28. The atmosphere changed and we were very conscious of the presence of God. Something happened – it was as if the power of God swept through the house. Most of us sensed the awesome change and a number came under deep conviction of sin.

After the cottage meeting I endeavoured to leave for home, but on looking around, outside the house, I noticed a man praying by the side of the wall. Shouts and heavy sighs were heard from the people within, as if crying for help. I could not restrain myself any longer and touched that godly man. In a broken voice I told him that I wanted to get right with God before it was too late. As he turned I saw Christ in the very expression on his face. In compassion he took me by the hand and led me into the prayer meeting.

At about midnight, Kenneth MacDonald from Shader was praying and the presence of God overwhelmed me. It was as though God came upon me and His presence went through me. I was suddenly released. I knew that I was forgiven and had peace with God.

An appeal was made at about 1.00 a.m. There would be a prayer meeting in a bedroom which was cleared for that purpose, and those who were concerned about their souls should go to the bedroom for prayer. Six of us went to the room. It was here in this house that I yielded to the Saviour and found the peace which He alone can give. There were at least six converts that night.

That was the beginning of the response in the meetings in Arnol. The meetings were held in April 1950, when we were busy with the spring work on the crofts. The night after I came to the Lord, my mother was saved, and during that week my father also trusted Christ for salvation.

Meetings

After two weeks in Arnol the meetings moved elsewhere. We were all fired up and followed the meetings wherever we could. John MacKenzie took us all in his truck. At one stage he put a canopy on the lorry which he used to transport the tweed, to protect us from the weather, and drove us to wherever the meetings were held. We went along the west coast to Ness, and on the other side to Point or to Lochs.

Generally it was Duncan Campbell who spoke at the meetings, but he was sometimes away from the island and when this happened others took his place. The Spirit of the Lord moved among the people whoever was speaking. Normally the first hour would be given to prayer and the singing of the Psalms. He would then speak for an hour, after which someone would be called upon to pray before the closing Psalm would be sung.

At different missions, Duncan Campbell would often use the same texts and the same sermons. His comment to someone who noticed this was, 'You never throw away a bait as long as it catches the fish.'

Prayer

Mr. Campbell involved both seasoned intercessors and young converts in his meetings. On one occasion he took a team of us to the island of Bernera. I learned much from his methods, for we were brought alongside him in ministry.

He would call us to prayer at 4.00 p.m. and we would pray through for the meeting in the church building and also for the after-meeting in one of the homes in the village of Tobson on Bernera. It was during the second week that we became aware, one afternoon, of God moving in a remarkable way in the prayer meeting. Mr. Campbell said, 'There will be a break tonight; God is going to bless His people.' And it happened. He knew!

The Lord descended upon the united prayers and fellowship of the people whose hearts God had touched. I saw how Duncan worked – it was a team effort. On occasions I was one on whom he called to lead in prayer in the meetings.

On one of these occasions – it could have been in Bernera or in Point – as I was praying, the power of God came on the meeting and some people fell down and were prostrated in the pews, that is, they lent heavily over the pews in front of them. For some time there was such a stillness when God dealt with people and many came under deep conviction.

On another occasion, this time in Bernera, Duncan Campbell found preaching difficult. The atmosphere was hard, and I, together with others, was burdened that he should get through in the spiritual realm. Mr. Campbell eventually stopped preaching and asked me to pray. That morning, at family worship, we had been reading in the book of Revelation. When I stood to pray it seemed as if I were looking through an open door and gazing at heavenly realities, just like John in the Revelation. I saw these heavenly things and declared them in my prayer. I saw the Lord with the keys of death and hell, and I said so. I saw that there was power there and I cried to God, 'Lord, let it loose.'

When I said 'Amen' and looked around me, I was amazed, for people were on their faces in the pews. Many were bent over the pews. There were also those who went into trances or fainted. The power of God was intense. It was a wonderful evening of the revelation of God's presence and power.

That night, and during that time of divine visitation, a number of people came to Christ in the little village of Kirkabost a few miles away where I was staying in the home of Findlay MacDonald. A number of the houses there had someone who became a Christian at that time.

Mary remembers but Donald does not recall all the occasions when the hand of God was manifestly upon him as he led in prayer. He was at the time a shy country lad, but when called upon to pray, one could sense the oneness of heart among the Lord's people and their expectation and joy in seeing one so young upon whom the Spirit of the Lord rested so convincingly. He was mightily used in prayer at that time.

Who will ever forget those divine moments in the church on the island of Bernera during a communion season when Donald led us to Calvary. In his prayer he described the scene and then said, 'I can hear the thud, thud, thud as with a hammer, they drove the nails into His hands and His feet!' He paused and then cried out, 'It was my hand that held the hammer!' How we wept!

On another occasion in a house meeting in the police station in Barvas, Donald was called upon to lead in prayer. (It was held in the police station as the policeman was an earnest Christian and opened his home to have meetings. The police station was not an imposing building but a home which was converted for administrative police use.) He stood to his feet, clasped his hands together and in his slow and thoughtful way of speaking, he began: 'Father,' he said, and I for one cannot recall the rest of his prayer for I, and others beside me, were overwhelmed with the reality of that one word! To think that I, who had been such a rebel, was now a child of God, and I, even I, could call Him 'Father!' Tears were painful, but oh, how sweet!

Called

It was at a communion service at Carloway that God called me into His service. The particular Scripture that Rev Campbell used that Sunday penetrated my heart and has carried me through the years of service. I had radical dealings with God concerning the mission field that day. I have been privileged to see Him work in Egypt, in parts of Africa and in the Yemen. But that Sunday the call came to me and has been with me from that day.

I recall the Scripture clearly – Jesus was coming into Jerusalem. He told two of His disciples to go into the village where they would find a colt tied. Mr. Campbell emphasized part of the text where Jesus said, 'Loose him and bring him hither.' Because they did what Jesus told them to do, He was able to ride into Jerusalem in triumph. When He reigns in our hearts, He will be able to lead us where he is to be glorified. The Lord had need of the colt, and the Lord had need of me. The message to my heart was as clear as a bell.

The battle raged within me. I was really convicted. I knew that I should yield to the Lord. I was sitting at the end of the pew and I felt so torn under the message, that I wanted simply to slip away from the meeting. I did not want to come to the decision that I knew I should make. Thankfully, the Lord won the battle and I yielded totally to Him. That moment has been with me through the years. It was about a year after my conversion.

Because of the revival several people visited the island. They had heard of my small part in prayer and came to see me. Among them was Arthur Wallis, the author of a book on revival, *In the Day of Thy Power*.

Time passed and I joined the army for my two years compulsory national service, spending most of this time in Germany. When I was discharged I went home and wove Harris Tweed.

The Battle

During 1955 and 1956 I helped build our house at No. 25 Arnol. I was rebelling against going to Bible College.

I had already met a few times with the Church of Scotland Candidates committee at their sessions in Stornoway, under the leadership, at that time, of Rev Horace Walker, but I had no liberty to proceed and apply for the Church of Scotland ministry.

I owe much to the discipling of Duncan Campbell at that time, for I was much on his heart. He sensed that things were not going well with me spiritually and he made the laborious journey from Edinburgh to come and see me in Arnol. He confronted me with my failure to enter the Lord's service and my apparent unwillingness to do so. It had been five years since God saved me and four since he had called me. It did not look very promising for me to leave the home scene and enter God's service.

He proceeded to ask me three personal questions. 'Is this true? Is this true? Is this true?' I admitted that they were all true. He said, 'The Lord has sent me from Edinburgh to come and speak to you because you are being disobedient to the heavenly vision. You are avoiding the vision and the call that God has given you. You are not obeying His voice.'

'Give me a week,' I said, and then I went through an enormous upheaval.

The spiritual turmoil lasted a month and at last I found peace when I wrote the letter of application to the Bible Training Institute in Glasgow. Thankfully I was accepted. Duncan Campbell, therefore, was instrumental in my conversion, consecration and call to the mission field, as well as in my being actually launched into God's service.

The Muslim Field

During the second year at Bible College I knew that I would be going to the Muslim field, so with this clear vision I was able to concentrate on the Arabic language. I completed the two year diploma course at B.T.I and then went to St. Colm's College and spent a year in Edinburgh doing Islamic studies with a few tutors, particularly Professor Watt. I was asked to consider doing a Ph.D. in a certain subject but I could not face such a hurdle.

I had six months before leaving for the mission field, so I spent three months in the Faith Mission Bible College, and three months in the Faith Mission work in both Northern Ireland and Troon.

In 1962 I went to Aden, Yemen, on probation responding to the invitation of the leadership of the Church of South Arabia and negotiating with Rev James Ritchie who presented this challenge to us when we were at Bible College.

I worked at a mission hospital founded in 1886 by Ian Keith Falconer, a Cambridge Professor of Arabic. This fell under the auspices of the Church of Scotland Overseas Council. On 26th March 1965, I married Moraig

Christine MacLeod from Dundee whom I had met at St. Colm's College in Edinburgh and who was the nursing sister at the hospital in the Yemen.

In 1972 the communists took over and circumstances changed. We have worked independently ever since and have been going back and forth to the Middle East for the last forty years. We are now resident in Stornoway, Isle of Lewis.

Features of the revival

Looking back over the revival, the first week of meetings would generally be hard in terms of worship and preaching. Mr. Campbell would preach so vividly and with such expression. He would thump the pulpit, wave his arms and shout. One could sense that he was struggling with his presentation.

Once the breakthrough came – usually in the second week – the whole presentation and communication of the message would change. His voice would change and one sensed he had the liberty of the Spirit. He himself testified that he was blessed anew and knew what it was to be released in the Spirit, God giving him the witness to that effect.

There were manifestations but these were more a recurrence of the 1939 revival than part of the 1949-52 awakening. The 1939 revival had little by way of preaching; it was a prayer revival, far reaching and effective but noted for manifestations. This seemed to be carried over to the 1949-52 revival by those who were affected then, but was not encouraged by Duncan Campbell.

It must also be said that it was the people who were saved in the 1939 revival who spearheaded the 1949-52 revival and who were the prayer warriors. It was these people who followed Mr. Campbell around the island and on whom he depended to pray through. They knew how to pray and to travail for souls.

The people of Ness are of a different temperament and there were no such manifestations among them. The conversions, however, were just as real and lasting. Manifestations took place in other parts of the island. Phenomena did not disturb the meetings and the Barvas minister, Rev James Murray MacKay, sought to keep the meetings under control, exhorting the people to remain calm.

One young girl from Carloway used to go into trances with her hands uplifted for the duration of the service. Her hands would go blue for lack of circulation and it was impossible to bring her hands down. She would later come out of the trance calmly and drop her arms – but this never disturbed the spirit of the meetings or the awareness of the presence of God.

Apart from the presence of God as a 'felt' reality, one was aware of the openness of heart among the people. It was easy to talk of the things of God. There was also a deep hunger to read and to hear the Word of God and an expectation of the moving of the Spirit through the Word.

I recall Rev James Murray MacKay saying to us, 'It is now 10 p.m. and you can go to any house and I am sure you will get your supper.' The people were 'given to hospitality'. Afterwards, he said, 'You can come back to either No. 10 or to No. 20 at 11 p.m. for the next meeting.'

It was spring time and we worked on the crofts but with one eye on the clock – waiting for the time of the meeting. The meeting would finish at 2 a.m. but even then the people would be reluctant to leave. Afterwards the Shader girls would stand outside at the road junction and the singing would begin – singing from the heart – spontaneous singing; with James MacKay in the midst of the congregation joining with them in newly composed hymns written during the revival. The singing would go on until 3.00 or 3.30 a.m. and no-one complained of being tired. They were reluctant to go to their homes. We never heard such singing!

One of our neighbours, Chirsty Maggie MacLeod, remembers a wonderful incident. She says, 'I recall one day, Duncan Campbell called at the house at 11 a.m. Of course when the converts saw him coming they also came in. We had started a prayer meeting when the door suddenly opened and our neighbour stood there, crying. He fell on his knees and we all dropped down on our knees. I will never forget that prayer meeting. The neighbour had just returned from Canada. He was converted and fifty years later, he is still following the Lord. That was only one incident of many.'

Duncan Campbell called this movement a spiritual awakening because the meaning of the term 'revival' can be confusing in some places. A revival in some parts of the USA is a short series of evangelistic meetings. This movement in Lewis was much more than that, and we give God the praise and the glory for all that happened.

17

MRS. FAY HAY
Carloway, Uig, later Missionary to Thailand

I had a dear friend who was a conductress on the buses and months before the revival, each time we met, her conversation was about spiritual things.

'I am worried about my soul, aren't you?' she would say. 'Well,' I would reply, 'Yes, sort of!'

She had a beautiful voice and used to sing at the concerts and she would say, 'I'm not going to sing any more.' Then I would say, 'You don't really need to be so drastic!'

'Yes,' she replied, 'this is something that requires drastic action. I want God to know that I am really serious and I am going to seek Him until I find Him.' Then she added, 'How about you?'

'Well,' I replied, 'I am beginning to agree with you. It is really serious. We ought to be thinking about our souls.' I realized that this was beginning to grip me too – this anxiety!

A curious thing began to happen to the dances; while I still enjoyed every minute I spent at them I found that the pleasure turned to very ashes in my mouth after I got back to the silence of my own room. What was I getting out of the giddy round? Absolutely nothing of any value! So the Spirit of God moves in answer to prevailing prayer.

When I went to church after that, I used to listen very carefully and often used to end up with quiet tears because the message was hitting home really hard. By then I was truly exercised – reading my Bible under the bedclothes each evening and gleaning but the one indubitable fact: I was a sinner and far away from God. I knew it sorely. Each church service now drove this fact home mercilessly. When the preacher would extol the loveliness of Christ, I would weep for sorrow that between us there was a 'great gulf fixed'. I had but one heart cry: 'What must I do to be saved?'

I will never forget one night. I sneaked into Martin's Memorial Church of Scotland. We weren't really allowed to go there, for we were Free Church!

It was a special meeting and they sang:

> Man of Sorrows, what a Name
> for the Son of God who came
> ruined sinners to reclaim;
> Hallelujah, what a Saviour.
>
> Bearing shame and scoffing rude
> in my place condemned he stood,
> Sealed my pardon with His blood;
> Hallelujah, what a Saviour.

I had never heard it before and it struck me with such force, which I now understand was the Spirit of God. I stood there and thought, 'It wasn't true; it wasn't for me.' It was for other people; and I wept!

I went back to the hostel and found a quiet place in a toilet – the only quiet place in the building. I wept because I had no share in what Christ had done. After that, strangely, I cut off the 'for Jesus sake' from my prayers, ending on a non-note. I had no share in what Christ had done. I could not 'cash in' on the blessings of redemption. It was not for me!

It was coming up to Christmas 1949, and there was to be a school concert in the Town Hall and a play was part of that. I was taking the leading role. That, to me, was wonderful. I loved acting and public performances of all kinds.

Someone told me that there was a revival in Barvas and that my friend, Chirsty Ann Martin, had been converted. I knew that that was what she wanted, and by that time it was what I too wanted. The discussion among the girls was about spiritual things – months before the revival. We would say, 'Yes, that is what we need and what we want.' We used to say in the study, 'What do Christians have that we haven't got?' None of us knew, but we all agreed that they had something that we didn't have and it was vital. We wished we had it. So God was definitely preparing us.

Anyway, someone said to me, 'Did you hear that your friend was converted?' I will never forget the feeling – this is a crisis time – a real pivotal time in her life and in mine. It needs to happen to me too!

Two or three days before the concert I went down town to look for her. I did not know what bus run she was on and I could not find her. The weather was bad and it was dark. I was churned up because of this concert that was to take place on Friday – rehearsing for it every spare moment and suddenly not wanting to perform in it. I was desperate to get hold of my friend to ask her what had happened to her. It was the very day of the concert, when I met her. She rushed up to me and flung her arms round me.

I said, 'You've got it.'

'No,' she said, 'we have been so stupid; it's not *it* – it's *Him*! It's the Lord Jesus!' I wept and wept on her shoulders and she said, 'Come with me now.'

'Oh!' I said, 'I can't. I've got this concert.'

'Concert?' she scornfully cried out.

'Yes, I can't let them down!'

'Tomorrow morning then,' she said.

I went to the concert on that Friday night and waded through my part. People whom I respected and my friends as well praised my performance but to me it was like my death knell. I hated to hear their praise – something that in the past was more precious to me than the whole world. Suddenly it was to me absolutely horrible. After the concert I rushed to my room, went to bed and buried myself under the clothes in my misery. The devil had a field day: 'You've had it! You've blown it! Your chance is gone! You chose to go to the concert.' And no matter how I argued that I couldn't let them down for I had no understudy to take my place, I was condemned.

'That's it,' said the devil, 'you've made your decision,' and I remember nearly going crazy. I finally prayed, 'Lord, please help me to sleep.' I fell asleep and on waking, I said, 'The first thing I'm going to do is to go to Shader with Chirsty Ann.'

Now looking back on the revival I am amazed. It was unlike any other thing I have ever known. Chirsty Ann's dear parents flung their arms around me and scooped me up saying, 'Oh! My love – you will not leave here until you find Christ!' I wept and thought this to be very unlikely after having chosen to be at the concert the night before.

They said, 'You sit there and we will send for John Murdo Smith,' who was next door.

'Pray for her,' they said – and he did, with great feeling and love.

The father prayed and we sang. All they did was pray for me and they sang, and all I did was to sit there and weep! Nothing mattered, not even food – only the one thing was needful. My friend returned from work and said to me: 'You will not leave here until you find Christ.'

Later on Catriona, John Murdo's sister, came in and asked if she could go with me to the meeting that evening. She was unconverted. 'No,' I said, 'I am going with Chirsty Ann's father.' I did not want anything to divert me from this one purpose. However, we all went together. The church was crowded. People sat in the windows and along benches in the passage way, even up the very steps to the pulpit!

O my! The Spirit of God was in the place. The difference is that everything is highlighted. The verses of the psalms were glowing with truth. Psalm 118:19 spoke to my heart:

> O set ye open unto me
> the gates of righteousness;
> Then I will enter into them,
> and I the Lord will bless.

How I longed to find a gateway to God! All the psalms were so alive – saying what my soul was saying! Oh! That I knew where I might find Him!

Then I remember Duncan Campbell. I remember his prayer. What he said was the cry of my heart. Then he began to preach from the Song of Solomon: 'My beloved had withdrawn himself and was gone'; then the voice of my Beloved: 'Rise up my love, my fair one and come away.' He talked about Him being 'behind the lattice; behind our wall' – the barrier between us. Did I not know that barrier between us! It was all blinding light on my condition and on my life. He then came to what the barrier was – sin! That was very clear to me as well. Yes, it was sin. Then the hopelessness of trying to reform – and what a hopeless undertaking that was. Mr. Campbell added how dishonouring to God it was for us to even try to reform when God's provision was so completely different. Everything he said was absolutely true. He came back to the point that we really were hell-deserving sinners. I agreed wholeheartedly that we were. We had never actually found this loving God. We did nothing but ignore Him and pass Him by. That we could ignore such a loving God, to me was so awful, so terrible. Mr. Campbell talked about hell being where God was not and for a moment I experienced it – total blackness – a place where there was no God or love or hope. It was horrendous for a minute.

Then Mr. Campbell said, 'Who His own self bare our sins in His own body on the tree…by whose stripes ye were healed' (I Pet. 2:24). He broke down the wall between us! Suddenly it dawned on me. I understood the gospel in a flash. 'Of course, just as Chirsty Ann had said, 'It's not *it* but *Him*! He is standing behind our wall and He is saying, "Rise up, my love, my fair one."'

'Fair one?' I said, 'I am the blackest of the black.'

'Look what I did for you!' – and it was so clear, so heavenly! Nothing but the grace of God! I fell at His feet in total adoration and blinding light. The thing that was so astonishing was that we knew this all along and we could have told the heathen in Africa all about it, but we couldn't apply it to our own hearts.

And oh! It was beautiful at the end of the meeting – the singing! Heaven came down and glory filled our souls. When I got out, Catriona met me at the door – and her face was glowing like the sun.

I said, 'Oh! I found Him!'

She answered, 'So did I.'

We fell on each other's necks. Quite a lot of people were saved on that night – maybe six or seven. Duncan Campbell asked us if we wanted to go back into the after-meeting. He read to us some beautiful verses such as 'my sheep hear my voice' – he used these verses quite a lot in encouraging seekers. Of course, I thought, that the Lord will keep us.

It was just before Christmas and I recalled that on every night of the following week I had either a social or a dance to attend. Oh help! What will I do? Mr. Campbell continued: 'You are sitting here and saying, "What on earth am I going to do this coming week?" ' It was no surprise to me to hear him saying that. 'I'll tell you,' he said, 'light will be given to you on each problem as you come to them. Trust Him. Don't worry about it. He will work it out for you.'

I said in my heart, 'Thank You, Lord!' and He did work it all out for me.

The news spread around and by Monday morning the school knew about my conversion. I went to the boy with whom I was going out to the dance. 'Have you heard?' I asked.

'Yes, I have heard,' he replied.

I said, 'Do you still want me to go out to the dance with you?'

'No,' he said.

That was the first problem solved. I was not any longer the kind of person with whom they wanted to socialize! Duncan Campbell was right!

Some were sceptical. I told the lady who was in charge of the hostel and she said, 'Time will tell' – which, of course, was right. She professed to be a Christian – but no help there!

Oh! The singing in Chirsty Ann's house that night! The rejoicing! It was just beautiful! Next Sunday when we went to church (we had been up late – Chirsty Ann and I – talking about these events) our ignorance was only too obvious. We did not have many answers. Duncan Campbell touched on so many of these problems and Chirsty Ann and I talked much together on these things. I owe so much to the praying people who carried me through these difficult times.

One night as the hymn was being sung – one I had never heard before, 'The judges of earth will be dumb when the One they killed stands before them, alive' – the Spirit of the Lord fell on us and I could just see the scene described in the hymn. I seemed to get a glimpse into eternity. There was a hush – a complete silence as the reality of the song sank in. But now there is a drought, a dreadful punishment from God.

Studying at Glasgow University, I met my husband, and later we spent years in central Thailand as missionaries, he, as a doctor.

Fay Hay – A Tribute (Stornoway Gazette)

The 6th of May dawned calm, still and peaceful; the waters of Loch Roag glistened like a mirror and even the touch of the breeze on our cheeks was gentle. Yet we were sad. With a certain sense of disbelief we made our way to Ceannlangabhat church to join with the hundreds who had come from near and far to pay their last respects to Fay Hay.

Her life had been characterised by boundless energy, and even in her illness, as her physical strength gave way to frailty, her mental strength remained unchanged, and her spiritual light shone even brighter. That inner glow which we loved radiated to all around her. Yes, it was hard to believe she had gone.

Her passing leaves a void in our community, to which she had contributed so much, in so many ways, but especially in the school. All her former pupils will remember her with fond memories and will not easily forget her inspiring teaching, her high standards, her insistence on diligence, school trips, school plays, sport, stories for the Mod. The list is endless. All of this, well mixed with a great deal of fun. Above all she would wish them to remember the Christian teaching which was so sincerely given and consistently lived out before them. Her interest, prayers and goodwill followed them into adult life.

Fay never did anything by halves. She gave total commitment to everything she undertook to do. Wholeheartedly and confidently she tackled work, leisure interest, domestic duties and every other call that was made on her – and they were many. A devoted wife and mother, her home was truly her castle where she dispensed hospitality to all and sundry. She loved cooking which she did with characteristic excellence and enjoyment. Nothing was ever too much trouble. A typical response to a request for any kind of help or favour was; 'No problem.'

Her strong faith, and love of God and His Word were central in her life since her conversion at the age of sixteen, while still a pupil at the Nicolson. From there she went to Glasgow University where, in the Christian Union, she met her future husband, John Hay. After their marriage, they went to Thailand as missionaries, and worked in Manoram for thirteen years. We thank God for their service there with OMF and their faithful witness here in Uig, where Fay's presence is so sorely missed in the church.

To John and the family: Marion, Peigi, Janet, Kirsty, Joy.

To the sons in law: Crispian, Neil, Murray, Angus, Peter and the twelve grandchildren who were such a source of joy to her, we extend our heartfelt sympathy. We also remember her sister Bella and brother Norman, who are mourning the loss of their loving elder sister.

Fay's life touched and influenced many others. Friends, neighbours and colleagues, while mourning her loss, are truly grateful for the privilege of her friendship and counsel.

Yes, we were sad on 6th May, but as we looked away from ourselves and sang the timeless words of Psalm 45:13-16, our spirits rose in praise, and we could only be still and give thanks for a life lived to the full, and worship the Saviour who moulded that life.

— Mrs M. Macleod

18

MRS. ANNIE MACKINNON
Formerly of Lochs, Lewis.
Now in the Mull of Kintyre, Scotland.

It took us about four hours to drive from Edinburgh to Tayinloan on the Kintyre peninsula to record Mrs. MacKinnon's story. Her life and witness is as a beacon of light in the whole area and we were anxious to meet and hear her.

There was an immediate oneness of heart and spirit, and in the conversation I said, 'It's wonderful to sense such unity in the things of God.'

'Ah,' she replied, 'Affinity of spirit; oh so precious and oh so rare.'

When leaving, we said our 'goodbyes' and stood just outside the back door. She had walked slowly with her sticks and stood in the doorway. Unwilling to part we were saying our last parting words when she raised one stick, pointed at the clouds and said, 'Behold, He cometh with clouds and every eye shall see Him.' It was a moment of God. Our hearts broke and we stood there weeping in His presence. We had read that verse scores of times, but suddenly God spoke it to us. What a moment it was!

We drove down the lane and stopped before we reached the main road. There we sat in the car and prayed and wept. On we went and for miles neither of us spoke as we did not want to break the wonderful sense of the Spirit with us in the car, despite the fact that we were driving through some beautiful country and would normally have remarked on it. It was a memorable day of spiritual enrichment.

At the time of the revival, in the cottage meetings, the people made themselves seats of a pile of peats (fuel) in order to have some measure of comfort through the long meetings. By today's standards they were very poor. The 1939 revival is very vivid with me; I was sixteen years old at the time. I left the island at eighteen. The 1949 revival was taking place when I went home on holiday. The Spirit was present then as in the 1939 revival.

1939

As I said, I was sixteen in 1939 and I was working in the shooting lodge. It was deer shooting and salmon fishing. I will never forget how the 'gillies' would come home in the morning — radiant. 'We were not in bed last night. We had an all-night prayer meeting and we are not even tired,' they said.

I wasn't saved at the time — not until I was twenty-nine, but I will never forget that atmosphere. It was the presence of the Lord! The conversation centred on the revival and my memory is that I felt as if the Spirit of the Lord was in the very air one was breathing — and it was just wonderful! The atmosphere was not just in the church but everywhere.

The revival actually started in a home in Crossbost. The minister felt it first. He was aware of the stirrings of the Spirit and he called the elders to hold prayer meetings. At that time there was such opposition that the elders said, 'No, there will be no prayer meetings! It is a busy time of the year, and people need their sleep!'

However, two of the elders were determined to hold prayer meetings. They set off to go to another village but the Lord turned them back. Mary Jane, who told me this story, said that they met her father and asked him if they could hold a prayer meeting in his home.

'There were only eight of us,' said Mary Jane — but the singing was 'out of this world!' That night, four out of the eight were saved — including Mary Jane herself. It was a sensational revival — just before the war and many of our lads left for the services and some did not return. Rev. Murdo MacAulay wrote a book entitled *The Burning Bush* highlighting the revival.

I recall how that in the church in Kinloch the conviction of sin was so intense that some of the people collapsed in their pews. They had to be carried out of the church at the close of the service. There was an element among the people who doubted the genuineness of the work but the fruit of the revival remained.

In the village of Carloway, as recently as thirty years ago, friends from Campbelltown returned to the island to find that every member of the football team, who were all saved in the revival, in their youth, were present in the church as members and the captain of the team was the preacher at the service. He was none other than Rev Murdo MacAulay! He was the minister of the Free Church. That was some of the abiding fruit of the Spirit's visitation.

Some people had such visions of hell and a lost eternity that they were even collapsing on the dance floors! These were never seen on the dance floor again! Lochs and Carloway were deeply touched but other villages were bypassed.

There was a godly woman in Lemreway. She was not able to attend church but on the night of the prayer meeting she was at the well to fetch a pail of water. The prayer meeting was about to start and she was looking at the meeting house and saw a cloud resting above the building. That was the night when the revival broke out in the prayer meeting in Lemreway.

There were prayer meetings every night in the home of one of my relatives during that revival. She said that a godly man had a significant dream before the revival commenced. He saw an angel passing over the villages, and the villages where the angel tarried were the villages where revival came and the ones the angel bypassed were not visited.

Sometimes the ministers could not preach. There was such a sense of the Lord's presence! I recall (years later) being home on holiday before my mother died and sorrowing over the fact that there were no new faces in the prayer meeting. I said to my mother, 'Remember the revival?'

'Oh,' she said, 'the revival. One night there was a gale blowing and you just couldn't stay at home despite the gale and my objections.' One could not resist the drawing power of the Spirit to the centre of worship. And yet I did not get saved! You can be in a move of the Spirit and miss out!

The two elders, who originally arranged the prayer meeting in Crossbost, never lost their desire for a repeat of the revival but prayed continually to their dying day. They kept the fellowship meetings going. Those who are saved in revival never seem to lose the glow.

1949

During the 1949 revival I was home on holiday in Lewis. The same wonderful Spirit was present. It was the same beautiful atmosphere. The revival centred in Barvas but it was also in Lochs. The crowds were there and queues of cars at the meeting places in Kinloch. As in the 1939 revival, the only subject of conversation was the revival. The singing is not like singing down here at all! (The custom in Gaelic Psalm singing was that the precentor, as he is called, sang the first two lines. The congregation joined in as soon as they recognised the tune. Thereafter the precentor 'chanted' the next line and the congregation repeated that line in the original tune – and so on until the end of the stated verses. But in the revival the congregation took over and joined the precentor as he led the singing. It was a spontaneous reaction to the liberty of the Spirit – so evident in the atmosphere of revival.)

In revival the Spirit comes down upon the people. It isn't something which man can produce. A minister who visited there stated that at that time the very fields were hallowed. The sea was hallowed. Wherever people worked, they prayed. The place of solitude was precious to them. Out on the moor, caring for the cattle, they prayed. Prayer was not a burden to them but a delight. They loved to pray; they were constrained to pray.

In 1939, the people were poor. They had to pray for every meal. I recall being on holiday at home in Lewis. I met a godly widow who later lost three beautiful sons in the war. She was left with two daughters. She was known in the community as the elect lady. Her daughter met me and said to me, 'You must come and visit my mother.' So I went with my brother. Her five children were in school and she told us that on a certain day she had potatoes for their meal but she had nothing in the house to cook with the potatoes. About midday she had a conviction that if she went down to the shore she would find a skate (a fish) on a certain rock. In obedience to this conviction she sent the boys to the rock – and there they found the skate! The meal was provided for the children!

Later on in life the Lord saved my husband and me, and He gave me a word. 'Feed the flock of God that is among you.' I knew then that I must start a prayer meeting in my home and it continues to this day. To begin with it was held monthly but now it is every Tuesday.

At one stage there was an attack on this prayer meeting and it was stopped – supposedly never to be held again. However, I received a letter from the godly factor's widow (in whose house we now reside). This letter was written on the anniversary of his death. I read it in the kitchen and suddenly the Lord spoke to me as clearly as on the day I was saved. She wrote, 'I am praying day and night for a weekly prayer meeting for the believers in Tayinloan' (the village where I now live). I lifted up my hands and began to pray and praise the Lord in my kitchen. The power of the Lord was present in such a manner that I could hardly prepare my son's dinner for his homecoming. Three months later two Faith Mission workers came and conducted a mission and were instrumental in starting our weekly prayer meeting again and it has continued ever since. That was in 1960.

I praise the Lord for the privileges in experiencing revival even though, at the time, I was not converted. God had mercy on me and brought me into His fold and has made me a witness in this area for His glory.

19

NORMAN MACLEAN ('Paddy')
Church of Scotland Missionary

Affectionately known as Paddy, Norman MacLean had a unique story to tell. He was brought up in a godly home and had the privilege of being the son of a praying mother. However, Norman had no appetite for religion and at an early age he gave in to 'peer pressure', finding satisfaction in what the world had to offer him under the name of pleasure.

During the war he had a close brush with death when his ship was torpedoed. Twenty-seven of his mates died but he was able to run to safety away from danger. His salvation he attributed to his own smartness. Later he realized that he was saved by Divine intervention in answer to the prayers that were constantly offered on his behalf by his parents. Here is his story:

I came back from the war unscathed and wasted no time in making known to my parents that I despised their authority and that I had no intention of remaining with them. Wisely or unwisely, my father gave me a car – no doubt in the hope that this would anchor me at home. There were very few cars around at that time.

I indulged myself in strong drink to such an extent that there were times when I had to look outside in the morning to see whether or not I had brought the car home! My companions were the boys who survived the war with me and we would celebrate together, drinking and dancing.

Thank God for parents who loved me despite my waywardness! I would come home at 3.00, 4.00 or 5.00 in the morning. My mother would tell me in the morning what time it was when I came home. I used to take my shoes off so that she would not hear me – but she did! Why? Because she was watching and praying! It was amazing to me that I came through those years without an accident.

I had no respect whatsoever for the Word of God. I recall one evening being at home by myself and I was going to light a cigarette but I didn't have a match. I went to the drawer and discovered there an old Bible. I took out a page, rolled it up and went to light it in the fire – but I couldn't. I didn't believe in God or His Word but I unrolled the page and put it back in the Bible. Later I was astounded at my behaviour; imagine it!

I wasn't in the habit of going to church. I used to travel around in a van, selling goods in order to make a living. One day, as I drove, I came across two young girls and I stopped to give them a lift. This was not unusual in a close knit community. Such kindness was part of island life.

'Where are you going?' I asked.

'We are going to a meeting,' they replied. The argument started! They wanted me to come to the meeting with them – but I was armed with excuses. However, when we came to the church, they said, 'You must go into the church,' but I said emphatically, 'No! I'm not going!' They persisted until I promised to attend on the following night. At the back of my mind I thought, 'I will go, but I will go to mock or at least just to see what is going on.'

I kept my promise. The following night I went into the church and sat in the pew. Then I heard the minister begin to preach, as we never hear preaching today! His subject was *sin*, and the wages of sin. My attention was drawn to one of the elders, and he was smiling. I thought to myself, 'These girls told him that I was coming tonight.' I also thought that he had told the minister because his preaching was directed at me, as if I were the only person there! It was all about my sin – sin – sin!

This experience was common with many people in the revival as the Word of God, the 'sword of the Spirit', found its mark and God's arrows pierced the hearts of the King's enemies.

After the service I promised myself that I would stop boozing and begin going to church. 'Then,' I thought, 'I will be as good as they are! That,' I thought, 'is all that is necessary!' I arrived home, went to bed, but couldn't sleep. I couldn't get rid of my sin!

I continued from that time on to attend the meetings but I had to go to the town of Stornoway every day on business and there I met one of my boozing companions who invited me to join him for a pint of beer. 'No,' I replied, 'I'm not going in there any more!'

'What's wrong?' he asked.

I replied, 'I'm not going in, I'm in a hurry.'

'Ach,' he said, 'we'll go in and have one.'

Alas, one is not enough, and one is too many. We were there in the pub until we were kicked out! We took a bottle of whisky with us and on our way home we drank it. We both had cars and when my friend came out of the car he fell in the ditch. I tried to pull him out but in my drunken stupor I too fell in. A passerby saw our plight and came to the rescue – but he also reported us to the police.

I decided that my friend was not fit to drive, so I took him in my car. The police were on our track but they failed to catch us! I was already on their books, charged with drunken driving.

I deposited my friend home and, taking the floor, I preached to him all that I could recall from the sermon of the previous night! Why did I do that? It was because it stuck to me. I could not get away from it. The lady of the house said later to me: 'You know, you nearly converted me that night!'

I wanted to go to the meeting that evening but my wife wouldn't let me go. The following night, however, I went, and the theme was the same as before. My sin, my sin, my sin!

The following day I went down to the village, and who did I meet but another of my boozing pals. 'I hear you've been converted,' he said. When I heard that I cursed and swore so that he would understand that he hadn't lost me – for I was the leader of the gang. I didn't know that Peter the disciple had done this!

As I travelled home that evening after work, a fear gripped me that Christ would meet me on the road and condemn me to hell.

Suddenly, in the middle of the moor, in the dusk, a light shone on the windscreen of the car. I didn't know what it was, but it forced me to stop. The sound of the engine was in my ears as sounds from hell itself and the noise was so fearful that I would not wish a dog to spend a day there, never mind eternity!

I managed to move on and who should I meet but the minister. I stopped and asked him where the meetings were to be that night. There would normally be at least two meetings each evening, one in the church and one in a home.

The minister answered that he was not sure whether it would be in Barvas or in Arnol, but he said that if I inquired at the Police Station, they would tell me. (The policeman at that time was a believer and his own home was open for house meetings.)

I said to myself – a policeman and a minister! The very ones I tried to avoid! There must be something wrong with me!

I went to fill up with petrol and then popped into the shop next door for something to eat. The liquor bottles on the shelves seemed to cry out to me, 'Take me, take me! And you will be all right.' However, I managed to overcome the desire. I was gripped with fear and a sense of condemnation.

The meeting was in Arnol. It was a house meeting and I slipped in the back door, assured that I would be unnoticed, but again the preaching was directed at me. I knew, however, that the minister was not aware of my presence.

Afterwards, as was the custom, tea was served and I stayed for that. Then the singing began. A young girl sang in Gaelic, 'A Thighearna cuidich me, s'aithne dhuit m'fheum' ('Oh Lord, help me, You know my need'). The words gripped me and I have been singing them now for over forty years!

I left the meeting with a friend whom I thought had become a Christian. I felt on my part that I was doomed – lost for all eternity. When I arrived home I said to myself, 'I am not going into my house, nor will I lie on my bed until I find a resting place for the God of Jacob.' I did not realize that I was quoting from Psalm 132. This was a psalm that was often used to bring the services to a close. To hear an awakened congregation singing this psalm in an atmosphere pregnant with the presence of God was an experience which one could never forget. But I was now in the shed in the middle of the night.

I fell flat on my face on the concrete floor of the shed and I cried, 'Lord, this is as far as I can go. Do what you please.' What do you think a God of love, a Christ of love would do? He put His hand on me and peace flooded my soul. I stood up, a new man, and I went into the house and I cried, 'Get up, get up – at 2.00 a.m.! We're going to praise God!' I didn't need to tell mother what had happened – she already knew! She knew her prayers were answered!

My life was transformed. God had in His mercy saved me and already the reality of my conversion was evident in the desire to see others coming to the Saviour. On being asked later to drive a coach of young people on a May Day excursion, I said that I would, but only on condition that I could take my Bible and preach to the passengers.

I was burdened especially for one young man who seemed to be resisting the Spirit of the Lord. I had a conviction that this young man's death was imminent, although I did not know when. I pulled the coach to the side for them to enjoy a picnic tea on their way to the Butt of Lewis lighthouse, and turning round to face the passengers I began to preach, directing a special warning to this young man.

I felt extremely uncomfortable and fearful. I desperately wanted the trip to be over but as they were about to leave, after they had seen inside the lighthouse, another coach arrived, blocking our exit. The young people were persuaded to join the occupants of the other coach for a game of football and fifteen minutes later a young lad rushed to tell me that Bobby, the lad for whom I was so burdened and to whom I had preached, had gone over the cliff as he chased the ball. He died later in hospital.

A day of joy and revelry was turned into a day of sorrow and mourning and I was given the sad task of passing on the news of Bobby's tragic death to his parents. Some of those who were on board the coach later came to Christ as I preached at a house meeting nearby.

My goal was set from that hour and my mother's prediction was realized as I dedicated my life to the service of my Saviour and Lord. I have been telling the wonderful story for a long time now and as long as God spares me I will continue. Praise His Name!

Norman was one of these 'characters' who grace the church from time to time. He was no theologian, nor was he an academic. His preaching was from a heart aflame for God and his presentation of truth was without polish or apology. His illustrations were down to earth although obscure at times. There was no doubting his zeal and deep love for his Saviour and he died as he lived, trusting in the finished work of Christ.

20

REV. ALISTAIR MACDONALD
Ness

In trying to recall the revival in Ness, my mind goes back to the winter of 1949. At that time I was conscious of an aching void in my life which I could not explain.

In December 1949, the Rev Murdo MacSween, who was a minister in Broadford on the Isle of Skye, was invited to preach at a series of special evangelistic services in the Church of Scotland in Ness. There was evidence of a movement of the Spirit of the Lord in the district. Each evening from Monday to Friday the church was packed with young and old alike. Seats had to be brought in from the church hall and placed in the aisles. Young people sat on the steps leading up to the gallery. At the close of the service a prayer meeting was held but few left the church on the first evening. It was then decided, in view of this, that on the remaining nights the prayer meeting would follow the benediction without a break.

On the Friday evening Rev MacSween said to the local minister, Rev Calum Smith, that if he became aware of a breakthrough, he must feel free to send for him. Later on, during the Christmas holidays, Mr. MacSween's brother John, who was then a headmaster in Broadford, was asked to come to Ness to conduct further services. Again, the people crowded to the church as before and later in February Rev. MacSween returned and several people professed faith in Christ.

In the spring, the meetings in Barvas with Rev Duncan Campbell continued and several young men and women from Ness came to know the Lord. There were several of my friends who were seeking, but they were not willing to make this public. We hired a van one evening and set off for Barvas, fifteeen miles away. Everyone in the van that night was unconverted at the time. What was it that persuaded young people to travel thus to a place of worship? There is only one answer to this question and that is, that the Spirit of the Lord was at work.

Afterwards, Rev Duncan Campbell came to Ness and again the people were drawn to the sanctuary. Every evening the service at the church was followed by a house meeting. On one occasion this latter service was conducted in a meal store. Souls were being saved day after day and the general conversation among the people, saved and unsaved, centred on the Scriptures and on what God was doing in the community.

Some who had not attended church for years were now drawn to hear the Word of God. There was a Christian lady in Swainbost who had been bedridden for several years. For some time she seemed to be in a coma but on the outbreak of the revival she suddenly recovered. She could tell us who the next convert would be and on hearing the door opening, although she was blind, she would greet each visitor with a very apt and suitable verse from the Word of God. Her recovery was remarkable – nothing short of a miracle.

A friend of mine had been a prisoner of war for many years in Japan. He had worked on the infamous Burma railway where so many British soldiers had died of starvation and ill-treatment. He came home an atheist. He maintained that if there was a God He would not have allowed these dreadful sufferings to continue. His mother, a woman of prayer, pleaded with him to go with others to hear Duncan Campbell. Finally he agreed and went on a few occasions to hear Mr. Campbell. One evening he and a friend were standing, talking together on the road, when they were approached by Mary MacDonald from Swainbost. She told them both to go to the service as the Lord was going to deal with one of them that night. They obediently went and from that time Calum's life was transformed.

Wonderful conversions took place. Some families who previously had no interest in spiritual matters were now to be found eagerly attending church. One such family was a local schoolmaster's. Previously they were taken up with worldly pleasures but all that changed on the occasion when Rev and Mrs MacLennan entered the dance hall in Carloway. (The account of this is recorded in the next chapter.)

Duncan Campbell's preaching was indeed challenging. He did not shun setting before us the whole counsel of God. He made it clear that there was a Heaven to gain and a Hell to shun. We were often reminded that our privileges would one day be held against us when standing condemned before the throne of God's judgement. There was, he would say, only one way of salvation and that was through faith in Jesus Christ.

People travelled from all over the island in any mode of transport they could find. The inclement weather or discomfort in travel was a trivial matter and of no consequence. From Ness we would travel across the island to Carloway, Bernera, Lochs and other places where services were held. Usually we did not return home until the early hours of the morning, but still we went to work at 8 a.m. without feeling tired. One seemed to have received supernatural strength!

For the young converts, older Christians were there to encourage them in their spiritual life – and how we loved these old saints! One can mention Angus MacDonald, an ex-sergeant of the Seaforth Highlanders. He was a good soldier of Jesus Christ. Very frequently he would be the only one to attend the weekly prayer meeting in the small church near to his home, but Angus would go through the normal pattern of worship as if the hall was full. He was overjoyed when at last God answered his prayers and the little church was filled with converts of the revival. Angus was blessed with a musical voice and he frequently led the singing of the Gaelic psalms. People wanted to sing, indeed they could not help but sing.

Only eternity will reveal the full story of the revival and its extent. Like the ripples of the ocean as it ebbs and flows without restraint, so the fruits of the Lewis revivals touch the far ends of the earth through the lives of those who, hearing the call of God, have gone forth, bearing the message of the gospel to distant lands.

21

REV. JACK MACARTHUR
Galson, Lewis; Glasgow

When I was a teenager in Barvas, in Lewis, years after the revival, I was visiting an old elder – Roddy Alex – a man who had known revival, not just once but several times. He had suffered the consequences of this knowledge in some ways because the impact that it made upon him meant that he was not an easy person for a minister or a kirk session to handle.

I loved to spend Sunday evenings with him. I remember one Sunday evening walking down from the thatched house where he lived. As we passed the Barvas Church something happened that I will never forget. Roddy was sharing with me experiences of a revival in Lewis in the 1930s in the parish of Lochs and he was describing what happened in the meetings. It was very much a revival among lay people. During it, on calm summer evenings folk came out of their houses, miles away across the loch, to hear the people singing at the close of the meetings. As he spoke and shared, I learned a lesson that I will never forget.

The person who was speaking was not somebody who had been there thirty years before, but someone who was present in the recounting of what he had experienced. That road became alive with the presence of God, and what was spoken of was not something historical but something gloriously real. There was a stillness and a quietness. Indeed I think that Roddy walked back to the schoolhouse with me, and we walked back again and again to enjoy the sense of the glory of God.

I have been asked many times to speak on the subject of revival. Maybe increasingly, I have been hesitant to accept the invitation. I am conscious that I am not speaking about what Duncan Campbell did or what I experienced, but when I speak about it I am speaking about revival as the sovereign, glorious work of the Holy Spirit. I am conscious that for some, revival has become something of an academic interest – wondering what it must have been like – and even in our prayers, praying as if the God of revival was somehow totally different from anyone we have ever known. That is just not true.

The God who worked in Lewis, the Holy Spirit present in those years is here now. There are not two Holy Spirits, there are not three Holy Spirits; there is one Holy Spirit. I have puzzled over the years theologically to try and work out what it is that happens when God comes in revival. Is it something that happens within God in His response to us or is it something that happens in us in our response to Him?

My memory of the revival is the memory of a boy who was not brought up in a church home. It is the memory of someone who did not have the experience that others had in terms of seeing what was happening. What happened in my life and in our home was something that happened in a home that had, to a large extent, pushed God out.

In Lewis at that time, most people would go to church, if not on Sunday morning, they would try to go on a Sunday evening – the real pagans would at least go on the communion Sunday evening. If you didn't go then, you would really be a marked person. The biggest infidel in the place would come out on the Sunday evening of the communion. We didn't! I think I had been once inside the church when I was eleven!

I had heard other boys speaking of strange goings on in the church, but I did not know what they were talking about. There was not much talk about it in our home. Yet one morning when I woke up, I knew something had happened totally out of the blue.

To begin with, I thought someone had taken ill. Indeed the atmosphere in the home was such that I thought someone had died. There was a quietness, a stillness. As I was getting up, my sister said, 'You'd better be quiet and don't make a noise. I think Alan Ian was converted last night.' She might as well have told me a scientific formula; I might have understood it better than the word 'converted'!

My mother and father had been running a concert; a voluntary thing, the previous night in Carloway, in another part of the island. They had gone to enjoy themselves. My elder brother was the Master of Ceremonies (M.C.) on that occasion. In the early hours of the morning, the local minister walked in. (You might be used to some ministers attending dances, but they don't go to dances in Lewis!)

There was consternation! My brother, who probably had had more than tea or coffee in the course of the evening, got very annoyed, and as the M.C. was likely to have to throw him out. He confronted the minister and asked him for his ticket.

Mr. MacLennan had the Bible in his hand and he showed it to him. He said that he was the parish minister and that that was his ticket. Mr. MacLennan was a very fiery minister – red haired – and on occasions he could be very fiery indeed. But that night he was very quiet, very gentle, very non-judgmental. He said that he had heard a girl singing a Gaelic song as he was passing and he wondered if she would lead in the singing of a psalm. My brother was almost hysterical. My mother, trying to be the peacemaker, said to him, 'Just let him carry on. Let him have his say. The sooner he has it, the sooner he will be out of the door and you can carry on with the proceedings. You lead the singing and we will all help you.'

Mr. MacLennan very briefly spoke about what had happened that night in Barvas. The piper, who was to have played that night at the dance, had stopped off at the meeting and had been converted. Then he said that he wondered if they would be as happy in the morning as William would be – how many sore heads there would be in comparison with the sheer joy which William was now experiencing. He spoke very gently, very quietly, pronounced the benediction and went home. He lived but a short distance from the hall.

My brother, who had been so angry, could not be found anywhere. Ultimately they found him in the back of the bus that brought them to the dance – broken before God. The Holy Spirit in revival does not just use one individual. He mightily used Duncan Campbell, but he comes into a community, and where He is, others are used as well. That night, Murdo MacLennan, who had been such a faithful supporter of Duncan Campbell and was such a hungry person for revival himself, was used gloriously in the hand of God. The revival was not contained within a meeting here or a meeting there. It was something that had broken into the community.

The following night my father searched for a Bible. He remembered that an old missionary had sold him one a few years before. He had it for emergencies or in case someone died, or to have for a minister when he visited. It was still in its tissue paper. I did not know what was happening as he gathered the family round. My father was still unconverted, but he knew that something had happened and that a place had to be given to God – but then, he didn't know what to do. He knew that he could not pray, so he said the Lord's Prayer. He prepared to go to church on Sunday. In a few months, both he and my mother were converted and the hall beside us which had been used for concerts and dances and all kinds of things became a place used by the Holy Spirit. Duncan Campbell himself came to stay with us and for several weeks held meetings in the hall.

The house that had known nothing of God became a place where everything else became secondary. My mother did not get much sleep for many nights. She had a family of eight and it was the days before washing machines and dryers and all the other gadgets. To get to school, to prepare for the meetings, to wash Duncan Campbell's clothes. If you had seen Duncan Campbell at the end of the meetings you would know that he put everything into it! He was wet through! You could wring his clothes from his vest to his jacket and sometimes every stitch he was wearing. After the service the clothes were washed and hung up for the next day!

Night after night people came. Nobody asked the question, 'I wonder if anyone will be converted tonight?' You sensed that those who were praying were looking around and thinking, 'Who is going to be saved tonight?' And as they noticed that God was using the proclaimed Word and folk were responding, they prayed that these individuals would come right through – and they did! In revival, God is working sovereignly in those who as yet had not bowed the knee.

I recall a butcher from Ness called Calum. He had a van which he used during the day for selling meat. He was not a church person, but he was fascinated by what was happening. Every evening he would go and scrub the van out and would fill it with people and bring them to the house meeting. He would be there to all hours in the morning. I do not know if that man ever bowed the knee to Jesus Christ. I trust he did, but there was a compulsion to do something about it. I do know that one night he got as far as the door of the prayer meeting. Duncan Campbell did not make an altar call; he did not call for decisions, but at the end of a meeting he would announce that there would be a time of prayer afterwards and add; 'If you are concerned about your soul tonight, come in to the prayer meeting.' They were not dealt with individually, but as other folk prayed, the Holy Spirit would deal with people who were broken under conviction of sin. One night Calum got as far as the door and, I remember them saying, he actually put his hand on the knob and turned back.

Another aspect of revival, and I believe you will find the same historically in revivals, for instance with those associated with Whitefield and Wesley, is that there can be a hardening amongst those who reject, in the midst of that situation, which is different to the rejection under normal preaching. There is a judgement in revival. There is an opportunity given. There is a reality. It is as if you see things clearly and you know that if you go this way there is something that will happen, and if you go that way there is something else that will happen. Sometimes there is a settling of issues: time for blessing, time for rejection.

There were those who said the revival was not genuine. For one thing there was suspicion about the denomination (the Church of Scotland) where the revival meetings were held. Then there were physical manifestations – things which some people could not understand. Then there was the accusation that Duncan Campbell was an Arminian. Booklets were written, including one by Kenneth Macrae, the godly minister of the Free Church in Stornoway, called *The Resurgence of Arminianism*. It was distributed widely. Yet Duncan Campbell was not Arminian. A strange feature of such divisions is that all too often those who profess to be Calvinistic act as if they were Arminian because they want God to work within their own particular framework – and if He moves out of that, He can't be God! And many who would be named Arminian know full well that they cannot do a single thing without the power of God moving through them.

Revival totally transformed the situation. Glorious things happened. Men recognized that although God had come and revival had come, it did not absolve them from further prayer. It placed them under a burden to pray more, for they knew that it was only God who could do anything for them. On some nights Duncan Campbell would be going from one main service to another somewhere else. People would ask, Where is Ruairidh Alex? Where is the blacksmith? They would normally be in every meeting. On one occasion, someone said, 'O they came off the bus at one of their houses.' The first meeting had been hard. A new situation – opposition to the gospel – a real hardness. So these two men went to their home, for they knew that they had a mission to fulfil. So when Duncan Campbell was preaching, they were at that house praying through, broken before God – supporting Duncan.

Another important lesson I learned was the reality that children can understand the gospel. We think today that children cannot understand. Yet I cannot remember ever not understanding what had been said when I heard the gospel at the age of eleven. There were no children's meetings. The doctrine of sin, the justice of God as judge, the holiness of God, my responsibility; this is what came to me. The fact that I was eleven and not seventy did not make one single iota of difference. The Holy Spirit was working. No one is going to tell me that the Holy Spirit cannot communicate to a child.

There is one other aspect of revival that I will touch on briefly. One feature associated with revival is a thrusting out of people to a variety of areas of Christian work. For example, some of the great missionary movements have been born following times of revival. But I have to confess that, as I see it, this did not happen with the Lewis revivals. There was a thrusting of some men into the ministry at home, and a few who went further afield. I have come to this conclusion, that revival is not the panacea for everything, and neither is everything put right by revival. So I don't like speaking of 1949 or 1953, as if that was the end of the story. The fruits of that revival, I believe, are hundreds and hundreds of people who have come to know Christ in parishes throughout Scotland. God did not go on holiday in 1953. His work continues and will continue until the end of time. Praise His Name!

22

REV. JOHN MURDO SMITH
Barvas, Lewis

I don't believe that there is any greater need in God's church today than the need for revival. This is not something new in the experience of God's people.

As far back as the days of Habakkuk in the Old Testament, the cry went up: 'Revive Thy work in the midst of the years' (Hab. 3:2). Even further back, in the days of King David the cry was, 'Wilt Thou not revive us again: that Thy people may rejoice in Thee?' (Ps. 85:6).

The word 'revival' was a very familiar word in our household in my childhood days, possibly because both my parents were Christians. They had seen revivals, had come through revivals and had tasted of the sweet fruits of revival. They longed to see another one before passing to their Eternal Home and, no doubt, certainly hoping that the five members of their own family would be among the first converts. The words that often came from my mother's lips were:

Oh! For the floods on a thirsty land
Oh! For a mighty revival
Oh! For a sanctified fearless band
Ready to hail its arrival!

And there was at that time, a sanctified fearless band, ready to hail its arrival. What a difference that makes!

My own first encounter with revival was before the Second World War, the 1939 Revival. I remember being in meetings when revival was taking place, a year or two before 1939. I was young at the time, yet, the amazing thing was, that although I was unconverted, I was conscious of the presence and power of God in the meetings – explain that as you will, but I was very conscious of God's power. The revival before the war was very different from the 1949 revival. There was not any special preacher as there was in the 1949 revival. Most of the meetings were held in the homes of the people, though there were many in the churches. I remember being in some house meetings where there were physical manifestations – perhaps prostrations, people raising their arms, crying to God. In some of the meetings, while someone was praying, one of the converts would stand up and pray loudly. These things happened in the first revival I experienced in 1939.

The 1949 one was different. The war years brought many changes, and the war seemed to have a blighting influence on the life of the nation. People, especially the young, began to drift away from the ordinances of the church. It seemed as if true spirituality had gone by the board. Certainly, in the island of Lewis, the gospel was still faithfully proclaimed. Family worship was conducted in most of the houses, but yet there was little response to the proclamation of the gospel. Nevertheless there were 'watchmen on the walls of Zion' who resorted to prayer and would not accept things as they were. Prayer meetings for revival were held in various Christian homes. Christians bombarded heaven with their prayers. The cry that went up from many hearts was 'O that Thou wouldest rend the Heavens and that Thou wouldest come down' (Isa. 64:1).

No revival is of a sudden origin. There must be a preparing of the way. That is what happened at Pentecost. The people were of one accord in one place, united and waiting for the coming of the Holy Spirit. 'Tarry ye in the city of Jerusalem until ye be endued with power from on high' (Luke 24:49). They were waiting, like what happened when Lazarus was raised from the dead. Christ said to those around Him, 'You move the stone. I'll bring the dead to life. You have some part in this.' Just as He said to those at the wedding in Cana of Galilee, 'Fill the water pots with water. Leave the miracle to me!' They had a hand in it. God's people, those who engaged in prayer and who believed that God would answer, continued to pray until the power of God came.

How did the revival begin? I have heard and read many distorted accounts about how the revival began. We know of those who heard of the two ladies who prayed. I spent many hours with them, but more people than those two ladies were constantly praying. I met them, I saw them and heard them and I know how diligently they prayed that revival would come. When Rev. James Murray MacKay was parish minister in Barvas, he was asked to send for Rev Duncan Campbell because there were those who felt that he was to be a channel through which revival would come. He was in the middle of a mission on the island of Skye and felt that he could not come in response to that call from the parish of Barvas, but eventually he felt compelled to come.

He arrived in Barvas on 7th December 1949, and began his meetings that night. For the next few nights, nothing happened – there was no break. On Sunday, 11th December, the morning service was held in the Barvas church – still no break. In fact Mr. Campbell was contemplating leaving the island and going back to Skye.

I'll leave that for a moment and tell something of my own experience. In the mid-forties I was called up to the RAF and after my initial training in England I was sent with many of my colleagues to the Middle East. I was demobbed in 1948 and returned home. I felt very unsettled at first. When you had been with colleagues like that for years, you had your routine. You knew what you were going to do. I felt very unsettled. I took a job for a year after I came home, intending to join the merchant navy in order to see more of the world. But my thoughts were not God's thoughts neither were my ways His ways (Isa. 55:8).

Now to go back to the 11th December. Duncan Campbell was preaching that evening in the village church in Shader. I went to that service because my parents were constantly telling the members of the family about the great preacher who had come to the parish and the wonderful meetings they were having. That evening I went, more to please them, but also out of curiosity to hear this wonderful preacher that they were speaking about.

Mr. Campbell preached a very forceful sermon. I felt as if he knew my life story. I was greatly challenged but I did not commit my life to Christ at that meeting. I went home after church. It was intimated that there would be a house meeting in the village. I had no intention of going.

A school pupil who was in High School in Stornoway at the time came to our house and she asked me if I would accompany her to the meeting in the Post Office House, as we called it. I 'hummed' and 'hawed' and tried to make every excuse until she said, 'Well, I have no one to go with me, why not come.' Eventually, I went. When we arrived at the house, it was filling up with people.

During the course of the evening, I felt very convicted. It was near Christmas and the New Year. Our Christmas and New Year parties were already arranged. I was to supply the accordion music. The Lord said, 'Tonight.' The devil said, 'No, not yet, you cannot let your friends down. You must be at the Christmas and New Year parties that have already been arranged.' A battle was raging within my soul – whether I would yield myself to Christ that night or procrastinate. Procrastination never landed anyone in Heaven, but it has doomed multitudes to a lost Eternity. I thought I was young enough. Sometime in my declining years I would yield myself to Christ – at the eleventh hour. But the danger is that so many who leave it to the eleventh hour die at half past ten!

I decided then and there, this is the night!

> 'Tis done, the great transaction's done,
> I am my Lord's and He is mine.
> He drew me and I followed on
> Charmed to confess the Voice Divine.

> Take the world, but give me Jesus
> All its joys are but a name,
> But His love abideth ever
> Through Eternal years the same.

I remember a verse that came to me: 'Who shall separate me from the love of Christ?' and I spoke these words quite openly. They were heard by those present. The school pupil who took me to the meeting was converted, as were another four school girls. That was the beginning of the Lewis Revival.

The following day, word went round the whole island. There was to be a meeting in the Barvas church the following evening. Buses came from all over the island to that meeting. The church accommodates about 500 people and it was crowded. The schoolgirl who invited me to the meeting the night before had gone back to Stornoway. Her friends immediately saw that there was a great change in her. 'What has happened to you? You are different!' Like the woman of Samaria, she said, 'Come and see!' and a lot of her friends came to the meetings and were converted. What an ambassador she was for Christ!

Among those whom she brought to these meetings was one who later went as a missionary to Thailand – the late Fay Hay who became, latterly, the doctor's wife in Uig, Lewis, but who spent many years with her husband as missionaries in Thailand. Another of the schoolgirls went as a missionary abroad, but many others became bright witnesses in their own respective parishes.

As the meetings went on, night after night, it was not a question of 'Were there any converted?' but 'How many were converted?' Each night, as the number of conversions increased, Duncan Campbell would ask them to remain behind after the rest had gone and often he would speak from John 10:27: 'My sheep hear my voice. I know them and they follow me and I give unto them eternal life and they will never perish, neither shall any man pluck them out of my Father's hand.' He would expound that verse to the new converts. Or perhaps he would speak from Isaiah 55: 'Seek ye the Lord while He may be found. Call ye upon Him while He is near.' He was so encouraging to the new converts. He wanted to encourage them to go on with the Lord.

My late brother, who had been a piper with the Royal Scots during the war, was going to be one of the pipers at a concert and dance in Carloway. But he said to my parents, 'I'll go first of all to the meeting in Barvas and later on join the concert party in Carloway.' He and the other piper who was to play went to the first meeting, intending to go to the concert afterwards – but they never reached that concert! They were both converted in Barvas Church. What a night! Rev Murdo MacLennan left the meeting and went to the Carloway concert hall to tell the news! (This story is told elsewhere in the book.)

People flocked to the meetings from all over the island and later on Mr. Campbell moved from parish to parish at the invitation of other ministers – to Ness, Carloway, Lochs, Point. Further invitations came and, wherever he went, people were converted.

The amazing thing was that most of them were in the age group eighteen to forty. There were certainly some younger and some older, but so many of those who were converted were young. So many of them are still officebearers in the churches in Lewis.

The following features were the outstanding *features of the revival.*

There was a universal consciousness of *the presence of God* – a sense of the Lord's presence was everywhere. On the streets, in the shops, in the school – wherever people gathered, revival was the topic of conversation. It was by no means confined to revival gatherings – wherever people met, even in the public houses, the revival was the topic of conversation. Converts sang spontaneously in the buses, praising the Lord and praying as they went from one parish to another. It had a great influence on those who travelled in the buses, whether they were converted or not. I know of two of the bus drivers who were converted. It was so easy to speak about God. You felt free to talk to anyone about Him. Everyone seemed to accept the fact that the Lord was working in the parish – a universal consciousness of the presence of God.

And then the *expectancy* that prevailed at the time. God's people were waiting and longing, just as they were at Pentecost – united and waiting for the coming of the Lord in their midst. I wonder if there is that spirit of expectancy nowadays. The empty pews in our churches today is tragic evidence of the lack of expectancy.

Another feature was the *power of God in the preaching*. Mr. Campbell would preach with great power. Very often, before he would commence to preach, he would ask one of the prayer warriors who were present to engage in prayer and one would feel the power of God coming down. Mr. Campbell was ready to preach then – preaching so often on repentance – the need for repentance. Yes, but also that God was a loving God, a God who would forgive.

Yet another feature was *the power in the prayers*. You felt that as people got up to pray the power of God was coming. I recall one man saying, 'You know, when I got up to pray I felt the Holy Spirit coming down as if He was pouring corn seed out of a barrel. It was so real that I felt I could reach out and handle it and I felt so uplifted and inspired.' Then there was the power of God in *the singing*! A foretaste of Heaven! Such a hunger and thirst after God among the people. People were longing to get to church whereas previously the difficulty had been to get any to church. The difficulty now was to get them out of it! I wish that this were true in our day and age.

Yet another feature was the *rejoicing* among the Lord's people: 'Wilt Thou not revive us again: that Thy people may rejoice in Thee?' I have never in my life experienced such rejoicing – it must have been similar to what was happening when Philip was preaching in Samaria. During the revival, we were told that there was great joy in that city. What brought that joy? A man called Philip came and preached Christ to them. When we consider our own cities today there is not much cause for rejoicing. Gloom and doom when we read the papers and watch television! What a difference in Samaria! A man called Philip came and preached to the people. There was great joy among the people – and that was true in the revival. When Mr. Campbell was preaching and people were converted, what rejoicing there was among those who were praying and labouring for this to happen! When they saw it happening, they rejoiced. When the prodigal son returned home the elder brother had no part in the rejoicing. Why? He was unconcerned about his lost brother. Only those who were burdened and concerned about the lost rejoiced.

Others were *sceptical*, bitter, doubting. They lost so much blessing on account of this, but those who were praying fervently and earnestly and were burdened about lost souls rejoiced, and it was amazing to see how the older Christians cared for the converts. They were so supportive, so caring. They were so well nurtured and the young converts desired to be in the company of older Christians whenever they could.

I think a lot of the young converts nowadays miss out on that. They don't desire the company of older Christians. They were our College, our Theological College. We learned so much from them. One thing the young do not have is experience. We gained so much.

From that revival there were at least eight ministers as well as many lay missionaries, officebearers and members. There were five members in our own family. Three of us were converted in the revival. The other two were later converted – I believe as a result of what happened to their brothers and sister. My mother used to say when she saw the five of us converted, 'I feel like Simeon when he got the child Jesus in His arms, "Now lettest Thou Thy servant depart in peace for mine eyes have seen Thy salvation."'

After my conversion I felt called to the ministry. In 1950 I began my course, which I finished in 1956. I then spent thirty-seven years as a parish minister. I am now retired, but I can never forget those days. Every time I speak about the revival I feel as if I am back there and my greatest desire is to see another revival before I pass on.

What we need today, said someone, is a revival that comes through heaven-anointed men rather than human appointed machines. My own cry is still, 'Wilt Thou not revive us again that Thy people may rejoice in Thee?' I can truly say that, after fifty years as a Christian, 'every day with Jesus is sweeter than the day before'.

23

MRS. MARY ANN MORRISON
Uig

Rev. Angus MacFarlane came to Baile na Cille (near Uig), in the summer of 1951, and later, in October, he invited Rev. Duncan Campbell to the parish for a mission. He remained in the parish for about three weeks ministering to a congregation of eager listeners, people who were in the habit of attending church. It was the custom for the majority then to come to at least one service on the Sabbath.

Revival was already 'in the air' and there was much expectation among the Lord's people who could be described as being in a lively state. God was at work in other parts of the island and this fired their expectation and strengthened their faith.

The first mission in Uig was in the Baile na Cille congregation and the following year the meetings were in the Uigean Church where Rev. Norman MacLeod was the minister. God's people were ready and prepared, and souls were saved in both missions. It was a glorious time. People from both congregations attended the meetings, irrespective of which church building they were in.

For my own part I was very pleased to learn that we were having a mission in Uig. I had been in school in Stornoway in 1949-50 and had seen a number of my friends in the hostel converted. When they returned every Monday from weekends in Barvas, Carloway and Lochs they were full of news of the revival. I listened avidly to their stories and to their witness, and having been brought up in a godly home and surrounded by a Christian influence all my life I understood what they were saying. In fact it made a deep impression on me and convicted me. So when the mission began in Uig I eagerly attended the meetings with my parents, neighbours and friends. There was no age gap! We would walk across the bay when the tide was out and walk round it when the tide was in. No obstacle stood in our way; we were there in every meeting whether they were in the church or in one of the village mission halls. There was a wonderful spirit of praise and prayer, and a sense of oneness as the community gathered nightly in God's house and afterwards in the house meetings.

Youth Club meetings in the school were forgotten. Soon there were conversions and the services in the church were followed by special meetings for seekers. Mr. Campbell would then expound the Scripture for a short time, concentrating especially on those who were in distress and anxiously seeking the Lord. Who can ever forget the atmosphere in those after-meetings? The thundering of God's judgment gave way to the comfort extended to the penitent. He dealt so tenderly with the seekers. It was beautiful! These after-meetings were so comforting and special. Often God's people were present at these after-meetings and they were all blessed.

I was being convicted about my sin but it was in the meeting-house in Crowlista under the preaching of our own minister, Rev. Norman MacLeod, that I committed my life to Christ and found peace. I could no longer contain myself but came right out on the Lord's side.

The main focus of attention in the community was on spiritual things. The staff at the Youth Club were all converted and the Club ceased to function.

I recall my parents' joy on the night of Dolligan's conversion. All the men in Timisgarry were saved, and nearly all at the same time. Ian William who had been a godly member of the church for many years was wonderfully blessed. He was radiant and filled with the Spirit of God. He loved the fellowship and was a great help to the young converts. He loved to be with them. He frequently requested that my mother, who had a sweet voice, should sing one of the lovely Gaelic hymns which gave expression to the longings, aspirations and praise so deeply felt by awakened saints and sinners.

Some English hymns were also sung from memory. Faith Mission workers in years gone by had left this legacy to the boys and girls who attended their services. So now in their teenage years they sang from their hearts what had previously been meaningless to them.

The time had come! The flood-gates were open and the prayers of years were answered. Words are inadequate to describe what it was like. Above everything on earth we would love to experience this again and to see our own families coming to know the Lord. They cannot imagine what they are missing! The Lord's Spirit touched everyone, even those who did not come through for salvation.

People went to the meetings in any mode of transport that they could find. Others walked many miles in inclement weather. Nothing would stop them. We often returned home in the early hours of the morning and were ready for work as usual the next day.

There was nothing in the meetings that would have distracted anyone. There was no crying out. There was just the sense of awe and solemnity which surrounded us everywhere. Silent tears were shed and deep conviction was experienced but the atmosphere was under the control of that awesome felt presence of God.

Among the converts were the young, the middle-aged and some older folk. Many had been good church-goers, others less so. Numbers of couples were saved and in one case, both parents, two sons and one daughter came to faith in Christ. What a season of joy we had. Nothing on earth can compare with this!

24

Two Ladies From Berneray

We will but glean from two interviews on Berneray, off North Uist, normally known as Berneray, Harris. The island is now connected to North Uist by a causeway, but at the time of the 1949 revival there was no causeway.

Mrs M. MacKillop

Her husband was very closely involved in the movement of the Spirit at that time and had great memories of the revival, but is unfortunately deceased. His testimony is lost. She, however, has given us some insights.

It was to this island that Duncan Campbell came from the Bangor convention which he suddenly left as he felt that the Lord wanted him here. He had been invited many times to come to us and at last God brought him.

At that time we did not have a minister residing on the island. Both my husband and I were converted then. The presence of the Lord was everywhere and it was just a wonderful time of enormous blessing.

Most of the islanders attended the meetings. It is just a small island and when sixteen came forward to the first communion during that time, it made a tremendous impact on the island.

When Duncan Campbell was away, the minister from Tarbert, Harris, came with one of his elders to conduct the services, and the Spirit of revival was still abroad. People were so hungry that they would gather in homes after the church meetings for more ministry.

Mrs Jane Maclean

I was one of a number of young people converted at the time of the revival with Duncan Campbell. There was a tremendous hunger for the Word of God and after the church services we would gather in the homes of the people.

I felt the power of the Lord in the meetings but also afterwards when I was alone. God was everywhere! You couldn't miss Him! Older believers helped the fresh converts and there was great joy among the people of God.

The preaching was stern. God's holiness was clearly illustrated from Scripture, as were His judgments and His wrath against the ungodly. There was no escape; no refuge for those who were thus exposed to the fiery preaching of God's Word.

Hector MacKinnon, the postman, was a man of prayer and a powerful orator. He sometimes took meetings when the minister was absent. He became a writer of some remarkable and very inspiring hymns. At the beginning he was not able to write but he retained his compositions in his mind until he came to someone who could put them down on paper. He died on his knees at a spot on the shore which he frequented for his sessions of prayer. *(Mary has sung some of Hector's spiritual songs on the Gaelic BBC.)*

I just thank the Lord that I was able to be present at this remarkable time of God's favour.

*Oh that Thou wouldest rend the heavens, that Thou wouldest
come down, that the mountains might flow down at Thy presence
(Isa. 64:1).*

Other Books of Interest
from
Christian Focus Publications

Revival Man

The Jock Troup Story

George Mitchell

Jock Troup's story is quite simply extraordinary. From a childhood in the Far north of Scotland he went to work in the fishing industry and then on to service in the First World War. It was during the war that the major turning point in Jock's life arrived - his conversion.

Jock went on to become an Evangelist, but no ordinary Evangelist. To quote a neighbour *'he had huge hands. He could pick up a fully inflated football easily with one hand. He had sixteen-inch biceps, un-expanded, and a neck like a prize bull'*, and to match this formidable physical presence he had a fire for reaching the lost with the Gospel.

George Mitchell gives fascinating insights into the lives of the fisher folk on the East coast of Scotland, and Glasgow life in Jock Troup's time. He includes many testimonies of those influenced through the ministry of Jock Troup and looks at the ingredients of revival, providing a useful lesson to the Church today.

'From one who has gained so much from the legacy he left in my own life, I can do no better than recommend this book to all, praying that the passion and fire for souls that he had for his day, will once again be experienced in our day.'

Bill Gilvear, Evangelist

Dr. George Mitchell is author of *Chained and Cheerful: Paul's Letter to the Philippians* ISBN 1 1-85792- 666-8 (Published 2001), his autobiography, *Comfy Glasgow* ISBN 1-85792-444-4, was published in 1999 and was a best seller.

ISBN 1-85792-728-1

"What an extraordinary book!
Real encouragement and inspiration"
Dr Patrick Dixon

THE
SPIRIT
OF
REVIVAL

**A first hand account of the
Congo revival of the 1950s**

Compiled and edited by Norman Grubb

The Spirit of Revival

A First Hand Account of the Congo Revival of the 1950's

edited by Norman Grubb

When you read this book, any scepticism about whether there are still genuine revivals post Pentecost will fade away. The events narrated in this book are understated and utterly genuine. There is no evidence in these first hand accounts of the hype and hyperbole that surround so called 'revival' reported in many corners of the Christian press today. You will be amazed and humbled and, more importantly, inspired.

"Nothing is more needed today than the powerful presence of God active in the people of God. Here is a story of expectant people visited by God in revival power. It has much to teach us about the importance of handling such holy things with care, weighing all things by the standard of Scripture, while being prepared unconditionally for God the Holy Spirit to deal with us as He wills. May this eyewitness account of revival awaken that deep desire for His coming that will prepare us for another awakening in our day!"

R T Kendall

"What an extraordinary book! Real encouragement and inspiration from those at the heart of a great move of God. This important book sheds clear light on recent events, and has a wonderful message for the new millennium."

Patrick Dixon, author of Signs of Revival

"This story is a powerful testimony to God at work in incredible ways. The insights to the holiness of God are awesome and terrifying. He is unique and sovereign…We need revival when we are not living in a revival lifestyle. Be challenged! This book could change your life."

Evan Davies, International Director, WEC International

"I read this book as a young Christian when it was first published in 1954. It has been a continuous stimulus and inspiration since that day to seek and never lose sight of the need for revival and for God's presence among His people."

Roger Forster

ISBN 1-85792-611-0

Christian Focus Publications

publishes books for all ages

Our mission statement –

STAYING FAITHFUL

In dependence upon God we seek to help make His infallible Word, the Bible, relevant. Our aim is to ensure that the Lord Jesus Christ is presented as the only hope to obtain forgiveness of sin, live a useful life and look forward to heaven with Him.

REACHING OUT

Christ's last command requires us to reach out to our world with His gospel. We seek to help fulfill that by publishing books that point people towards Jesus and help them develop a Christ-like maturity. We aim to equip all levels of readers for life, work, ministry and mission.

Books in our adult range are published in three imprints.

Christian Focus contains popular works including biographies, commentaries, basic doctrine and Christian living. Our children's books are also published in this imprint.

Mentor focuses on books written at a level suitable for Bible College and seminary students, pastors, and other serious readers. The imprint includes commentaries, doctrinal studies, examination of current issues and church history.

Christian Heritage contains classic writings from the past.

For a free catalogue of all our titles, please write to
Christian Focus Publications, Ltd
Geanies House, Fearn,
Ross-shire, IV20 ITW, Scotland, United Kingdom
info@christianfocus.com

For details of our titles visit us on our website
www.christianfocus.com